ISSUES *in* CONTEXTUALIZATION

ISSUES *in* CONTEXTUALIZATION

CHARLES H. KRAFT

WILLIAM CAREY
LIBRARY

Issues in Contextualization

© 2016 by Charles H. Kraft

No part of this work may be reproduced, stored in a retrieval system, or transmitted in any form or by any means—electronic, mechanical, photocopy, recording, or otherwise—without prior written permission of the publisher, except in brief quotations used in connection with reviews in magazines or newspapers.

Published by William Carey Library, an imprint of William Carey Publishing
10 W. Dry Creek Circle
Littleton, CO 80120 | www.missionbooks.org

Andrew Levin, editor
Rose Lee-Norman, index

William Carey Library is a ministry of Frontier Ventures
Pasadena, CA 91104 | www.frontierventures.org

23 22 21 20 19 Printed for Worldwide Distribution

Library of Congress Cataloging-in-Publication Data

Names: Kraft, Charles H., author.
Title: Issues in contextualization / Charles H. Kraft.
Description: Pasadena, CA : William Carey Library, 2016. | Includes bibliographical references and index. | Description based on print version record and CIP data provided by publisher; resource not viewed.
Identifiers: LCCN 2016019372 (print) | LCCN 2016018622 (ebook) | ISBN 9780878088867 (eBook) | ISBN13: 9780878084920 (pbk.) | ISBN10: 0878084924 (pbk.) Subjects: LCSH: Missions--Theory. | Christianity and culture. | Intercultural communication--Religious aspects--Christianity. | Communication--Religious aspects--Christianity.
Classification: LCC BV2063 (print) | LCC BV2063 .K728 2016 (ebook) | DDC 266--dc23
LC record available at https://lccn.loc.gov/2016019372

CONTENTS

PREFACE..vii

THE BASICS

1. THE INCARNATION AND INSIDER MOVEMENTS 3
2. CULTURE, WORLDVIEW, AND CONTEXTUALIZATION.................... 13
3. MEANING EQUIVALENCE CONTEXTUALIZATION 25
4. APPROPRIATE CONTEXTUALIZATION................................ 41

WHAT WE ARE TO TAKE

5. CONTEXTUALIZATION IN THREE CRUCIAL DIMENSIONS 55
6. DON'T TAKE YOUR RELIGION, TAKE YOUR FAITH 73
7. WHY ISN'T CONTEXTUALIZATION IMPLEMENTED? 89

TYPOLOGY AND DYNAMICS

8. A TYPOLOGY OF APPROACHES TO CONTEXTUALIZATION 105
9. DYNAMICS OF CONTEXTUALIZATION 111
10. CONTEXTUALIZATION AND TIME: GENERATIONAL APPROPRIATENESS... 125

RELATIONAL ASPECTS

11. APPROPRIATE RELATIONSHIPS 147
12. PARTNERING WITH GOD 165

CONTEXTUALIZATION OF POWER

13. SPIRITUAL POWER. 173
14. APPROPRIATE CONTEXTUALIZATION OF SPIRITUAL POWER 189
15. POWER ENCOUNTER 211

APPENDIX: THE DEVELOPMENT OF CONTEXTUALIZATION THEORY
IN EURO-AMERICAN MISSIOLOGY 223
REFERENCES. 241
INDEX 247

PREFACE

What follows is not all new. Those who have read the book I edited, *Appropriate Christianity* (2002), will have noted that I wrote eleven of the twenty-eight chapters in that book. Those chapters, lightly edited, plus five new ones, are presented here in response to requests for just my thoughts and a shorter volume.

Contextualization is an important topic. In Jesus, God contextualized Himself in a particular society at a particular time in order to reach a particular people in the most appropriate and impactful way. This is an "insider" approach to communicating and expressing the gospel. In going about His communication this way, Jesus set an example for us to go as far as we can go to work inside other cultures in order to incarnate ourselves and His message today. Though we cannot totally incarnate ourselves as He did, still He says, "As the Father sent me, so I send you" (John 20:21). Our goal, then, is to go as far as possible to "fill His shoes." He is our model for both communication and expression of Christianity. We are sent by Him to extend His kingdom in today's cultural worlds. And I would contend that we are to carry out that mission in as much an insider way as possible.

One day in 1959, one of our Nigerian village evangelists returned from a witnessing trip to a place where the gospel had not yet been proclaimed. The people of that area had, however, heard some of the Christian songs the believers had produced in their words, put to their traditional musical forms. Their young girls had been singing them at the full moon dances for months. And the elders of those villages had one question: "Who is Yesu Kristi?" The message was new, but the cultural forms in which that message came were theirs, and the songs spoke loudly about someone named Yesu Kristi. Was this the missionary that the young girls were singing about? Or was it someone else?

The music was stopped and the evangelist was asked to explain, which he gladly did. For the message had preceded the evangelist. And it had come to this distant people packaged in what were to them familiar forms—their language, their music. And now, over fifty years later, the estimate is that that whole tribal group of between 500,000 and a million is 95 percent Christian. The message had come to them in appropriate ways as an insider thing, and they responded big time. Christianity is now theirs, in their cultural forms.

"As the Father has sent me, so I send you" (John 20:21). Like Jesus, we are to incarnate ourselves and His message as best we can so that all peoples can experience a Christianity that is *theirs,* not someone else's—a Christianity that springs from seeds, not a transplanted tree that first sent its roots into another soil and comes to them half-grown. Contextualization/incarnation is God's way. And that's what this book is about. May God bless it to the end that more of this world's peoples will be able to know and commit themselves to Yesu Kristi as *their* Savior and Lord without the requirement that they convert to another culture.

NOTE: As I was writing and revising for this book, a very important book dealing with contextualization was published by A. Scott Moreau of Wheaton College. He is also the editor of *Evangelical Missions Quarterly,* giving him access to the best of evangelical scholarship on contextualization published there. The title of his book is *Contextualization in World Missions.* This is a magisterial piece of work that surveys, summarizes, and evaluates nearly everything that has been written by evangelicals on the subject. I am pleased and honored that Scott has referred to my writing often, though not always positively.

I have decided, however, not to interact with that book here for at least two reasons. First, Moreau's book is so good and comprehensive that it deserves to stand by itself without the detractions that an evaluation would raise. Second, the purpose of that book is different from the purpose of this one. Moreau's aim is to evaluate writings that have contributed insights, mine to present insights that come from my own understandings.

I recommend that book highly for everyone seriously interested in this topic. Perhaps my book can stand beside it to provide a more comprehensive view of our subject than either provides by itself.

Charles H. Kraft
March 2016

THE BASICS

CHAPTER 1
THE INCARNATION AND INSIDER MOVEMENTS

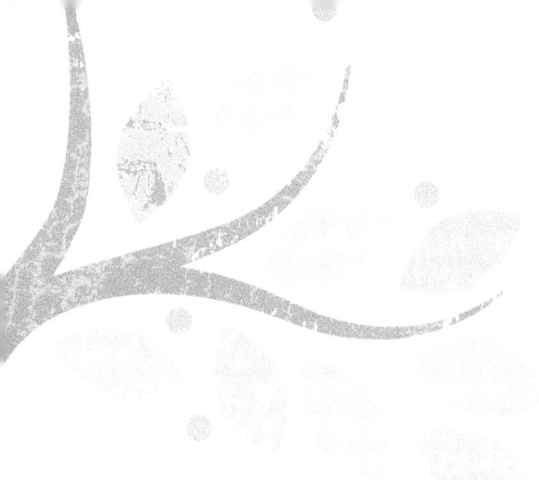

There are two major issues we want to deal with in the pages that follow. They are *communication* and *expression*. Much of what is dealt with here is communication. Jesus came to communicate God and in the process to show us how to communicate God. The other main topic is expression. I will contend that our model for the expression of the gospel is also Jesus. An insider movement starts with incarnational communication and continues inside a society as an insider activity expressed in insider ways to honor Jesus.

To attempt to understand the implications of insider strategy I present the following discussion of incarnational communication in culture.

HALFWAY BRIDGE COMMUNICATION

Years ago, I was riding with a friend in an American city and saw what to me was a strange sight. As we drove along a river, I noticed a bridge that went halfway across the river. I asked my companion if I was seeing correctly. He assured me that I was, and told me that the bridge was started in 1934 without a proper plan to connect it to the opposite side of the river. Construction was well on the way when the engineers realized that there was no way to connect it on the other side. Some people found the halfway bridge a good place to jump from to commit suicide. But no one could use it to get to the other side.

As I have been teaching missionaries on communication over the last fifty years or so, this picture has come to me over and over again as a way of looking at how we often attempt to communicate Christ. Whether we think of missionary communication or what goes on weekly from our pulpits, much of our communication is like that halfway bridge. We communicate in our language and concepts halfway across the communicational bridge and expect those who listen to build the other half of the bridge to understand what is being said. For many, the communicators are speaking what might be called "theologese." The listeners have to learn the language and concepts that the preacher is using in order to understand him/her, building the other half of the communicational bridge. On the mission field, the missionary may use words and concepts that were appropriate at home but are known on the field only to those who have been to seminary and learned the meanings that those concepts are intended to convey. The schooled ones may be able to build the other half of the communicational bridge, but the common people may not have a clue what the communicator has said.

I once listened to a prominent American pastor speak in Japan (through an interpreter) to an all-Japanese audience. But his illustrations were all taken from the American context, and they could only make sense to an American or one who had spent time in the United States. These were the same illustrations he had used many times in the States in a set speech. But he lost his listeners—except, perhaps, for those few who had traveled to the US. Only this small group was able to build the other half of the communicational bridge and understand what my friend was saying.

When we communicate in a culture other than our own, it is possible not only for our words to make no sense, but for our very lives to hinder effective presentations of our message.

THE GOSPEL IS A PERSON MESSAGE

We lose a lot when we reduce the gospel to words. The usual translation of John 1:1, "In the beginning was the Word . . . ," misleads us into a kind of static, word-oriented concept of God's communication. How much better does J. B. Phillips get across the truth of the dynamic character of our faith when he translates John 1:1 as "At the beginning, God expressed Himself." We then recognize the fact that God wrapped that message in a Person, a real live human being who Himself *is* the Message from God. Jesus showed us both the message and the method. *The message is a Person; the method is incarnation, insider communication.* Jesus not only came, He *became*. Indeed, He became so much an insider that many did not even notice His presence. Or they noticed Him but would not take His presence seriously. Or they discounted Him because he spoke a non-prestigious dialect (Galilean Aramaic).

Communication specialists tell us that *the communicator is the major part of his or her message.* Following this principle, God's supreme method of communication is in the incarnation of the *person* of Jesus Christ. Incarnation focuses on the communicator becoming a part of the culture of the people he or she seeks to win. *Incarnation is by definition, then, an insider approach to getting God's message across.*

Jesus is the Message. When He is communicated properly as an insider, several things come into focus.

A FOCUS ON FAITH, NOT RELIGION

Incarnational, insider movements focus on the essence of what it means to follow Jesus. We take our faith, not simply our religion. The underlying fact here is that the term "religion" refers to a cultural thing. It connotes a system made up of such things as belief in God or spirits, rituals used to express an allegiance to that God or spirit, doctrines, often a holy book or books, plus a whole lot of other cultural items and beliefs.

Religions, because they are cultural things, can be *adapted* to new cultures. Adaptation is an external thing resulting in smaller or larger changes in the forms (including rituals) of the religion. *A religion cannot be contextualized, only adapted.*

Biblical faith, however, can be *contextualized*, a process in which appropriate meanings may be carried by quite different forms in various cultures. The reason it can be contextualized is the fact that none of the cultural forms in terms of which the essential gospel is expressed are required. All of the cultural forms employed in the expression of Christianity in one culture can be substituted in another culture because essentially the biblical relationship is a faith, not a religion.

In contrast, each religion requires some cultural structures borrowed from the original expression of that religion. Islam requires the Arabic language, pilgrimage to Mecca, praying in a certain posture and in a certain direction, recitation of a statement of allegiance, etc. Buddhism requires cultural elements from the country of origin, as do Hinduism and Shinto. Only animism does not require the same cultural elements wherever it is practiced. Animism can be contextualized and frequently is.

A faith, though it lies beneath the cultural structuring of a religion, is something quite different from a religion. A religion involves one in activities of various kinds. The essence of faith, though, is the commitment to something or someone, a commitment that may or may not be religious. When talking about a faith, it is the commitment or allegiance that is in focus, not the cultural structuring in terms of which that commitment is expressed. Most faiths can be expressed through a variety of cultural structures.

The faith commitment can be to an idea, such as communism or evolution, or it can be to a person, such as the leader of a movement or Jesus Christ. A faith can even be an allegiance to a cultural entity such as an organization or even a religion. But that faith can be expressed in many different ways. It can, therefore, be as differently expressed from culture to culture as any belief or commitment.

The gospel requires none of the original cultural forms. That's how it has historically been "captured" by the West and can be considered Western even though its origin is not Western. *The biblical way is an allegiance, a relationship, from which flow a series of meanings that are intended to be expressed through the cultural forms of any culture.*

These forms are intended, then, to be inside, chosen for their appropriateness to convey proper biblical meanings in the receptors' contexts.

Jesus spoke of our faith as a seed, not a tree. We have often taken full-grown trees to other peoples, trees that were at home in their native soil but are out of place in the new context. What Jesus meant by picturing our faith as a seed is that the tree or bush that springs from that seed does not look like it came from another place. It is chosen to serve inside, nourished by the new soil, the new water. It is meant to look like it belongs. This is, in fact, what He Himself did in becoming an insider.

As for the differences between a religion and a faith, I offer the following chart (to be discussed further in chapter 6).

A RELIGION (STRUCTURAL)	A FAITH (PERSONAL)
Structural, Cultural/Worldview	Personal/Group/Social
Rituals, Rules	Relationship
Beliefs	Commitment/Allegiance
Perform	Obey
Adapt	Contextualize
Borrow/Accept/Imitate (e.g., worship forms)	Create/Grow (e.g., new cultural forms)
"One size fits all"	Cultural varieties of expression
Like a tree that must be transplanted	Like a seed that gets planted
Like a loaf of bread that gets passed on	Like yeast that gets put in raw dough
An Institution	A Fellowship

TABLE 1.1. A religion vs. a faith

INSIDER MOVEMENTS ARE APPROPRIATE

An insider movement is a movement that is by definition a culturally appropriate expression of a commitment. It is "inside," appropriate to the culture in which it is planted rather than to some outside culture. The judgment as to whether a movement is appropriate or not is to be made by insiders. So such a movement is to be expressed in terms that are understandable by insiders who have not become bicultural through being able to function in another culture.

In Japan (and many other places) it is easy to identify Christian church buildings. They look like they have been imported from eighteenth-century America. They don't look Japanese. Nor do they look to the Japanese like power places. In a Japanese context it is required that a place that purports to serve a religious function look like a place of power. If the buildings are to be interpreted as representing the High God and understood as power places, they will need to be built in Japanese style with something that looks to Japanese people like a shrine (a spiritual power source) on the premises.

Now we know that people regularly adopt foreign customs. One or two or a few customs can easily be borrowed from another culture without upsetting things. But if people need to adopt a hundred poorly understood foreign customs to practice a new faith, the situation is quite different. Then the religion feels foreign to insiders. It's as if they were learning to follow a foreign Christ and to speak their language with a foreign accent.

Many who follow Christ in our day have converted to a Western cultural religion as well as to Jesus. They may be called "*Western* Christians," since they have adopted a Western form of the Christian religion, the religion of the visiting carriers of Christianity. A savvy missiologist of yesteryear looking at this problem asked, If Africans poured their full-fledged Africanness into their Christian expression, would the rest of the world even recognize it as being Christian (Taylor 1963)? Perhaps not. There are some African movements to Christ that present just such a challenge to us Westerners.

I believe that *our expression of Christ-centered faith should be as different from culture to culture as our cultures are from each other.* When this is not the case, I believe we are insulting the God who came all the way from heaven to be an insider, to reach others who would accept the faith and express it in insider terms and practices.

OUR MESSAGE IS A PERSON MESSAGE

We tend to think of our message as it is formulated in words. We may even back up that understanding of the gospel by referring to the traditional translation of John 1:1. But seeing the message as primarily a word message is a problem.

Communication theory tells us that *a person is himself or herself the major part of any message he or she brings.* Communication depends on relationships. The message, then, involves the content of the message wrapped in the relationship between the communicator and his or her audience. The relational part of the communication interpenetrates every part of what is said and done, influencing powerfully every aspect of the way the event is interpreted by the receptors.

The scary thing here is that each of us *is* our message, and how we relate to those who receive messages from us is a crucial part of the message we seek to put across. How sad it is when we hear of missionaries who define their ministries in terms of words or tasks. They have been influenced by our society to "wordify" the message. Much of our theological training is word, proposition, and information oriented.

These wordsmiths often carry our society's baggage when they see themselves as specialists rather than as persons. We can weep when we hear of Bible translators or development workers or teachers, or even pastors and evangelists, who carry out their specialties with precious little focus on how they are relating to the people around them. This is an outsider approach, and their relationships—or lack of them—carry a very loud message about Christianity. Their behavior, as opposed to their words, says, "Our faith stands for a distant God, an uninvolved God, a God who speaks about or specializes in what He thinks is important but pays little attention to what His actions communicate."

How different is Jesus, who spent thirty-three years among us communicating that when God gets close, it's good news rather than bad news. This is the insider approach. How different was the message of His person, the One who gave Himself to us and for us, the One whose whole ministry was couched in a close relationship with the Twelve and many others (e.g., the women, the family of Lazarus). The Apostle Paul articulated this message when he said, "Imitate me just as I imitate Christ" (1 Cor 11:1).

The point is, the message, the gospel, is not simply *about* Jesus. Jesus *is* the message, the gospel we seek to contextualize, and we are the personal representatives of that message today. *We are Jesus today.* So, to contextualize Jesus, we must contextualize ourselves. And this involves both *being* (who we are) and *doing* (what we do). Our being is to be like Jesus. Our doing is to demonstrate God in the midst of human life.

Jesus' message was a *life message,* not simply a word message. He said that he had come to bring life, abundant life, and that he was the way, the truth, and the life (John 10:10; 14:6). And life can only be communicated through *life rubbing against life to produce life.*

Relationship, then, is the key—from God's early relationship with Adam to His relationship with Noah, Abraham, Joseph, Moses, David, and everyone else in Scripture and beyond Scripture. So Jesus tells us to abide in Him and bear fruit (John 15)—fruit that is the demonstration of God. This is fruit that *demonstrates* God's love, His compassion, His mercy, His grace, His righteousness, indeed His very character. It was carried in the person of Jesus and is today carried in our persons.

The first name given to Jesus was Emmanuel, "God with us." So to communicate Him we have to be genuinely *with* those we seek to win and disciple. Contextualization, then, is the process by means of which Jesus in us is lived in such a way that people *feel* His incarnation, His life being lived among them. All else that we talk about in contextualization studies is derivative of this *presence communication,* this insider focus. *To contextualize the gospel is to bring Jesus' presence into the lives of a people.*

OUR FAITH NEEDS TO BE DEMONSTRATED, LIVED

The most effective way of communicating anything is to demonstrate it. And demonstration is an insider thing. In order to demonstrate the message, we need to get close enough to the people for them to touch us. Insider communication is incarnational.

In His incarnation, Jesus was the *demonstration* of God the Father, living among us. As Jesus says to Philip, "He who has seen me has seen the Father" (John 14:9). I find it interesting (and disturbing) that our word-oriented Bible publishers put the words of Jesus in red. That's not where His main message lay. Jesus actually said very little that was totally new. *The newness of His messages sprang more from Who said those things than from what was said.* His primary message was not in His words but in who He was (His being) and what He did (the way He demonstrated God).

And Jesus' message was from inside, an insider approach to the message, leading to an insider expression, bringing His presence into the lives of the people He worked with. If we are to communicate a *life* message, we must get close enough to the receptors for them to see our life firsthand.

One thing that needs to be demonstrated is that the *gospel message produces a faith, not simply a religion*. And as a faith it needs to be growing—it is intended to be dynamic—as it was in New Testament days. When it is alive, people are growing, changing, creative. When revival hits, we can count on movement and creativity, even heresy.

Most people and groups that come to Christ start out with at least some very sub-ideal beliefs and practices. Their churches may be too Western (C1 or C2) or too indigenous (what some critics consider C5 to be). In either case, there may be need for movement, say from C2 to C3 or from C5 to C4, if the people in these churches are to understand and relate to God better.

Much of the criticism of approaches to contextualization that advocate insider movements, a C5 variety of Christ-following, seems to be based on the fear that if people start one way, there is little hope of them ever maturing into something better. The assumption seems to be that if people start with sub-ideal customs (e.g., polygamy, reverence for ancestors, common-law marriages), they will continue in those customs forever.

Such an attitude, however, demonstrates our unwillingness to trust both the Holy Spirit and the people who turn to Christ. Our tendency is to treat both people and God as if they can't handle the faith without our control. But biblical discipleship is to be a dynamic thing, starting inside, perhaps with help from outsiders, and continuing to change and grow.

Part of our demonstration should be, then, to help people to recognize that religious expression should not be set in cement. Biblical discipleship needs to be seen as a process in which people engage under the direction of the Holy Spirit, not simply a product produced in one society and transported into another, the way a postman might transport letters and packages. We are to seek to plant seeds, not to transplant whole trees. Insider movements are about seeds, not trees.

OUR FAITH IS MEANT TO UNITE HUMAN AND SPIRIT LEVELS

Although to most of the peoples of the world there is but one world with a human part and a spirit part, to Westerners there are two realms: the human realm and the spirit realm. This means that insiders are often more keenly aware of the spirit world than we Westerners are. Unfortunately, we often challenge their perceptions by introducing a secular, human-focused Christianity.

Everything in human experience has ramifications in both realms and can therefore be said to have two expressions, a human one and a spiritual one. We live and function at the human level. But everything at the human level has a spiritual counterpart, whether we know that part of it or not.

Our lack of awareness of the spiritual dimension often puts us in a poor position to help non-Westerners experience a faith that unites the two foci. Though these two levels function as one, we Western humans are often only aware of what's going on at the human level. The fact that we often do not see what's going on at the spirit level, however, does not mean that the spirits do not exist or are not active in our lives. It is like the law of gravity: it powerfully affects us whether we believe in it or not.

The presence and involvement of the spirit world is constant, and it is widely recognized by insiders. If we from the West want to attract insiders, it is incumbent upon us to present them with a powerful faith rather than the powerless variety practiced by most churches in our home countries.

Insider movements will give an important place to spiritual warfare—war against the gods and spirits the insiders have been serving. Our Master paid a lot of attention to the enemy and what he was doing. He spent a lot of time freeing people from this enemy. Insider movements spend a lot of time and energy confronting what the enemy has been doing. Jesus came to destroy the works of the enemy (1 John 5:8). This should be an important focus of insider faith in Christ.

HOW NOT TO CONTEXTUALIZE

There are many emphases that fight against contextualization, some of which I have mentioned above. When we see these symptoms, we know that a disease that we may call "anti-contextualization" has set in. All of these symptoms are outsider symptoms. I will enumerate them so we can see the contrasts clearly.

1. Create things that cost a lot of money to maintain (e.g., hospitals, schools, mission stations, church structures) and then "graciously" turn them over to the nationals. All of these are outsider structures, understood by the outsiders but often not by the insiders, except by those who have westernized. None of them are incarnational, though sometimes they do good things for people. When these institutions are turned over to nationals, they are usually too expensive for them to maintain. An insider approach would focus on developing appropriate technology that the people can afford, will use, and will be able to repair when it stops working.

2. Avoid the spiritual stuff. Create or go along with a secular mentality that deals with human problems as if there was no spiritual dimension to them. Don't deal with demonization and spiritual infestation, the major problems of the people. These are insider problems that we leave to the nationals. An insider approach would give the same priority to spiritual issues as Jesus did. Healing and deliverance would be prominent in church activities.

3. Wordify everything. Treat ministry as primarily a talking thing, as we have learned in school. Create a separate theological reality and train the national leaders to do the same. Focus on the propositional nature of some of the Scriptures, and ignore the life-related majority of them as mere illustrations of the words and theological logic on which we focus. We often ignore the "insiderness" of Scripture in favor of our choice to deal with outsider issues that concern us rather than the insider problems that Jesus dealt with. Jesus educated with an insider method: apprenticeship. He healed and delivered and cleansed, dealing with spiritual problems in insider ways.

4. Focus on foreign structuring of church. Avoid doing things as insiders would in favor of establishing our type of organizations. In doing so, we are focused on Christ following as a religion rather than as a faith. A religion is a cultural thing in competition with other cultural religions. A faith is a supracultural thing that can be expressed in any of a number of religious structures, borrowed from the culture itself rather than imported from overseas. An insider approach would assist the nationals in growing their cultural structures to fit their expression of the faith.

5. Turn the focus of worship to a lecture rather than to experiencing the presence of Jesus with us when we gather. The church service and what goes on there has so often been patterned after a school classroom rather than after what the insider practice would be. And the messages have so often been intellectualized as in school that school and church are seen as the same thing to many. Jesus story-told rather than intellectualized. An insider approach would have people meeting in a traditional way in a traditional place, using a traditional communicational approach (e.g., dialogue rather than monologue, storytelling rather than sermonizing). An insider approach would see Scripture as what it is—a divinely inspired casebook full of true life stories of God-man interactions rather than a theology textbook, working with the culture of the receptors rather than against it.

In short, traditional mission has propagated an outsider thing in spite of Jesus' example of working as an insider. Biblical faith, however, is an insider, incarnational thing, claiming the insider's culture for the structures through which it is expressed.

INSIDER = INCARNATION

My point is this: Ours is an incarnational faith. Jesus, in the incarnation, became an insider, using His culture and way of life to serve God. He did not start things too complicated for His followers to continue. He did not import foreign customs that signaled that what He established would forever be labeled "foreign." He fought against rules, regulations, and practices that had been instituted by and for earlier generations, and the arrogance of those who, considering them sacred, imposed them on the people. Indeed, Jesus did not do anything that His followers could not continue.

By contrast, we have often proclaimed a message that says, "Become like us culturally and God will accept you." As one of my missionary colleagues put it, "We have had two thousand years of experience with Christianity; we know how things ought to be run." My response was that we have not had one year of experience in this culture. We need to find out how God wants to work with these people. Our job is seed-sowing, not tree-planting.

Incarnation is an insider thing, focused on faith, not on religion, seed-sowing rather than tree-planting, dealing with the receptors' needs in ways that they understand as representing an insider Jesus. Like Jesus' message it is accompanied by power demonstrations exhibiting the love of God and His desire to free captives from the grip of Satan. We are to imitate Jesus in every way. His way is to be an insider, endorsing even disrespected Galilean culture and language as fit vehicles for God's messages.

Though we who are outsiders cannot be born into another culture, we can approximate Jesus' approach by identifying with our receptors, learning their ways and dignifying their language and culture as we demonstrate how they can be used by God for God's purposes.

The cultural structures we recommend may already have been used to express other faiths (e.g., Islamic faith, Buddhist faith, animistic faith). Our faith can use the same cultural structures as these faiths have, but in allegiance to the true God. Our faith is an insider thing at the core.

CHAPTER 2
CULTURE, WORLDVIEW, AND CONTEXTUALIZATION

If we are to work inside of culture, we need to understand culture and worldview. A key question for those who work cross-culturally and attempt to work inside the receptors' culture is, what is God's view of culture? Is Jewish culture created by God and therefore to be imposed on everyone who follows God? Or is there some indication in Scripture that God takes a different position? I believe we have our answer in 1 Corinthians 9:19–22, where Paul articulates his (and God's) approach to cultural diversity. Paul says, "While working with Jews, I live like a Jew" but "when working with Gentiles, I live like a Gentile." His approach, then, is what we now call "an insider approach" to "become all things to all men, that I may save some of them by whatever means are possible."

The early Christians were Jewish. It was natural for them to believe that the cultural forms in which the gospel came to them were the only right ones for everyone. So, they believed, everyone who comes to Jesus must also convert to Jewish culture. But God used the Apostle Paul, himself a Jew, to teach his generation and ours a different approach. In the above verses, he articulates God's approach. Then in Acts 15:2ff we find him arguing fiercely against what was the majority position of the early church for the right of Gentiles to follow Jesus *within* their own sociocultural contexts. God Himself had shown first Peter (Acts 10), then Paul and Barnabas, that this was the right way by giving the Holy Spirit to Gentiles who had not converted to Jewish culture (Acts 13–14).

But the church has continually forgotten the lesson of Acts 15. We have continually reverted to the assumption that becoming Christian means becoming like us culturally. When, after New Testament times, the church required everyone to adopt Roman culture, God raised up Luther to articulate God's approach for Germans: that God could accept people who spoke German and worshiped in German ways. Then arose Anglicanism, showing that God could use English language and custom, and Wesleyanism, to let the common people of England know that God accepted them in their culture. And so it has been that there are major cultural issues in the development of every new denomination.

But sadly, the problem of the communicators of the gospel imposing their culture or denomination on new converts continues. So we attempt to apply anthropological insight to missions, to enable us to protect the people to whom we go from our own inclination to require them to be like us. If, then, we are to take a scriptural approach, we are to *adapt ourselves and our presentation of God's message* to the culture of the receiving people. We should not misrepresent God as most of the early Jewish Christians (Acts 15:1) and others did who used their power to require that converts become like them in order to be acceptable to God.

CULTURE AND WORLDVIEW DEFINED

The term *culture* is the label anthropologists give to the structured customs and underlying worldview assumptions in terms of which people govern their lives. Culture (including worldview) is a people's way of life, their design for living, their way of coping with their biological, physical, and social environment. It consists of learned assumptions (worldview), concepts, and behavior, plus the resulting artifacts (material culture).

Worldview, the deep level of culture, is the culturally structured assumptions (including values and commitments or allegiances) underlying how a people perceive of and respond to reality. Worldview is *not separate* from culture. *It is included in culture* as the structuring of the deepest level of presuppositions on which people base their lives.

A culture may be likened to a river, with a surface level and a deep level. The surface is visible. Most of the river, however, lies beneath the surface and is largely invisible as we look at the surface. But anything that happens on the surface of the river is affected by such deep-level phenomena as the current, the cleanness or dirtiness of the river, the presence of other objects in the river, and the like. What happens on the surface of a river is both a reaction to external phenomena and a manifestation of the deep-level characteristics of the river.

So it is with culture. What we see on the surface of a culture is patterned human behavior. But this patterned or structured behavior, though impressive, is not the most important part of the culture. In the depths are the assumptions we call *worldview*, in terms of which the surface-level behavior is governed. When something affects the surface of a culture it may result in a change at that level. The nature and extent of that change will, however, be influenced by the deep-level worldview structuring within the culture.

Surface-Level Culture (Patterned Behavior)
Deep-Level Culture (Worldview Assumptions)

FIG. 2.1. Levels of culture

Culture (including worldview) is a matter of structure or patterns. Culture does not *do* anything. Culture is like the script an actor follows. The script provides guidelines within which actors ordinarily operate, though they may choose on occasion to modify the script, either because they have forgotten something or because someone else changed things.

There are several levels of culture (including, of course, worldview). The "higher" the level, the more diversity is included in it. For example, we may speak at a *multinational* level of culture such as "Western culture (or worldview)" or "Asian culture" or "African culture." Such cultural entities include a large number of quite distinct *national* cultures. Within *Western culture* there are varieties called German, French, Italian, British, and American. Within *Asian culture* are varieties called Chinese, Japanese, and Korean. These national cultures, then, can include many *subcultures*. In America, for example, we have Hispanic Americans, American Indians, Korean Americans, and the like. And within these subcultures we can speak of *community cultures, family cultures,* and even *individual cultures*.

In addition, the term *culture* can be used to designate groupings that sometimes are cross-cultural because they have similar strategies for running their lives. For example, we can speak of such entities as *a culture (or worldview) of poverty, deaf culture, youth culture, culture of factory workers, taxi drivers' culture,* even *culture of women*. Identifying people in this way is often helpful in working out insider strategies for reaching them for Christ.

PEOPLE AND CULTURE

Just as in drama we must recognize the difference between actors and their scripts, so also with culture. It has been common for both non-specialists and specialists to refer to culture as if it were a person. We often hear statements such as "Their culture *makes* them do it," or "Their worldview *determines* their view of reality." Note that the italicized verbs in these statements give the impression that a culture behaves like a person.

As in drama, the patterns are there and the actors ordinarily follow them by habit. But the "power" that keeps people following the script of their culture is the power of habit, something inside of people, not any power that culture possesses in itself. *Culture (including worldview) has no power in and of itself.*

People ordinarily follow the patterns of their culture, but not always. People regularly modify old customs and create new ones. Although the habits that result in great conformity are strong, we can change our customs. Cross-cultural witnesses must recognize the place of habit in cultural continuity, but they must also recognize that people can change their habits.

The distinction we are making is embodied in the contrast between the words *culture* and *society*. *Culture* refers to the structure; *society* refers to the people themselves. When we feel pressure to conform, it is the pressure of people (i.e., social pressure) that we feel, not the pressure of cultural patterning (the script) itself.

Table 2.1 summarizes the distinction I am making between the behavior of persons and the cultural structuring of that behavior.

SOCIETY (PEOPLE)	CULTURE
Surface-Level Behavior What we do, think, say, or feel either consciously or unconsciously, mostly habitually but also creatively	**Surface-Level Structure** The cultural patterns in terms of which we habitually do, think, say, or feel
Deep-Level Behavior Assuming, evaluating, and committing, mostly habitually but also creatively: 1. Concerning choosing, feeling, reasoning, interpreting, and valuing 2. Concerning the assigning of meaning 3. Concerning explaining, relating to others, committing ourselves, and adapting to or deciding to try to change things that go on around us	**Deep-Level Structure (Worldview)** The patterns in terms of which we carry out the assumptions, evaluations, and commitments of deep-level behavior. Patterns of choosing, feeling, reasoning, interpreting, valuing, explaining, relating to others, committing ourselves, and adapting to or deciding to try to change things that go on around us.

TABLE 2.1. Society vs. culture

CULTURES AND WORLDVIEWS ARE TO BE RESPECTED

Cultural/worldview structuring functions both outside of us and inside of people. People are totally submerged in it, relating to it much as a fish relates to water. And people are usually as unconscious of it as fish must be of the water or as people usually are of the air they breathe. Indeed, many people only notice culture when they go into another cultural territory and observe customs different from their own.

Unfortunately, when we see others living according to cultural patterns and worldview assumptions different from our own, we often feel sorry for them, as if their ways are inferior to ours. If we are able, then, we may seek ways to "rescue" them from their customs. An approach that seeks to extract people from their culture is typical "outsider" behavior, the result of ethnocentrism. One of the tragedies of American (including missionary) attempts to help other peoples is that we have so often shown little respect for their traditional customs.

The way of Jesus is, however, to honor a people's culture and its incorporated worldview, not to wrest them from it. Just as He entered the cultural life of the Jews in order to communicate with them, so we are to enter the cultural matrix of the people we seek to win. Following Jesus' example, we note that working from within a culture will involve acceptance of their customs as starting points but will reserve the right to eventually suggest biblical critiques of certain of their customs and worldview assumptions.

But if we are to witness effectively to human beings, we have to speak and behave in ways that honor the only way of life they have ever known. Likewise, if the church is to be as meaningful to receiving peoples as Jesus wants it to be, it needs to be as appropriate to their cultural lives as the early church was to the lives of first-century peoples. We call such appropriate churches and insider movements "dynamic equivalence churches" (Kraft 1979), "contextualized churches" (see below), or "inculturated churches."

CHARACTERISTICS OF CULTURE (INCLUDING WORLDVIEW)

A number of characteristics of culture and worldview may be listed, but space does not allow us to do so. A fuller discussion of them may be found in my book *Worldview for Christian Witness* (2008).

CHARACTERISTICS OF CULTURE AND WORLDVIEW

1. A worldview consists of the *assumptions (including images)* on which all cultural values, allegiances, and behavior are based.

2. Worldview assumptions and images *underlie our perception of reality and responses to it.*

3. There are two realities: REALITY as God sees, and perceptual reality as we with human limitations see (1 Cor 13:12). Our worldview provides us with *the lens, model, or map* in terms of which we perceive, interpret, structure, and respond to God's REALITY.

4. Worldview assumptions or premises are learned from our elders, *not reasoned out, but assumed to be true without prior proof.* It seldom occurs to us that there may be people of other groups who do not share our assumptions.

5. We organize our lives and experiences according to our worldview and *seldom question it* unless our experience challenges some of its assumptions.

6. Culture/worldview provides a *total design for living,* dealing with every aspect of life and providing people with *a way to regulate their lives.*

7. Culture/worldview is a legacy from the past, *learned as if it were absolute and perfect.*

8. Culture/worldview *makes sense to those within it.*

9. But *no culture/worldview seems to be perfectly adequate* either to the realities of biology and environment or to the answering of all of the questions of a people.
10. Culture/worldview is an *adaptive system*, a *mechanism for coping*. It provides patterns and strategies to enable people to adapt to the physical and social conditions around them.
11. Culture tends to show *more or less tight integration* around its worldview. The worldview assumptions provide the "glue" with which people hold the culture together.
12. Culture/worldview is *complex*. No simple culture/worldview has ever been found.
13. Cultural/worldview practices and assumptions are *based on group or "multi-personal" agreements*. A social group unconsciously agrees to govern its life according to their cultural patterns.
14. Culture (including worldview) is *structure*. It doesn't *do* anything. People do things either according to their cultural script or by modifying that script. Any supposed power of culture or worldview lies in the *habits* of people.
15. Though analytically we need to treat people and culture/worldview as separate entities, *in real life people and culture/worldview function together*.
16. In cross-cultural ministry, *the problems that arise from differences in worldview are the most difficult to deal with*.

THE SUBSYSTEMS OF CULTURE

With worldview at the center, influencing all of culture, we can divide surface-level culture into *subsystems*. There are many cultural subsystems, some of which are diagrammed below. These subsystems provide various behavioral expressions of worldview assumptions.

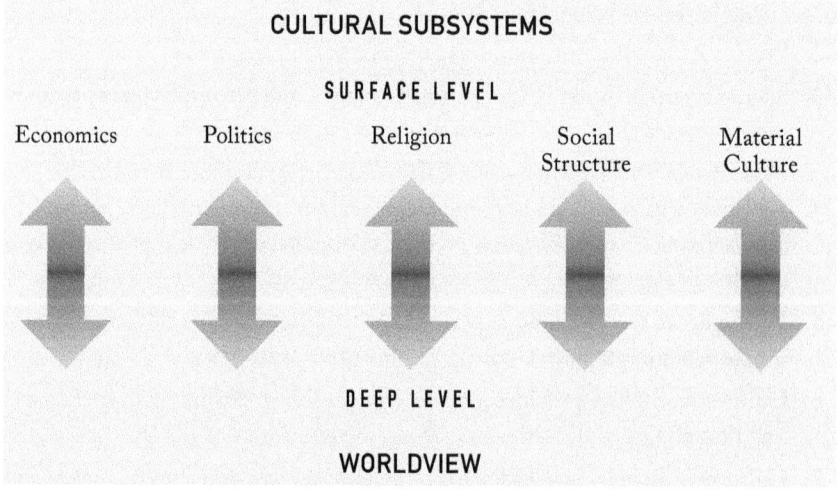

FIG. 2.2. Cultural subsystems

Although it is tempting to present Christianity as the replacement of a traditional religion with the religious forms of Western Christianity, this is the wrong way to go at witness. For Christianity is to be directed to the worldview of a people so that it will influence each of these subsystems from the very core of the culture. Truly converted people (whether in America or overseas) need to manifest biblical Christian attitudes and behavior in all of their cultural life, not just in their religious practices.

If we are to reach people for Christ and to see them gathered into Christ-honoring but culture-affirming churches, we will have to deal with them within their culture and in terms of their worldview. We will do this either wisely or unwisely. It is hoped that by understanding more of what culture and worldview are all about we can deal with them more wisely than might otherwise have been the case.

WORLDVIEW AND CULTURE CHANGE

Significant culture change always involves changes in the worldview. Just as anything that affects the roots of a tree influences the fruit of the tree, so anything that affects a culture's worldview will affect the whole culture and, of course, the people who operate in terms of that culture.

Jesus knew this. When He wanted to get across important points, He aimed at the worldview level. Someone once asked Jesus, "Who is my neighbor?" In response, He told them the story of the Good Samaritan and then asked the audience who they thought was being neighborly (Luke 10:29–37). He was leading them to reconsider and, hopefully, change a basic value down deep in their system.

On another occasion Jesus said, "You have heard that it was said, 'Love your friends, hate your enemies.' But now I tell you: love your enemies and pray for those who persecute you. . . . If anyone slaps you on the right cheek, let him slap your left cheek too" (Matt 5:43,44,39 GNB). Again, the seeds were being planted for change at the deep worldview level.

When there is change at a deep level, however, it frequently throws things off balance. And any imbalance at the worldview center of a culture tends to cause difficulty through the rest of the culture. For example, when we in the US believe at the worldview level that we cannot be defeated in war but then cannot win in Vietnam, a deep sense of demoralization ripples throughout the society, contributing greatly to the present disequilibrium in our land.

Major worldview problems can be caused when even good changes, introduced by well-meaning people such as missionaries, are applied at the surface level without due attention to the deep-level meanings people attach to them. For example, the almost universal missionary requirement that Africans who come to Christ but have more than one wife divorce the "extras" before they can be baptized has led both Christian and non-Christian Africans to certain undesirable worldview assumptions concerning the Christian God. Among these are: God is against the real leaders of African society; God is not in favor of women having help and companionship around the home; God wants men to be enslaved to a single wife (like whites seem to be); and God favors divorce, social irresponsibility, and even prostitution. None of these conclusions is irrational or far-fetched from their point of view. Though we believe that God intends that each man have only one wife, missionaries forced this change too quickly, unlike God's patient approach in the Old Testament where He took many generations to do away with the custom.

As mentioned above, even good changes if they are introduced in the wrong way can lead to cultural disequilibrium and demoralization. Among the Ibibio people of southern Nigeria the message of God's gracious forgiveness resulted in many people turning to the Christian God because He was seen as much more lenient than their traditional god. But the converts saw no need to be righteous, since they believed God would always forgive them, whatever they did.

In Aboriginal Australia, among the Yir Yoront people, the introduction by missionaries of steel axes to replace the traditional stone axes had a powerful disruptive effect simply because the axes were given to the women and younger men, who traditionally were required to borrow axes from the older men. This change, despite providing the people with better technology, challenged their worldview assumptions, leading to the destroying of the authority of the leaders, widespread social disruption, and the near extinction of the people.

Add to such examples the enormous damage (both cultural and spiritual) among non-Western peoples that has been done through the influence of Western schools (including those run by missions), and you will understand that there are at least a few valid reasons (among the invalid ones) for certain anthropologists to be critical of missionary work.

CONTEXTUALIZED (APPROPRIATE) CHRISTIANITY

The aim of Christian witness is to see people come to Christ and be formed into groups we call churches that are both biblically and culturally appropriate. The process by means of which the church becomes "inculturated" in the life of a people has been called "indigenization" but now is more frequently referred to as "contextualization."

The contextualization of Christianity is part and parcel of the New Testament record. This is the process that the Apostles were involved in as they took the Christian message that had come to them in Aramaic language and culture and communicated it to those who spoke Greek. In order to contextualize Christianity for Greek speakers, the Apostles expressed Christian truth in the thought patterns of their receptors.

Indigenous words and concepts were used (and transformed in their usage) to deal with such topics as God, church, sin, conversion, repentance, initiation, "word" (*logos*), and most other areas of Christian life and practice.

The early Greek churches were in danger of being dominated by Jewish religious practices because those who led them were Jews. God, however, led the Apostle Paul and others to struggle against the Jewish Christians to develop a contextualized Christianity for Greek-speaking Gentiles. In order to do this, Paul had to fight a running battle with many of the Jewish church leaders who felt that it was the job of Christian preachers to simply impose Jewish theological concepts on new converts (see Acts 15). These conservative Jews were the heretics against whom Paul fought for the right of Greek-speaking Christians to have the gospel expressed in their language and culture. We conclude from such passages as Acts 10 and 15 that it is the intent of God that biblical Christianity be "reincarnated" in every language and culture, at every point in history, and that Christianity be an insider movement.

Biblically, the contextualization of Christian faith is not simply to be the passing on of a *product* (a religion) that has been developed once for all in Europe or America. It is, rather, the imitating of the *process* that the early apostles went through. To return to our tree analogy, biblical faith is not supposed to be like a tree that was nourished and grew in one society and then was *transplanted* to a new cultural environment, with leaves, branches, and fruit that mark it indelibly as a product of the sending society. The gospel is to be *planted as a seed* that will sprout within and be nourished by the rain and nutrients in the cultural soil of the receiving peoples. What sprouts from true gospel seed may look quite different above ground from the way it looked in the sending society, but beneath the ground, at the worldview level, the roots are to be the same and the life comes from the same source.

In a truly contextualized church, even though the surface-level "tree" may look different, the essential message and meanings will be the same, and the central doctrines of our faith will be in clear focus since they are based on the same Bible. But the formulation of that message and the relative prominence of many of the issues addressed will differ from society to society. For cultural reasons, such things as what the Bible says about family relationships, fear and evil spirits, and the advocacy of dance and prescribed rituals will be much more in focus in contextualized African Christianity than they might be in America.

God intends today's Christian faith to be "meaning equivalent" to New Testament faith, perceived by people today as excitingly relevant to the problems they struggle with. Though many non-Western churches today are dominated by Western approaches to doctrine and worship, it is not scriptural that they remain so. There are, of course, similar basic problems (e.g., the problem of sin, the need for a relationship with Christ) that peoples of all societies need to deal with. But the ways those problems manifest themselves differ from people to people and need to be approached in different ways, culturally appropriate ways, for each cultural group.

CONTEXTUALIZING CHRISTIANITY IS VERY RISKY

There are great risks involved in attempting to promote a Christian faith that is culturally and biblically appropriate and an insider thing. The risk of *syncretism* is always present. Syncretism is the mixing of Christian meanings with those worldview assumptions that are incompatible with Christian faith so that the result is not biblical.

Syncretism exists whenever people practice rituals because they consider them magic or use the Bible to cast spells on people or, as in India, consider Jesus just another of many human manifestations of one of their deities or, as in Latin America, practice pagan divination and witchcraft right in the churches. It is also syncretistic to insist that people convert to a different culture to become Christ-followers. In America it is syncretistic, unbiblical faith that sees "the American way of life" as identical with biblical faith, or that assumes that by generating enough faith we can pressure God into giving us whatever we want, or that we should out of love and tolerance allow homosexuality and even homosexual "marriage" to go unopposed in spite of clear biblical condemnations.

There are at least two paths to syncretism. One is by importing foreign expressions of the faith and allowing the receiving people to attach their own worldview meanings to these practices with little or no guidance from those who are practicing a mature faith. The result is a kind of "nativistic" Christianity or even, as in Latin America, "Christo-paganism." Roman Catholic missionaries, especially, have fallen into this trap by assuming that when people practice so-called "Christian" rituals and use "Christian" terminology, they mean by it the same thing that Euro-American Christians mean.

The other way to syncretism is to so dominate a receiving people's practice of the faith that both the surface-level practices and the deep-level assumptions are imported. The result is a totally foreign, unadapted kind of faith that requires people to worship and practice their faith according to foreign patterns and to develop a special set of worldview assumptions for church situations that are largely ignored in the rest of their lives. Their traditional worldview may remain almost untouched by biblical principles. This is the kind of Christ-following that evangelical Protestants have most often advocated, probably out of a fear of the first kind of syncretism. In many situations, this kind of Christ-following attracts some of those who are westernizing. But the masses of traditional people find little or nothing in such faith that meets their needs, simply because it is presented and practiced in foreign ways to which they cannot connect.

Though we must be cautious concerning syncretism, there is a middle road that involves deep trust in the Holy Spirit's ability to guide and the receiving people's ability to follow that guidance. We are to always point to the Holy Spirit (not ourselves) as the Guide while participating with them in discovering His leading. Practicing this approach, missionary Jacob Loewen chose to never answer directly any questions from the Christ-followers such as, "What should we do?" Instead, he would ask them, "What is the Holy Spirit showing you?" Only after they had struggled with the answer to that question would he participate with them in seeking guidance, and even then his approach was to offer them at least three alternative approaches from which they might choose. In response to this approach they usually developed a fourth alternative that was uniquely their own. If that approach worked they would continue it. If it did not, they felt free to change it, since it was their own and did not come with the prestige that often accompanies the suggestions of respected outsiders.

The risk of syncretism is always present when Christ-followers attempt to inculturate the faith, but it is a risk that needs to be taken in order that people might experience New Testament Christianity. Whether in a pioneer situation or after a foreign brand of our faith has been practiced for years, the quest for a vital, dynamic, biblical, contextualized faith will require experimenting with new, culturally and biblically appropriate ways of understanding, presenting, and practicing the "faith which once and for all God has given to his people" (Jude 3 GNB). It will especially require attention to what is going on at the worldview level. To this end the insights of anthropologists into culture and worldview can be harnessed to enable us to advocate a Christianity that is truly contextualized, truly relevant and meaningful, and genuinely insider.

UNDERSTANDING CULTURE AIDS CONTEXTUALIZATION

Understandings of culture and worldview such as those presented above have helped us greatly in our attempts to understand what biblical and cultural appropriateness means. Among the understandings that have come from such studies are the following:

1. God loves people as they are within their cultures. As we see from the Bible, He is willing to work within everyone's culture and language without requiring them to convert to another culture.

2. The cultures and languages of the Bible are not special, God-made cultures and languages. They are normal human—indeed, pagan—cultures and languages, just like any of the more than six thousand cultures and languages in our world today. The Bible demonstrates that God can use any pagan culture (even Greek or American) with its language to convey His messages to humans.

3. The Bible shows that God worked with His people in culturally appropriate ways. He took customs already in use and invested them with new meaning, guiding

people to use them for His purposes and on the basis of new worldview understandings. God even discarded some customs He Himself had once endorsed. Among the customs used by pagans that God adapted or adopted are circumcision, baptism, worship on mountains, sacrifice, the synagogue, the Temple, anointing, and praying. God wants churches today to be culturally appropriate, using most of the customs of a people but attaching new meaning to them by using them for God's purposes. In this way, people get changed at the worldview level as well as on the surface.

4. But God's working within culture never leaves that culture unchanged. God changes people first, then through them the cultural structuring. Whatever changes are to take place in the structures are to be made by the people themselves on the basis of their understanding of the Scriptures and God's workings in their lives, led and empowered by the Holy Spirit, not pressured by an outsider.

5. Though contextualization within a new culture risks a nativistic kind of syncretism, equally syncretistic is a Christianity dominated by foreign cultural forms with imported meanings. We must therefore follow Scripture and risk the use of receptor-culture forms, because God favors insider approaches.

CHAPTER 3
MEANING EQUIVALENCE CONTEXTUALIZATION

Some of this chapter may seem academic. It is. Even so, I invite you to think of the subject of communication in insider/outsider terms. What goes on in the minds of those to whom we go to communicate Christ? How can we use the language and culture vehicles at our disposal to lead people (insiders) to Christ and help them develop insider structures, so that they can serve and grow in Him?

For the last several years, it has been commonplace to speak of contextualization, localization, or inculturation as the ideal toward which we strive in the planting and nurturing of Christian churches. By this we mean that it is important for people to receive and express Christianity in culturally appropriate ways—insiders making Christianity their own.

Our discussions of this topic, however, have all too often tended to focus on finding the appropriate cultural *forms* (see below) through which to express either theological truths or things we outsiders see as structural necessities. Well and good. Finding the proper forms is absolutely crucial to the conveying of the proper meanings. The wrong cultural forms in the receiving society result in the wrong meanings in the minds of the people.

But it is because of our concern for meanings that we must be so concerned about the forms. The forms are not important for their own sakes. They are important for the sake of the meanings. When, for example, the form of a church building, or the music or rituals used therein are interpreted by the people of a given society as foreign (outside) and not their own, we say that the wrong forms are being used. But this is not because there is anything inherently wrong with those forms. Indeed, they may be just the right forms in another sociocultural context. The problem is that the use of those forms signals certain meanings that are theologically wrong since they are not what the Scriptures show to be God's intent.

CULTURAL FORMS (OR CUSTOMS)

Culture is made up of what we call "cultural forms." Forms are the customs, the ideas, the patterns and structures in which we live and move and have our being. In language, words, sentences, and paragraphs are cultural forms. Beyond language, material objects such as chairs, pencils, cars, and dishes are cultural forms. So are non-material items such as ceremonies, ideas, and beliefs.

Cultural forms are used by the people of a society in the living of their lives. We often refer to them popularly as customs. We may speak, then, of forms or customs that are linguistic, religious, political, economic, family, educational, etc. We may even speak of deep-level, largely subconscious worldview assumptions as cultural forms.

Forms, then, are the vehicles of culture and worldview. By definition, every custom, whether visible or invisible, is a cultural form. The forms are the basic elements of culture. Cultural forms are what people use to live their lives. How we use each cultural form provides the basis on which people interpret what we are doing.

Any given form can be the vehicle of more than one meaning, since meaning stems from the interpretation of the receptors. For example, an automobile may mean such things as transportation from one place to another, status for those who buy expensive cars to show off their prosperity, trouble and expense when it needs fixing, freedom from dependence on other people and other means of transportation, coming of age for young people just getting their licenses, danger to those crossing the street, and perhaps several other things. A form we call "wedding ceremony" can mean different things to the bride, the groom, the bride's parents, the attendants, the musicians, the pastor, the janitor, and those in the audience. The same musical forms can mean one thing to the members of the younger generation and quite another thing to their elders.

People choose the language forms they use on the basis of the meanings assigned to those forms by the people using them. For example, I am attempting to be careful as I write to use just the right language forms to enable you, the reader, to understand what I mean.

THE INPUT OF COMMUNICATION THEORY

A major assist in understanding the dynamics of contextualization and insider Christianity comes from the field of communication theory. It is axiomatic that the response we seek from the receptors of gospel communication will be based on the receptors' interpretation of the life and messages coming from those seeking to communicate Christianity. If we are to guide that interpretation so that our receptors understand and work toward appropriate contextualization, we ourselves need to understand the process of communication and to be able to use the principles effectively.

There are two primary areas of understanding to be gleaned from communication theory. Those areas concern *receptors* and *meaning*. What follows is a listing of several important principles relating to each of these areas. For more detail, see my books *Communication Theory for Christian Witness* (1991) and *Communicating Jesus' Way* (2000).

RECEPTORS

The following are some characteristics of receptors.

1. Receptors are *parts of reference groups*. Receptors (like all humans) are never alone, even when they are "by themselves." Whether one lives in an individualistic society like we Americans do or in a strongly group-oriented society like those of most of the Two-Thirds World, we always consider the reactions of others when we make decisions. Whenever an appeal is made to people to consider a change of opinion or behavior, their basic question is, "What will the people in my group think?"

All humans are related to reference groups whose opinions strongly affect the choices they make. Any change a person contemplates and/or carries out is, therefore, made in relation to the person's perception of the desires of such a group. If the person feels his or her reference group is likely to react negatively to a given decision, it is probable that the person will turn away from that decision. Or the person may make the decision, later discover that his or her group is against it, and go back on the decision.

2. Receptors are *committed to their group and to the values of that group*. When people are approached to make changes in their attitudes and/or behavior, it cannot be assumed that they are not already committed to competing attitudes and/or behavior. People do not operate in a vacuum. People not only exist in groups, they are committed to those groups and for what they stand for. This is a deep-level commitment. And people often feel they are being asked to be disloyal to family and society when approached with the challenge to make a total commitment to Jesus Christ. This fact is especially relevant when considering insider interpretation of allegiances, messages, and practices coming from outside of their society and culture.

People are usually more open to changes that appeal to their own self-interest. If a new commitment can be presented in such a way that the receptors feel their position in life will be improved if they make that change, they are likely to be more open to it—that is, if it isn't perceived to cost them too much socially. Christ's way, of course, offers quite a number of good things that can appeal to receptors' self-interest if presented rightly. Many people are looking for such Christian benefits as more meaningful life, peace, forgiveness, freedom from fear, release from physical, emotional, or spiritual captivities, and the like, not to mention eternal life. To appeal attractively for people to give up previous commitments to gain these benefits is one of the greatest challenges of the Christian communicator.

3. If Christian appeals are to be attractive, they need to be addressed to *the felt needs of the receptors, the insiders*. An important thing to recognize, though, is that human beings never seem to be fully satisfied with whatever their state in life. And no sociocultural system seems to adequately provide for every need felt by the people

within that system. Those leftover problems, therefore, provide fertile ground for any communicator prepared to discover and provide answers for them. Like Jesus, we are to allow receptors to articulate their need (e.g., the rich young man in Matt 19:16–22; blind Bartimaeus in Mark 10:46–52; and the Samaritan woman in John 4). We then can deal with whatever the receptors are conscious of and thus gain their permission to deal with the deeper needs that may be on our agenda.

The appeal to needs perceived by receptors is a crucial dimension of effective communication. We cannot, however, assume that those we seek to reach understand life in exactly the same way we understand it. We need, therefore, to do whatever research is necessary to discover where our receptors are and what cultural insiders perceive their needs to be before we attempt to speak to them. Only when we have a fair idea of what they see to be their unanswered problems should we seek to discover how to apply scriptural answers to them. Merely applying answers, even scriptural answers, to questions they are not asking seldom works well.

4. Receptors are *always interpreting*. And everything about the communicational situation gets interpreted. The communicators' words are, of course, interpreted. But so are their relationships, their tone of voice, their gestures, use of space, and general appearance. Interpretation is clearly one of the most important, though least conscious, of the receptors' activities. And most of it is based on what the receptors have learned through past experience, rather than on their experience in the present situation.

When my wife and I went to Nigeria as missionaries, we were interpreted at least partially in terms of the impression previous American missionaries had made on the receptors. They had had some experience with Americans and factored that strongly into their interpretations of us. I realized early on that one of my concerns should be to prove myself out of the stereotype so that they would interpret me differently from other Americans, as "one of us" rather than "one of them," an insider rather than an outsider. When they nicknamed me "Albino" instead of "White Man," I felt that I had achieved something important. I was regarded by them as at least partially inside.

5. These interpretations feed directly into the most important of the receptors' activities: that of *constructing the meanings* that result from the communicational interaction (see below on meanings). It is messages, not meanings, that are transmitted from person to person. These messages are usually in linguistic form. And the meanings exist only in the hearts and minds of people, not in the vehicles of communication or in the words (cultural forms) used to convey the messages.

Contemporary communicologists see communicators with meanings in their minds that they would like to transmit to receptors. Communicators take these meanings and formulate them into messages that they then transmit to receptors. Receptors listen to the messages and construct within their minds sets of meanings that may or may not correspond with the meanings intended by the communicator.

6. Receptors either *grant or withhold permission* for any given message to enter what might be termed the receptor's "communicational space." Receptors may be pictured as encased in a kind of bubble that only they can give permission to enter. Therefore, when someone wants to negotiate some form of communication, he or she needs to gain permission for the interaction from the receptor, the only one who can control access to that bubble. The transactional nature of communication requires that each participant gain the permission of the other in order to either initiate or continue the interaction.

The attitude of the participants toward each other is, of course, crucial to the nature of the interaction. Permission may, for example, be more readily given to persons of higher prestige than oneself, to persons whom one trusts, to those in authority over oneself, to those with greater expertise than oneself, to those whose favor one seeks, or to those whom one perceives as interested in oneself.

Whether or not a receptor grants permission for a message to enter also relates to what may be termed the "range of tolerance" of that receptor for the particular type of message presented and/or the person presenting the message. Communicators need to give high priority to winning the permission of their receptors.

That permission may be complete (e.g., openness to dealing with any subject) or partial. Once permission is gained, however, it is not certain that it will be retained until the end of the interaction, for receptors *evaluate* as the interaction continues and sometimes take back permission (whether complete or partial) once granted before the event is over. Sometimes such withdrawal can be read in the receptors' behavior as feedback.

7. Closely related to the activity of giving permission is that of *evaluating the message*. In any communicational interaction the participants evaluate each component of that experience. The communicator, the message, and the receptors are all evaluated, and so is the total situation in relation to similar experiences the participants have had in the past and whatever expectations they have concerning the future. From this evaluation the participants construct an overall impression of the situation, an impression that has much to do with how they interpret what goes on in that situation.

I once listened to the president of an institution I was attending laud the virtues of leading a seminary that was theologically liberal. I felt he should be ashamed to be a liberal! And this personal evaluation resulted in my not taking his words seriously.

8. Another closely related kind of activity in which receptors are engaged is the matter of *selectivity*. People are selective in the kinds of things they allow themselves to be exposed to. If they fear something, it is unlikely that they will allow themselves to be exposed to it unless they are forced to be. If they allow themselves to be exposed to something, however, and then find that it is disagreeable, they can refuse to pay attention.

Even if people are paying attention, though, they may or may not perceive what is being communicated in the way the communicator intends. People tend to perceive messages in such a way that they confirm already held positions, whether or not the communicator intended them that way. This is usually done unconsciously and relates to their overall evaluation of the situation and its various components. It also relates strongly to the persons' past experiences and their perception of how the new information relates to what they already know.

Political messages, for example, may be intended by the sender in one way but interpreted in quite another way by the receivers. The use of the term "Christian" is another example and one major reason for an insider approach. To many people, especially Muslims, that word connotes Hollywood immorality, misuse of power, polytheism (they see the Trinity as the worship of three gods), support of Israel, and other anti-God behavior. Inviting them to become "Christians," then, is interpreted as an insult.

9. Receiving communication is a risky business, so receptors are *continually seeking to maintain their equilibrium* in the face of actual or imagined risk. Whenever people expose themselves to communication they are risking the possibility that they might have to change some aspect of their lives. People ordinarily seek at all costs to maintain their present equilibrium, to protect themselves from assimilating anything that is perceived to possibly upset their psychological balance.

MEANINGS

There has been a great deal of discussion down through the years concerning meaning. Some have claimed that meanings are simply contained in the linguistic and cultural forms people use to convey them. It is, however, obvious that different people regularly assign different meanings to the same cultural forms. And if we expose people of widely different cultures to the same forms, the interpretations differ widely. Meanings, then, are the result of the interpretation of cultural forms. The meaning Muslims assign to the word "Christian" is quite different from that assigned to the word by Western Christians.

Meanings are assigned by people and in a sense "flow" through the forms as people interpret them. Whenever people use cultural forms in the presence of others, meanings are attached to them first by the person(s) who originate(s) the forms and then by those who hear or observe those people.

Meanings lie within people, not in either the external world or the symbols we use to describe that world. Meaning is a personal thing, internal to persons rather than either a part of the world outside or of the symbols people use. Meanings, being personal, are attached by people to message symbols according to cultural rules in their minds.

This fact is well stated by David Berlo when he says,

> Meanings are in people, [they are] covert responses, contained within the human organism. Meanings . . . are personal, our own property.

> We learn meanings, we add to them, we distort them, forget them, change them. We cannot find them. They are in us, not in messages. Fortunately, we usually find other people who have meanings that are similar to ours. To the extent that people have similar meanings, they can communicate. If they have no similarities in meaning between them, they cannot communicate. (1960, 175)

Contrary to some understandings, communication is not the transmission of meaning. For meanings are not *contained* in forms, though they are *conveyed* by them. As Berlo has said, meanings are in people. It is people who attach meanings to the linguistic, religious, political, economic, and other forms of culture they use. Meaning is, therefore, a function of personal interpretation on the basis of social agreements rather than something inherent in the forms themselves.

Meanings are not transmittable, not transferable. Only messages are transmittable, and meanings are not in the message; they are in the message-users. Meaning is the result of interpretation. And interpretation is the subjective interaction of one or more persons with a situation. What that situation means to the person is what he or she comes away with from that situation. And persons attach their meanings independently of each other, though ordinarily in keeping with habits that they have learned to share with other members of their community.

But forms and meanings always come together in real life. Only as we analyze the communication process do we distinguish between the two. There are no forms that people don't attach meaning to—no forms without meanings as long as there are people around to interpret them. And there is no communication or understanding of meanings without cultural forms—no meanings conveyed in human life except through cultural forms.

The forms that are used are, therefore, extremely important to the communication process. They need to be the forms that the receptors will interpret as meaning what the communicator intended. If, therefore, a message generated by one group is to be effectively presented to another group, *the forms/symbols used to convey that message need to be those "owned" by the receiving group, whether or not they are the same as those preferred by the generating group.* For meanings are attached on the basis of group agreements developed from the shared life experience of the group.

These facts result in several implications of relevance to the process of contextualization.

1. The first is that in every communicational situation we can point to at least *three separate "realities" or views of reality*. The first may be labeled *Objective (or "capital R") Reality*. This is the Reality that God alone is able to see and know in an undistorted way. This Reality includes all that actually exists and happens in the world. It includes all that goes on, both external to and internal to the participants, in a communicational interaction.

Then there are two *small r*, perceptual realities. Each participant in a communicational situation has *his or her own perception of the Reality* of that situation. The communicator sees in terms of what may be labeled *the Communicator's Reality*.

The Receptor, however, sees in terms of a third reality. They understand in terms of their own reality. That reality, though, is likely to be different from that of the communicator—less different if they are a part of the same culture, more different if their cultures are different. And communicational interactants act and react in terms of their *perceived* reality, rather than according to the objective Reality of the situation. Both communicator and receptor, then, respond not to what is actually said or done, but to what each person *perceives* was said or done. *The materials with which each is working to construct meaning, therefore, lie not in the objective details of the interaction, but in their subjective interpretations of the situation.*

Meanings, then, "are the internal responses that people make to stimuli" (Berlo 1960, 184) based on their perception of the stimuli from within their own realities. On the basis of these meanings both the reality from which communicators respond and the reality to which receptors respond are constructed.

2. A second implication of this view is *the importance to the process of communication of the personal relationship between the participants*. The personal nature of the assignment of meaning requires that we give primary attention to the relationships between the participants. The dynamics of the relationship between the communicators and the receptors provide them with crucial information concerning how to interpret what is really meant by what each other says and does.

It is crucial that we keep ourselves continually aware of this factor. It is too easy to focus on the words we speak and to ignore the relational aspect of communication unless something goes radically wrong. When the relationship between the interactants is healthy, they may be quite unconscious of the part that relational healthiness plays in their ability to communicate effectively. If, however, the relationship is "sick," the interactants will be constantly hindered in their attempts to effectively convey content to each other.

Jesus, of course, based His whole ministry on the personal relationships He had with a fairly small group of followers. It was His life involvement with them that enabled His messages to get across at such a deep level. His example confirms a major insight of those who have studied communication theory. It also provides the right example for us to imitate. To work effectively both in winning insiders and in planting insider-sensitive Christ-following groups, one must recognize the importance of this principle and work in terms of it.

3. A third implication is that *those with similar perceptions of similar experiences are most likely to construct similar meanings*. It is not enough to have similar experiences. Persons must perceive them similarly if they are to come out with similar meanings.

The fact that people live in cultural groups within which they conduct most of their interpersonal interactions leads to the members of each group agreeing that given symbols are to be interpreted in the same way. This raises to a very high level the predictability of similar interpretations and responses to similar stimuli on the part of the members of any given group.

4. The personalness of communication results in the fact that *meanings are more felt than reasoned.* The immediate response of people to any given situation is more likely to be emotional than rational. If they think over the event, they may revise their earlier reaction on the basis of a more rational consideration. But in general, first impressions based on feeling are very difficult to shake, even when considered rationally.

5. A further implication derives from the nature of the Christian message. For *this message is far more than a verbal message—it is a "person message"* (see chapter 1). God specializes in messages that are personal rather than simply informational. Information messages such as those about scientific facts, world news, or the weather don't require good behavior on the part of the communicator to make them valid. God's messages, however, require a high degree of personal involvement. For in this kind of message, the person who brings the message is a major part of the message he or she brings.

God Himself is the message, and we are to respond to a person to properly attach meaning to that message. At the purely human level, we do the same thing with messages of love, care, concern, sympathy, and the like—we respond not simply to words but to the person who does the deed. Such messages are only conveyed effectively by life rubbing against life. The ultimate Christian message, then, is a person. And *anything that reduces that message to mere words stimulates, in the receptor, meanings unworthy of the message.* Our message is a message of life, and only life can properly convey it. Thus, only if that message is actually conveyed by life can it be properly understood.

Insider approaches in person form carry the best chance of being understood correctly. Those who do not truly get into the receptors' personal communicational space as insiders do, run a high risk of being misunderstood. Those who advocate insider approaches to expressing and communicating Christ as persons recommending a Person are likely to be correctly understood. Those who see their task as delivering an impersonal word message, or as focusing on structures, mislead themselves and others. Our focus must be on persons and person communication as insiders.

RECEPTORS AND CONTEXTUALIZATION

All of these principles apply to our task of advocating appropriate Christianity. The commitment of people to their reference groups is a major obstacle to any group, such as Christian groups, who seek to get them to change their allegiance. Allegiance to family is probably the major commitment of most of the peoples of the world, but Jesus demands that He be our primary allegiance (Matt 10:37,38). Getting this fact across in a winsome way to people who are exhibiting characteristics of receptors such as these is an incredible challenge, even for mature believers, and it is not to be laid on new converts.

We need, therefore, to discover a people's felt needs and present our messages in such a way that they will interpret what we say and do as relating to those needs. The messages they hear, however, will lead to the meanings they construct, largely from the materials in their own minds, with or without much understanding of where we are coming from. For example, the ready reception of schools by many of the peoples of East Africa is reported to have been based on their perception that schooling would give them spiritual power. They assumed that the power of the Europeans was spiritual power and that the way to obtain this power was through attending school. This misinterpretation resulted, of course, in a felt need for schools, a need that the missionaries were quick to take advantage of. What neither the missionaries nor the East Africans anticipated was the pervasive secularization that came with the schools.

Those attempting to work as insiders need to be constantly aware of the process of interpretation that is going on with receptors and the fact that they will interpret from their own point of view, whether or not that is even close to our intent.

When there is a wide cultural gap between those who bring the gospel and those who receive it, then, we can assume that the potential for misinterpretation is great. I found it a challenge, for example, to deal with Noah and his ark with northern Nigerians who had never seen a body of water larger than a flooded river that sometimes was big enough to cross in a canoe, small boat, or raft. Their word for those watercraft, therefore, basically means "canoe." The fact that we had come to Nigeria in a large ship (to them a canoe) tested their credulity. The story of how God got all those animals onto one canoe proved to be an enormous test of the Nigerians' faith.

A more serious problem exists in Japan, where the Japanese word *kami* is used for God. This is the word for any spirit. In the animistic perspective of the Japanese, such spirits are powerful, capricious, and dangerous, requiring constant vigilance and appeasement to keep them happy. The same spirits may be good at one time, especially if they are kept happy, but bad at another time, especially if displeased or neglected. Given that Japanese people, whether non-Christian or Christian, will attach their own meanings to this term, is it any wonder that there is in Japan widespread misunderstanding of the Christian God and how people should behave in relation to Him?

A major part of our job as contextualizers is, then, to do whatever we can to help people arrive at meanings that are as close as possible to the Scriptures by which we seek to be guided. This will, however, involve a process of redefinition of terms that are chosen as labels for elements of Christian faith. For those Japanese who are able to redefine in a scriptural direction the term *kami*, by adding "great" (*sama* = *kami sama*) to the term, that cultural form will be adequate to symbolize the biblical meaning. I'm afraid, though, that the pre-Christian associations of that term may greatly interfere with the understandings of those who use the term to refer to the Christian God.

A major problem, however, is this: if the word *kami* is not used, what term should be used? It is usually a poor choice to borrow a term from another language. In Hausa, for example, the word *ekklesia* has been borrowed from Greek to designate the Christian church. Had one of the Hausa words for a gathering or a fellowship been used, the people would be able to understand such groupings as normal. As it is, the taint of foreignness is always on the church because of its foreign name. Insiders may in time overcome that taint. But those outside the church will tend to regard that term as an intrusion into their society rather than an understandable expression of certain members of the society.

With regard to the word for "church" in Hausa, the choice of *ekklesia* is regrettable, since there are other possibilities from within the language. With *kami*, however, Japanese Christians feel there is no better alternative. So their choice is to work toward transforming the meaning of the word. They want to "capture" that word for Christ as the first century Christians did with *kurios*, the Greek word for "Lord." *Kurios* was used as the title of Caesar, signifying his deity. The Christians chose this word to apply to Jesus and were executed when they refused to use it to refer to Caesar.

God wants His people to capture customs as well. Throughout the Old Testament we see God using customs of worship and sacrifice that were also used by pagans. When God and Abraham began working together, the message to Abraham was, "From now on use your culture for Me." So God was worshiped in "high places," just as pagan gods were. And blood sacrifices were offered to Yahweh, just as they were by pagans to their gods. Indeed, God even reintroduced the ritual of circumcision that was practiced by the surrounding people but had apparently lapsed among Abraham's people. Although the universal meaning of the custom was initiation into the tribe, God gave it an additional meaning: commitment to Him.

In contemporary Japan, I have suggested that the Christians experiment with the development of Christian shrines. People go to shrines when they seek blessing, protection, healing, and supernatural answers to specific requests. Shrines are known as places of power, and people go to them at any time of the day, not just on Sundays. Given their concern for spiritual power, the Japanese are unlikely to go to churches when they feel the need for power since churches don't look like places of power. And anyway, the churches are usually not open except at specified times during the week. A shrine in which people meet Christians who would pray with them concerning their needs would soon gain a reputation as a good place (an insider place) to go for help. It would also provide a good first step into Christian groupings (hopefully contextualized) in which people could grow in understanding and commitment to Christ.

One of the most important dynamics of contextualization, and a major concern for insiders, is the capturing of such terms and customs to invest them with new meanings that serve the purposes of Christianity. If such terms and customs are to undergo the transformation required for this to happen, the Christian community must put constant pressure on its people to attach Christian meanings to the terms and customs. If such pressure is not put on the users of the terms and customs, the meanings will continue to be traditional, with little or no Christian significance.

Our respondents will be selective, often unconsciously, of what they allow themselves to be exposed to, and they will evaluate everything they hear and see—again in terms of their past experiences with similar activities. When they see Christian churches that look foreign and Christian people who behave strangely, they will be open or closed to them on the basis of their attitude toward that foreignness. And they either will or will not grant permission to those who represent Christianity to enter into their "communicational space." Unless they feel that the foreign organization will meet some of the needs they feel, they are most likely to attempt to maintain their equilibrium by staying as close as possible to their previous understandings and involvements. That is, there must be something that attracts them to the foreign organization for them to risk the possibility of change and perhaps social disequilibrium.

In order to cope with the challenges of new appeals, people often build "communicational walls" around themselves to protect their present customs. In this way, they can avoid anything they hear that would put pressure on them to change their lifestyle. They can refuse to take seriously whatever they choose to ignore, or they may pick and choose the things that require the least change. Effective contextualization takes all these communicational things into account both in the introductory stages of gospel presentation and in the continuing experience of the growth of the Christian movement. Insider movements make the most of these facts about communication.

MEANING EQUIVALENCE CHRISTIANITY

Years ago (1979), I suggested the concept of "dynamic equivalence" used in Bible translation as a useful label for what we intend by the term "contextualization." An alternate term for dynamic equivalence that I now prefer would be "meaning equivalence."

The idea is that what people do in response to Christ today should carry, as close as possible, the same meanings as the ideals presented in the Scriptures. Not that those ideals are always readily deduced—as some of my critics have pointed out, the Bible does not always show us how even the early churches worked out their Christian experience. We do, however, know some of the ideals. And it is these meanings that Christians are to exhibit in behavior and thought that are appropriate both to Scripture and to their culture. Insiders are to work out their own expressions with this goal in mind.

We know, for example, such things as that Jesus Christ is to be the center of Christian life for each person, whether we are alone, at home with our family, or at church. We are to be committed to Him and to strive to be like Him. We are to love

God with all our heart, soul, mind, and strength and our neighbors as ourselves (Matt 22:37,39). We also know that Christians are to meet together in groups for fellowship, prayer, and Bible study. The New Testament shows that Christian fellowship groups were organized and that they believed certain cardinal doctrines concerning God, Jesus (Phil 2), sin (Rom 3:23; 6:23), salvation (John 3:16; Acts 16:31), etc.

From many of the things the Apostle Paul and other New Testament writers mentioned, we know a lot of specifics concerning the kind of behavior Christians are expected to exhibit. We know that Christian groups are to stand for righteousness and to discipline their members who willfully turn from righteousness. We are to exhibit the fruit of the Spirit (Gal 5:19), we are to do the works that Jesus did (John 14:12), we are to live as dependent on Jesus as He was dependent on the Father, and so on. The ideals are fairly clear.

The problems lie in how these ideals are to be appropriately expressed in any given society. What, for example, is an appropriate expression of love—an expression that insiders will interpret as love? Mission history is full of attempts by outsiders to show love that were interpreted as something else by the insiders. In northeastern Nigeria, our mission was deeply involved in attempting to show love through schools, medical clinics, and hospitals. These efforts, however, were largely understood by the cultural insiders as ways missionaries make money (clinics and hospitals) or converts to Euro-American culture (schools). And the fact that schools were the primary ways of recruiting people for the churches led people to assume that one couldn't become a Christian unless he or she went to school or at least learned to read.

One medical effort of our mission did, however, seem to get love across. The mission in the early years started a leprosarium, a place where lepers came to live. At the leprosarium, people in great need—a need that traditional medicine was unable to meet—received loving treatment from doctors and nurses and soon became part of a meaningful community, even across language and culture barriers. The way they were treated in the leprosarium contrasted markedly with the way they had been treated at home, and the message of God's love came across loud and clear. Though the church at the leprosarium was only partly contextualized, it seemed to be less dominated by the missionaries than the other churches in the area.

The difference between the leprosarium and the other mission stations seemed to center on the fact that important needs—both medical and social needs—were being met and that more time was invested in those who lived there. A Christian community was brought into existence, and in that community many grew spiritually to such an extent that in the early 1950s, when, due to the advent of new medicine, most of the residents were released from the community, many went back to their tribal areas and became important witnesses for Christ.

Christian meanings seem to have gotten across better in the leprosarium than elsewhere in the mission area. Christian meanings also got across better wherever the missionary or Nigerian pastor spent a lot of time with the people. We have said that meanings are *in* people. Christian meanings are also *through* people. So when the advocates of Christianity are personal, the meanings are more likely to get across than otherwise. The key to contextualization as the key to communication, then, is the insider person(s) who relate(s) to the receptors.

Meaning equivalence contextualization, therefore, is first a relational thing before it is anything else. In 1 John 1:1–3 we get a glimpse of the impact Jesus as a person had on His followers. The experience of the Apostles was so intimate that John speaks of "handling" Jesus and implies that this closeness with the Master has left them radically changed and anxious to pass on the messages they have received from Him.

But Jesus was brought up in the sociocultural context in which He worked. We who come from outside need to learn the culture in which we work—or at least enough of it to be able to show love in ways appropriate to the insiders' frame of reference. Personal concern may, however, be more easily demonstrated than many of the other things we try to get across, since people are more alike than are cultures (Goldschmidt 1966). We may be able to tap into our basic human-beingness to get across such concern if we take the trouble to try to do things in their way rather than in ours.

On one occasion I was discussing with a group of young cross-cultural witnesses working in inner-city Los Angeles the fact that they were not getting across to an old woman they wanted to win to Christ. They had been trying to get her to come to their meetings. They had witnessed to her various times as they passed by her home on their way to their various engagements. But all she seemed to want to do was to sit on her porch and rock in her rocking chair. I asked the group if any of them had thought of sitting and rocking with her. They hadn't. They were too intent on bringing her into their orbit so they could talk to her on their terms. Considering the validity of her life and her ways of behaving and thinking, however, set this group to thinking differently—relationally rather than informationally. As someone has said, she didn't care how much they knew until she knew how much they cared.

Meaning equivalence Christianity will be rooted in relationships meaningful to the people we seek to reach.

CONTEXTUALIZATION IS A MATTER OF NEGOTIATION

It is clear, then, that whatever the cultural and linguistic forms used in the presentation of Christianity, it is the receptors who will attach the meanings. The meanings they attach to the various messages we bring can, however, be influenced to some extent, at least within an inner circle of friends. Meanings can be negotiated.

We do this all the time. Someone says something we don't quite understand and we ask for that person to repeat or to illustrate the point. As the point is worked through again, we may or may not get it. If we do, we may turn to something else. If we don't, we ask for more clarification. In this way we conduct a transaction that hopefully will result in a fairly good understanding of what the person is saying.

Such negotiation is not very effective when the means of communication is monologue. It is greatly increased when the interaction is give and take, question and answer, statement and explanation. And this kind of interaction is best when it takes place in small groups. I believe this is why Jesus worked primarily with a group of twelve. And even when there was a larger group, He permitted questions and negotiated with His audiences.

The discipleship group that gathers around an advocate of any new message serves several purposes. The Twelve got to spend more time with Jesus and therefore got to interact with Him more than others. Presumably, they also got to understand Him better. They could therefore interpret Him to those who did not get to spend as much time with Him. The fact that they were in contact with these others, then, enabled them to be able to communicate to Jesus what these others were thinking. See, for example, their statement in response to Jesus' query concerning what others were saying about Him (Matt 16:13–20).

In negotiating for the meanings of Christian witness, then, it is important for the advocates to have a group of close friends who will be able to function in the communication process as Jesus' disciples did. I was privileged to have five such men. We did all kinds of things together and got to know and respect each other very well. They learned a lot about what I was thinking and I learned a lot about what their life was all about. We trusted each other, and they, not I, led the church. They and I negotiated to achieve understandings of how to apply Scripture in their context. And they negotiated with their own people to implement those understandings both inside and outside of the church. What went on in the churches and in the individual lives of the Christians, then, served as a means of negotiation for certain meanings with the society at large.

CONCLUSION

The aim of meaning equivalence Christianity is to see expressed in the lives and cultures of the receptors the meanings taught in Scripture. If we are to participate effectively in bringing about that kind of Christianity, it is important for us to learn as much as possible about receptor-oriented communication. And having learned the principles, with the Holy Spirit guiding, we need to apply them in a relational manner, as Jesus did. The primary vehicles of meaning equivalence Christianity are Christian advocates themselves. The method is negotiation, grounded in respect for the receiving people and their way of life.

CHAPTER 4
APPROPRIATE CONTEXTUALIZATION

As can be seen from the historical overview in the appendix, it was orthodox for years to speak of *indigeneity* as the ideal toward which we strive. Those who discussed and advocated indigeneity, even in its most formal sense, were sincerely striving for a type of Christianity for their converts that would be both maximally meaningful to insiders within their cultural contexts and maximally faithful to the Scriptures. We do well, even when we see flaws in their conceptualizations and applications, to honor their intent.

Likewise with those who saw the flaws in the older concept (indigeneity) and came to advocate what seem to be more enlightened understandings, under labels such as *contextualization, localization, inculturation, incarnation,* or my *dynamic or meaning equivalence* (Kraft 1979). Over the years, there have been quite a number of helpful discussions of the concept of contextualization. See the bibliography for a listing of the more significant of these. We have been helped greatly by them and by current experiments with contextualization. I believe, however, that there is much more to be said and done in this area.

For one thing, it is high time we began to deal with the contextualization of the whole of Christianity, not just theology. Theology is important, but we err if we only deal with truth, knowledge, and information about our faith. As noted below and presented throughout this volume, any adequate and appropriate treatment of Christianity needs to deal also with the contextualization of allegiance (or commitment) and spiritual power. For allegiance to Christ is the basis for all we do that makes us Christian, and spiritual power is Jesus' supreme demonstration of the God who heals, delivers, and frees.

Jesus was very much into spiritual power. And in spite of the neglect of this area in contemporary evangelicalism, if we are to be truly biblical, we must deal with it—especially since it is this power that brings freedom. This topic will therefore be regularly referred to throughout this volume, in an attempt to deal with a more complete Christianity than that presented in treatments of the contextualization of Christian theology alone.

FIRST, A CHANGE OF TERMINOLOGY

Perhaps terminology is not a major problem. It is not difficult to read those who write of inculturation or of localization and simply convert that term in our minds to our preferred term. But since meaning is in the minds of people, we need to recognize that there will be a variety of understandings of any of the terms we use. And the more technical the term, the less likely non-specialists are to hold to similar understandings of it.

I recently participated in a large meeting to discuss the topic of contextualization. About two-thirds of the way through the week we began to realize that we were not all speaking the same language. So it became necessary to appoint a small committee to develop a definition of what *contextualization* means. Another committee was appointed to define what we mean by *gospel*!

Perhaps things like that occur because we have become too technical. If our concept is simple—and this one is, even though its implementation is often quite complex—let's keep the terminology simple. For example, not everyone is aware of the fact that contextualization means doing whatever is necessary to make sure Christianity is expressed in ways that are appropriate to insiders and their context. They may or may not realize that the *context* part of the word refers to the context of the *receptors*, the insiders. And they may or may not realize that, at least when evangelicals use the word, they are specifically assuming that the messages conveyed and the expressions that result will be true to biblical Christianity as well as appropriate to the hearers.

Some, in fact, mistake us to be referring to a new kind of theology when we talk of the contextualization of theology. One theology professor at a distinguished seminary, thinking that we were advocating some new and different kind of theology, asked in my presence, "What is the difference between systematic theology and contextual theology?" And then, when we answered him, he had a difficult time understanding that what we mean is the way God went about doing things in the Bible. It had never occurred to him that contextualization was God's way of dealing with theological truth in relation to human culture and language, and that it therefore ought to be a part of the teaching of his subject, systematic theology.

With this in mind, let me suggest that we move to a less technical and perhaps more vague word. This is the word we use when defining what we mean by contextualization. It is the word *appropriate*. When people ask us what our word means, we say, *appropriate to the cultural context of the insiders and also to the Bible*. Since what we all seek is *appropriate Christianity*—a Christian expression that is appropriate both to a given social context and to the Scriptures—why not just say that our ideal is appropriateness in both directions.

APPROPRIATE AT BOTH ENDS

One problem with terms such as *contextualization* (and the other terms listed above) is that, besides being too technical, they don't automatically signify accountability to Scripture. These terms come from a valid concern for the relationship between the gospel and the receiving culture. They represent the period in missiological thinking when we were emerging from the naïve assumption that communicating Christianity is largely a matter of exchanging our *Christian* culture for their *pagan* culture. To overcome that fallacy, we began to focus on the receiving culture while simply assuming that we knew how to be appropriate to the Bible in message and method.

Since questions continually arise concerning what we are recommending at both the cultural and the scriptural ends of our task, I suggest we move to a term that takes us beyond the single focus of the terms we have been using. The term *appropriate* does just that, since it necessarily raises the question, "Appropriate to what?" And our answer will be twofold since our subject is twofold: gospel on one side and culture on the other. *Appropriate Christianity* will, therefore, be a Christianity that is appropriate to the *Scriptures*, on the one hand, and on the other, appropriate to the *people*, the insiders, in a given cultural context.

Where the term *contextualization* has helped us is with regard to the inculturating of Christianity at the receptors' end. It assumes we know what we are doing at the Scripture end. But we can't use the word *contextualization* at the Scripture end except to point out that Scripture illustrates how God approached people inside their cultural contexts in this way. We can only say, as Darrell Whiteman has said, that *good contextualization* will offend people (1997, 3). What he means is that a properly scriptural set of meanings that are properly contextualized, when measured against the sociocultural norms of the receptor society, will not be agreeable to everyone in that society or to those who brought the message. But no similar measure is in focus for the scripturalness of the meanings to be conveyed. We simply assume, though we know we shouldn't, that everybody knows and agrees on what constitutes scripturalness.

With the term *appropriate* we seek to keep ourselves alert to the fact that we need a measure on either side of the equation. A diagram might help (note the arrows):

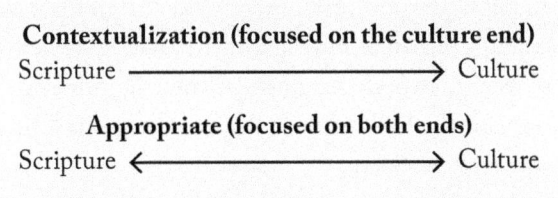

FIG. 4.1. Appropriate Christianity

APPROPRIATE TO SCRIPTURE

As noted above, I believe we have focused so much on appropriateness at the culture end that we may have neglected the Scripture end of our discussion. Several authors have written about this end of the process. Often, however, they have written more in a spirit of alarm than of helpfulness (e.g., Nicholls, Inch, Hesselgrave). More helpful—at least in outlining the approach we must take—has been the work of Paul Hiebert, especially in his article on what he calls "critical contextualization" (1984).

These authors and others have done a good thing to sound the alarm at this point, since liberals have often ignored biblical faithfulness in their attempts to be relevant to the receiving peoples. It is as if in this area, as in many others, they are wanting to do the Christian and biblical thing but are skipping the conversion step. For contextualizing, though properly biblical, is not truly Christian if the people experiencing it are not genuinely committed to Christ. I recently found students in India alarmed to hear me, an evangelical, espousing ideas concerning contextualization that they associated with some of the most liberal Indian theologians. They relaxed, however, when I made it clear that it is a relationship with Christ and not just with a brand of Christianity—in this case liberal Christianity—that I saw as at the center of contextualization studies. A firm and obvious commitment to the Bible as our standard and to a personal relationship with Christ as foundational distinguishes this approach to contextualization from that of the liberals.

In 1991 I published an article that focused on three encounters in Christianity: *allegiance, truth,* and *power* (1991, 258–65). Ours is a faith that has encounter at the core of it. It is not simply an "add on" to whatever a people already believes. And, as I pointed out in that article, it involves encounter in at least three areas. These areas of encounter I now see as representing three *crucial dimensions* of biblical Christianity. And these three crucial dimensions form a major part of the framework of this book. I will introduce them here and deal with them in more detail in chapter 5.

The dimensions may be labeled *relationship, understanding,* and *freedom*. Each proceeds from one of the encounters mentioned above. *Allegiance* is the basis for relationship, *truth* for understanding, and *power* for freedom. But these are dimensions, not separable entities. We cannot have Christian allegiance without some truth and enough power to allow freedom from our enemy, Satan. Nor can we experience God's truth without saving allegiance and, again, the freeing power of the Holy Spirit. Furthermore, the power we experience must be the true power of the true God, a power available to us only on the basis of our allegiance to Jesus Christ. It must never be the power of the counterfeiter, Satan.

If these dimensions are indeed crucial, each will be an area in which those members of a society who are serious about Christianity will confront their sociocultural ideals and behavior with the claims of Christ. I therefore suggest here that *appropriate to Scripture* should be understood to involve appropriateness in at least these three dimensions, two of which (relationship and freedom) have not been prominent, if mentioned at all, in the literature on contextualization. See the chart in chapter 5 for a summary of what each dimension includes.

Much of the discussion on contextualization seems to assume that the contextualization of the truth (theology) dimension is to be our major concern. Among numerous treatments of the contextualizing of theology, some may have mentioned thinking *about* one or both of these other dimensions of Christianity. The actual contextualization of relationship and freedom in appropriate ways, however, is seldom if ever referred to, at least in the literature I'm acquainted with.

Yet our concern here is the contextualization of Christianity, not just of Christian theology, though theological contextualization is an important part of the whole. But since our relationship with Christ is foundational, shouldn't we be also dealing with the contextualization of that relationship? We should not treat it as simply a byproduct of knowledge and truth (see chapters 10–12). Nor should we ignore the importance Jesus placed on the exercise of spiritual power in the communication of Christianity. Therefore, we speak of contextualization of spiritual power as well (see chapters 13–15).

APPROPRIATE TREATMENT OF TRUTH

Though more has been done in the area of contextualization of theology than in other areas, we need to question whether we have done enough. Have all of the nooks and crannies of this area been dealt with? For example, have we done enough with the judgment dimension of the use of Scripture? Have we held God's *TRUTH* up against cultural *truths* enough? Though we may have a fair idea of what the scriptural ideals are, have we adequately worked out the process by means of which we can attain such goals? In seeking to remedy this lack, I suggested in my book *Christianity in Culture* (1979) that God is willing to start at sub-ideal places and move people toward more ideal understandings and practices. Have we done enough with what might be termed *how to move appropriately toward God's ideals?*

This question points us toward what may be the greatest lack in theological thinking and instruction, both in cross-cultural contexts and at home: "How do we go about the process of theologizing?" In 1975, Daniel von Allmen wrote a seminal article entitled "The Birth of Theology," which is, I believe, still one of the clearest statements of the process by means of which theological thinking was developed during and after the New Testament period. Appropriate approaches to the truth/knowledge dimension of Christianity need to include biblically based treatments of the *process* of theologizing that can be taught in Western and non-Western theological institutions.

APPROPRIATE AT THE MEANING LEVEL

Let's be clear, though, that it is appropriateness of *meaning*, not simply of *form*, that we are advocating. But, as I point out below and in chapter 2, since meanings are in people, not in structures, our focus must be on people, not culture. So the question must be, do the meanings these people are attaching to the forms they are using correspond to the meanings God seems to have intended as indicated by the Scriptures? That is, are these meanings scripturally appropriate?

And here we are squarely into the problems of interpretation. "Scriptural by whose interpretation?" we may ask. "By the interpretation of the people themselves, not by that of outsiders," we should answer. A cross-cultural approach to hermeneutics thus becomes a pressing concern.

Alan Tippett had it right when he said that appropriate Christianity has come into existence when the meanings in the minds of the "indigenous people" have them seeing "the Lord as their own, not a foreign Christ" (1973, 158). Several years earlier, William Smalley also focused on meaning when he pointed to the fact that an appropriate (insider) church functions directly "under the guidance of the Holy Spirit [to] meet the needs and fulfill the meanings of that society and not of any outside group" (1958, 55–56). My own 1978 statement, likewise, points to the fact that appropriate Christianity "would preserve the essential meanings and functions [that] the New Testament predicated of the church, but would seek to express these in forms . . . appropriate to the local culture" (1978, 330).

So we are looking for appropriateness in the minds and hearts of the insiders who receive scriptural messages and who attempt to structure their responses in their own cultural patterns. The forms employed, then, need to focus on conveying the meanings that people, both inside and outside the churches, will attach to them. When outsiders look at church structures, are they attracted to them or repulsed by them? The meanings intended by the advocates could be scriptural, but the onlookers could perceive them either way, depending on the forms used.

Since it is the receptors, the insiders, who will interpret the forms and attach meanings to them, we must concern ourselves primarily with whether the meanings in their minds are scriptural or not. How will they interpret the forms used?

APPROPRIATE RELATIONSHIP

And what have we done about these other two dimensions? What does a biblically and socioculturally appropriate expression of commitment (allegiance) to and relationship with God through Christ look like for any given person or group in any given society?

Is the formal, seemingly nominal relationship to the church practiced by many in societies that consider themselves *Christian*, from State Church Europe to the South Pacific, an appropriate expression of Christian allegiance? What about the highly individualistic American evangelical Protestant version? Or the all-encompassing, total dedication of Japanese Pentecostals? And if any of these should be considered culturally appropriate, are they scripturally appropriate?

An Old Testament example of cultural appropriateness in relationship may illustrate what I have in mind here. God chose to define the relationship between Himself and the Jewish people in terms of socioculturally appropriate covenants. A covenant was a well-known type of agreement in Semitic societies involving the highest type of commitment. This was a two-way commitment, involving obligations on both sides, with the understanding that if one party to the agreement broke the agreement, the other was free of its obligations.

We learn about God's desire to be culturally appropriate from the fact that He chose this cultural form. Culturally appropriate? Very much so! Covenants and the processes in making and keeping them were well understood by the parties concerned. So God chose this culturally appropriate pattern for defining His relationship to the Jewish people and for enabling them to define their relationship to Him.

During the course of His relationship with Israel, however, we learn a very important fact about the character of God. This is that He chooses to patiently honor His agreements with humans for a long time even after human beings have broken theirs with Him. For even though the terms of a covenant allowed either party freedom from the covenant as soon as the other broke it, God did not exercise His right to be free from the covenant for a long, long time in spite of Israel's repeated unfaithfulness. And some of His covenants He has vowed to fulfill in the future anyway. What in today's societies are the culturally appropriate relationship structures that parallel Jewish covenants?

In asking about culturally appropriate commitments and the relationships flowing from them, we must distinguish between the ideal a people have for their commitments and relationships and the actual ways in which these are carried out in the society. Insight into cultural behavior worldwide indicates that actual behavior in every aspect of life will often be found to be sub-ideal. What we recommend as culturally appropriate, however, needs to be at the ideal level, no matter how infrequently such an ideal occurs in real life, since this is what the members of the society learn to aim at.

APPROPRIATE EXPRESSIONS OF SPIRITUAL POWER

With regard to spiritual power, the usual situation worldwide is that the enemy's power is not even contested. And when it is, that confrontation usually takes an imported form (as with Pentecostal missionaries in certain African Indigenous Churches), or it emulates shamanistic practices (as with some Korean Prayer Mountain deliverance practices). The latter is a worse scenario in that the *ministers* often beat the demonized in attempting to rid them of demons.

When spiritual power issues are not addressed, large segments of believers—many of whom have a genuine relationship with Christ—remain captive to the enemy in varying degrees. People who call themselves Christians faithfully attend church on Sundays but also seek the help of traditional healers and diviners operating under satanic power when they need healing, guidance, or any other power-related assistance. Although Jesus has promised that His power will accompany His followers (John 14:12), many of those Jesus-followers find no spiritual power in Christianity.

Given Jesus' promise, I assume that some sort of exercise of spiritual power is scripturally appropriate. But what would culturally appropriate spiritual warfare look like in any given society? For one thing, it would look like a challenge to whatever satanic systems are in operation. It would look enough like those systems to be recognizable by the people as well as by Satan as challenging them in appropriate ways.

The advocates of Christianity will need to learn to operate in the power of the Holy Spirit like Jesus did as he ministered with spiritual power in terms of the sociocultural realities of His time. In the same manner, Christian advocates today would need to work in spiritual power within their own sociocultural realities in order to free people from Satan's grip and demonstrate that God is alive, active, and using His power to communicate His love to them. The way such power is exercised would also be appropriate to the way God's power is manifested throughout Scripture. See chapters 13–15 for more on this subject.

APPROPRIATE TO PEOPLE

The terms *contextualization, localization, inculturation,* and especially the earlier term *indigenization,* fix our focus on culture rather than on people. Culture, in spite of the regular misuse of the term as a label for people, is a structural thing, not a people thing. And although the cultural forms employed for Christian purposes are very important, especially since people attach meanings to them, our primary concern has to be for the *people* who are observing, using, and interpreting them.

People and culture are quite different. For example, whereas people *do* things, culture doesn't do anything. As I have said before, culture is like a script, memorized by the actors but not necessarily followed by them in every detail. There are times when any actor forgets the lines he or she memorized. There are times when one actor makes a mistake and the other actor has to improvise. Or a part of the set may collapse, forcing the actors to scurry around seeking a solution to a problem that was not anticipated by the scriptwriter. In short, the behavior of actors illustrates quite well the ways in which personal cultural behavior relates to the cultural scripts we have been taught. Or, to use another analogy, culture is like a system of roads. The roads don't *go* anywhere; they simply lie there to be used by people. It is people who go places on (or off) the roads.

The point is, it is *people* who perform the activities we call cultural. Culture itself does not behave, people behave. So our approach to Scripture needs to be thought of as people-centered, not culture-centered. The technical word we use for people is *society*. A society is a group of people who habitually behave according to cultural patterns but who may change them at any time and in the process develop new habits to go along with the new patterns.

We therefore want a Christianity that is appropriate to the *people* and to their experience with God. This Christianity may or may not conform to the cultural patterns the people have inherited from their forebears. Indeed, they may be tired of at least some of those patterns and gladly adopt others. In any event, whether the people are seeking change or not, this appropriateness will commonly involve some, perhaps many, changes in the cultural structuring in terms of which they live their lives.

For some people, for example, it may be appropriate—and they even may desire—to become more westernized while they grow in their Christian experience. We outsiders may look at their churches and decry the fact that they are drifting away from their traditional customs. But again, much of the life and behavior of the non-Christians around them, especially those living in urban centers, doesn't look very traditional either. Our question, then, should be, what is appropriate for each segment of these people, given the sociocultural realities of life around them?

I'm afraid that in our conceptualizing of what contextualization means, some of us may have unwittingly fallen into the fallacy of what has been called *salvage anthropology*—an attempt at preserving the older way of life whether or not the people want it. Foreigners (especially Westerners) usually focus more on cultural structures than on people, and thus they are liable to lose sight of the more dynamic aspects of appropriate contextualization. Structures tend to be static. People are dynamic.

And yet, some people are not as caught up in modernizing as some others are. There are sizeable traditional populations in most of the societies of our world (including the United States). What is appropriate for traditional peoples may be quite different from what is appropriate for the westernizing segments of their own societies. It is inappropriate to offer people a Western variety of Christianity as their only choice. I wonder if this isn't a major problem with the non-Christian majority in Korea. While we rejoice in the fact that somewhere between 25 and 30 percent of the Korean population has turned to Christ, could it be that it will take a more traditional approach to Christianity to attract the other three-quarters of the population? And what about Japan, where Western Christianity has so far failed miserably to attract and keep adherents, even though polls show that Jesus has a very high reputation among Japanese?

On the other hand, when we offer only a traditional variety of Christianity to people who want to become more westernized, it is likewise inappropriate. There are places where the rural, more traditional form of Christianity practiced in the villages is totally inappropriate for the highly schooled, city-dwelling youth who grew up in a city and got schooled out of sync with their families. And yet, the imported Western Christianity of most city churches may be just as inappropriate to them as well. An appropriate alternative is in order.

We are trying to ask the basic questions concerning appropriateness to cultural structuring and to the people who use that structuring. We believe that God wants His church incarnated in the cultural way of life of every people group. Jesus fully participated in first-century Palestinian, even Galilean life, as an insider, not as a foreigner. He participated as a native son. So contemporary Christian communities should not be living like foreigners, outsiders, in their own lands, speaking their language with a foreign (usually Western) accent, performing foreign-looking rituals at odd times and in strange-looking places.

I believe we have been hurt by an overemphasis on the theological and structural concerns at the expense of the concern for persons. The appropriateness of cultural structuring, though very important, must always be secondary to appropriateness to the people.

Just as there are a variety of cultural approaches to life in any given sociocultural group, so there need to be varieties of Christianity. Each variety, each subculture, involves a culturally distinct approach to Christianity that is appropriate to its group but may be inappropriate to most of those in groups other than its own. And none of them should be imposed on any population as the only valid form of Christianity, though the more westernized of these types have regularly been so imposed.

COULD APPROPRIATENESS BE MEASURED?

An argument (though perhaps not a strong one) in favor of using the term *appropriate* instead of *contextualized* is that we may more easily think of measuring it. Things can be more appropriate or less appropriate either scripturally or socioculturally. The following diagram may help:

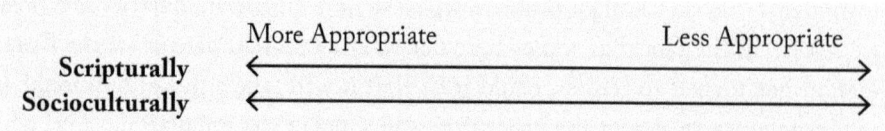

FIG. 4.2. Measuring appropriateness

As we have emphasized, we need to be concerned about practicing appropriateness at both the scriptural and the sociocultural ends of whatever we are dealing with. But as soon as we decide to speak of appropriateness, we raise the possibility of *more* or *less* in either area.

We may cite, for example, the many situations in which Christians go to native shamans to seek healing. We would have to say that such a practice, while *culturally* appropriate, is not *scripturally* appropriate. On the other hand, we frequently observe Christians meeting regularly on Sunday mornings for worship in foreign-looking meeting places. We can say that their practice of meeting regularly is scripturally appropriate, but that the foreignness of the place (and, often, of the time as well) makes their meetings culturally inappropriate.

An example of appropriateness at both ends of the spectrum comes from the experience of Bible translators Wayne and Sally Dye in Papua New Guinea. Three decades ago, the rather isolated Behinemo people (both Christians and non-Christians) would meet regularly on Sunday mornings to hear the latest translated portion of the Scriptures. Then their tribal leaders would lead them in discussions concerning the meaning and application of the passage read. This appears to have been appropriate both to the Scriptures and to the social setting at that time. Whether that approach is still appropriate among the Behinemo after three decades is another question.

COUNTEREXAMPLES?

In studying and advocating culturally appropriate Christianity, we dare not neglect the many churches in the world that appear to be counterexamples. In considering them, then, we can begin to look critically at our theories. We need to study what is really going on in the churches around the world even if they don't confirm our theories. Though we do not focus on this topic in the chapters that follow, we need to ask, where are the studies of counterexamples?

Such studies would look at many of the largest, apparently most *successful* churches (e.g., in Korea, the Philippines, Singapore, Nigeria) that appear to be poorly contextualized. We will need to ask, Are there factors that override cultural fit? If so, what are they? Are we missing something in our commitment to our theory?

A start toward dealing with the counterexamples would be to look at the relationship of spiritual power to the growth of these large, largely uncontextualized churches. To the casual observer it appears that most of them are healing churches, churches that regularly pray for healing and deliverance. Though these churches may be very Western in most features and even in some cases quite anti-traditional in culture, they would be speaking to a major felt need of most of the peoples of the world by involving themselves in demonstrating the power of God to heal and deliver. Perhaps the exercise of spiritual power is more important to people than cultural appropriateness. Should this be true, we ought to be aware of it.

But some of these churches, though large, are apparently not into spiritual power. They are just Western. Can their growth be attributed solely to the desire of their members to westernize? Or are there other factors we should know about?

I'll leave this subject here, not because it is not important but because we know so few of the answers we need to know if we are to write intelligently about the subject of counterexamples.

APPROPRIATE THEORY AND PRACTICE

In the chapters that follow, I attempt to speak for a number of us who have been practicing, thinking about, and teaching contextualization. We will attempt to deal with appropriate theory and practice for the pursuit of appropriate Christianity. We will attempt to deal with a number of issues related to this topic. This includes the relationship and power dimensions mentioned above, and also such topics as questions of timing, leadership, epistemology, renewal, and contextualizing in Western societies. It is our hope that the chapters in this book will help those who, like us, are striving towards appropriate *expressions* of Christianity among the peoples of the world. We further hope that our debate will be fruitful as we seek to learn and stimulate one another in our common pursuit of our God-given tasks.

WHAT WE ARE TO TAKE

CHAPTER 5
CONTEXTUALIZATION IN THREE CRUCIAL DIMENSIONS

It is obvious from what has already been said that much has been written on contextualization, including such synonyms as *localization, inculturation,* and *indigenization.* In spite of all this attention, however, I believe we have dealt too narrowly with our subject. Our bibliographies show that most of our studies have focused on the important *cognitive* and *structural* dimensions of our subject. But where are treatments of the more *experiential* side of Christian life and practice—theology as it is lived, not simply as it is thought about?

Given the fact that the Bible's primary concern is our relationship to God, a relationship that starts with commitment or allegiance to Him, where are the contextualization studies dealing with this issue? What are the culturally appropriate varieties of commitment and relationship to God through Jesus Christ? And since spiritual power is high on the list of concerns for most of the peoples of the world, where are the contextualization studies in this area? Doesn't the Bible have a lot to say about the exercise of spiritual power? And might there not be culturally appropriate differences in the ways God's authority and power are to be exercised from society to society?

In 1991 and 1992, I published articles dealing with three encounters that are crucial to the experience and communication of the gospel of Jesus Christ. I labeled these encounters *allegiance* (or commitment), *truth,* and *power.* As I have pondered these encounters, I have come to the conclusion that these areas are even more important than I had realized.

In my articles, I pointed out that each of these encounters leads to a very important dimension of Christian experience: *relationship, understanding,* and *freedom.* Each of these areas is a crucial dimension of the God-connected life. I now believe the areas of encounter are pointing to *three crucial dimensions* of Christian experience and witness. If they are this important, then, we need to theorize concerning contextualization in each of these areas, rather than dealing only with the truth (knowledge) area. We may diagram these dimensions as follows:

	leading to	
Allegiance/Commitment	⟶	Relationship
Truth/Knowledge	⟶	Understanding
Power (Spiritual)	⟶	Freedom

FIG. 5.1. Three crucial dimensions of Christian experience

WHAT I MEAN BY "DIMENSIONS"

A *dimension* is an aspect of Christianity that, though closely interrelated with the other dimensions, is quite distinct in its content and must therefore be defined and treated as a distinct entity. We can focus on this distinctness in several ways. One way is to look at the distinctness of the human problems in view under each category.

Knowledge, for example, is the appropriate antidote for ignorance and/or error. Spiritual power is what is needed when the problem is satanic captivity, harassment, or temptation. Allegiance/commitment to Jesus Christ is what is needed to replace any other allegiance that a person has made primary in his or her life. We cannot, however, fight a wrong primary allegiance simply with either knowledge or power. *We can only fight one allegiance with another allegiance.* Likewise, we cannot fight error or ignorance with either an allegiance or with power. *These must be fought with knowledge and truth.* So also with power. We cannot fight power with knowledge or truth, *only with power.* In other words, *we fight allegiance with allegiance, truth with truth, and power with power.*

There are those in the evangelical community who are *cult watchers.* Though they know a lot about cults, they often only poorly understand *power.* They are therefore very good at exposing the errors of the cults, but they may not be good at dealing with their power. In fact, some of these cult watchers, in their lack of understanding of power, actively condemn legitimate Christian power ministries along with the cult groups (see Priest, Campbell, and Mullen 1995).

Another way of distinguishing these dimensions is to look at the differences in the content of each dimension. I will go into greater detail below, but I here present an overview of these differences. In the relationship dimension we find things like love, the fruits of the Spirit, faith, repentance, prayer, fellowship, intimacy with Christ, and all of the other things in Christian experience that factor into our relationships with God and other humans.

These aspects of life are quite different in experience from the things we deal with in our thinking behavior. Although we can think about, talk about, and teach about relationships, none of these knowledge aspects of the subject is the same as *participating in a relationship.* Indeed, many who demonstrate a considerable expertise in thinking about relationships don't seem to do well in relating to others. Similarly, working in spiritual power is quite distinct from thinking about it. Spiritual power is also quite distinct from relating.

The truth/understanding dimension includes all of the cognitive aspects of Christianity. Doctrinal and theological tenets such as our understandings of God, Jesus, the Holy Spirit, humanity, sin, redemption, faith, Satan and demons, the church, the kingdom of God, and the rest of the things we believe fall into this category. So do the things we understand concerning the allegiance/relationship and power/freedom dimensions. This dimension is the easiest of the three to deal with since it largely involves the mere transmitting of *information*. And transmitting truth, though it is better done when people are free from satanic power and linked together in solid relationships, is not as complicated as either relating or dealing with spiritual power.

The spiritual power dimension involves working in the power of the Holy Spirit to bless, heal (both physically and emotionally), cast out demons, and challenge territorial spirits. As with relationships, it involves *doing* something, not just thinking and talking about it. Jesus taught and demonstrated that we are at war with a powerful enemy but that we have authority and power to defeat him (Luke 9:1). The exercise of that power under the direction of the Holy Spirit constitutes a dimension distinct from the other two but working in conjunction with them, since the power we use must come from the true Source of power and the authority to work in that power from our relationship with Him.

THE PROBLEM

In the aforementioned articles, I focused on the fact that most Euro-American evangelicals have known virtually nothing of the spiritual power dimension of Christianity. Unfortunately, in certain circles at least, there is also a tendency to degrade or ignore the experiential, relationship dimension as well (see Kraft 2002).

Church historians tell us that whenever there is renewal, the experiential component comes into focus in a major way. This focus tends to be maintained in pietistic and Pentecostal groups, though often allowed to dim in "more respectable" evangelical circles—except perhaps at conversion and revival times. In mainline liberal groups, experiential emphases tend to be discouraged or even castigated. The conversions involved in renewal movements, pietism, or the like, bring new people into the church on the basis of new relationships to God and the Christian community. And these newcomers need training if they are to move toward maturity.

The training we offer, however, tends to move the focus from growing in the allegiance/relationship dimension to acquiring knowledge in the understanding (cognitive) dimension. Unfortunately, this change of focus often does great damage by leading to neglect of the much more important process of growth in Divine-human and human-human relationships. Whether in pre-membership classes in our churches or in the classrooms of our Bible schools, Christian colleges, and seminaries, *people are weaned away from the centrality of their relational experience with God into an emphasis on learning information about the faith.* This is one of the main reasons why many "lose their faith" (that is, their closeness to Christ) in Christian colleges and seminaries. And because people lose their faith in academic institutions, many Christians, particularly those at the more conservative end of the spectrum and those who value the relational/experiential dimension most highly, have become anti-academic.

When the emphasis is on the truth/knowledge dimension, the focus becomes *knowledge about* Christian things, including the relational and the freedom dimensions, rather than *experience of* these things. The result is that many people who are well trained in Christian institutions can discourse very learnedly even about subjects such as relationship and spiritual power—subjects with which they have had little or no experience.

Evangelicals who come from this knowledge-oriented stance tend to make statements against emphasizing experience, as if experience is something to be afraid of, not to be trusted and, therefore, to be avoided. This has led to the experiential/relational dimension functioning largely underground. For example, even though all knowledge is grounded in experience and all interpretation pervasively affected by experience, many evangelical knowledge brokers perpetuate *the fantasy that what they are teaching is objective Truth unadulterated by their subjective interpretations*. Whether they admit it or not, however, all of what they teach as *objective* truth is strongly conditioned by their or someone else's experientially influenced interpretations. And both their experience and their interpretations are conditioned, perhaps unconsciously, by the kind of relationship they have with God and their fellow human beings.

The fact is that all we know is totally conditioned by both our conscious and our unconscious interpretation of our experience and our relationships. When someone teaches theology, for example, the real quality of what they teach is dependent on the nature of their relational experience with the God whose Truth they claim to proclaim. A distant relationship with God, the Source of theology, or with the subject being dealt with (e.g., pastoring, deliverance), yields a mere theoretical knowledge of those subjects that at least reduces, if not destroys, the relevance of what is being taught.

NEEDED: BALANCE

I am not contending that relationship and experience be emphasized more than understanding. However, given that there is no salvation without that relationship, we must give it proper priority. That relationship saves, whether or not we have a lot of knowledge to go with it. My plea is for balance, a balance that goes three ways. The academic nature of what we call theology, and the classroom context in which we teach, have led us to largely ignore two of these dimensions.

Jesus called the Twelve to first *be with Him* and only then to communicate and engage in power ministry (Mark 3:14). His teaching of Truth was, I believe, intended to serve these relational and ministry ends, not to be an end in itself. I have recently read and responded to two articles critical of some of what I am doing because, the authors contend, my theology may have some flaws in it. The impression I am left with is that these authors feel that what God really wants in this world is correct theology, whether or not people get helped. I am convinced, however, that Jack Deere was on the right track when he titled his chapter in *Power Encounters in the Western World* (1988) "Being Right Isn't Enough." By this he meant to indicate his repentance for seeking *right* theology over participating with God to bring freedom to those whom God loves.

My "encounter" articles point to an imbalance among evangelicals in our neglect of the power/freedom dimension of biblical Christianity. The additional neglect of the allegiance/relationship dimension may make the situation even worse than I suggested, at least among the academically inclined. Perhaps we may have done injustice to the relational dimension out of fear of anything that is not easily explainable in rational categories.

We have recommended allegiance/relationship experience as the way to salvation. But, at least in academic circles, we have often downplayed the validity of interpretations of Scripture and life based on experience. Instead, we go full tilt for the knowledge/understanding dimension as if that were the most important. But even in this knowledge/truth dimension we tend to go off the track because our understanding of knowledge and truth has been conditioned by Western Enlightenment rather than scriptural ideas. When we think of knowledge, for example, our *interpretational reflex* is to think of intellectual, theoretical knowledge. This kind of knowledge and truth is not, however, what the scriptural authors had in mind. The knowledge/truth spoken of in Scripture is *experiential truth*, not intellectual, theoretical truth/knowledge. If we are to be true to the original Greek (and the Hebrew worldview behind it), John 8:32 would need to be translated "You will *experience* [not *know in a theoretical sense*] the truth and the truth will set you free."

People die spiritually in seminaries and Bible colleges (not to mention churches) because the relational dimension that is so foundational to Christian experience is submerged, ignored, or even spoken against in our quest for *knowledge about* whatever subject we are investigating. Sometimes those subjects are relational things like conversion, spiritual growth, prayer, love, the fruit of the Spirit, faith, and any of the other aspects of Christianity that belong to this dimension. But knowledge *about* is quite a different thing from actually *experiencing* these aspects of allegiance/relationship. And the focus on knowledge *about*, plus the time and energy required in our schools and churches to learn information, militates against the practice of the very things we are learning about.

In order to further define what I see in these dimensions, I offer the following discussion.

THE ALLEGIANCE/COMMITMENT/RELATIONSHIP DIMENSION

The first and most important of the three dimensions is what I call the *relationship* dimension. This is the dimension the other two dimensions are intended to support. We may picture this fact as follows:

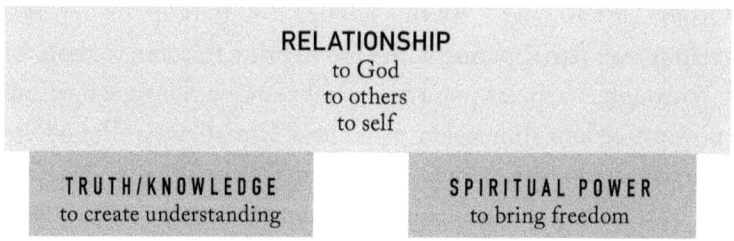

FIG. 5.2. Relationship supported by the other two dimensions

This dimension begins with an initial allegiance/commitment to Christ that we usually refer to as conversion, and issues in a continual growth in commitment and intimacy with Christ. The dynamic of this dimension is growth, a process that involves change toward Christlikeness on the part of the convert and movement into closer and closer relationships with Christ and with His people. As we grow, we are to become more and more conformed to the image of Christ, becoming more and more like Him to whom we have committed ourselves.

Our allegiance to Christ and the ensuing relationship is to replace any other allegiance/relationship that is primary in one's life. All other allegiances are to be secondary to this one. In His own family-oriented society, Jesus spoke in no uncertain terms of the need to put Him first, saying, "Whoever comes to me cannot be my disciple unless he loves me more than he loves his father and his mother, his wife and his children, his brothers and his sisters, and himself as well" (Luke 14:26). In this way, Jesus commanded those for whom allegiance to family was supreme to put family second and Himself first.

The allegiance/relationship dimension is quite distinct from the other two dimensions and in many ways more important than either of them. For no one becomes a Christian simply through knowledge or power. As James says, even demons have enough understanding to cause them to tremble in fear (Jas 2:19). They have all the knowledge they need but none of the relationship required for salvation. Yet we are often taught to witness primarily by increasing the person's knowledge, as if that knowledge is going to bring him/her into the kingdom. This is a radically different dimension from the knowledge dimension, though related to it. And we can't simply click into a relationship on the basis of what we know.

The problem we face, though, is how to cultivate and pass on this relationship. As Christians, we need to be constantly attentive to growing "in the grace and [experiential] knowledge of our Lord and Savior Jesus Christ" (2 Pet 3:18). For me, since I have learned well to read the Bible mainly for information, this has involved changing certain habits in order to *learn to read the Scriptures relationally. I have been teaching myself to experience the events of Scripture as I read them.*

The thing that propelled me in that direction is something we will discuss below under the power/freedom dimension. I began to experience the presence of Jesus in ministry. I began doing some of the *works* Jesus promised we would do in John 14:12, His works of power and of love. Participating with Jesus in doing the kinds of things He did while on earth has driven me ever closer to Him in the *abiding in Him* relationship He spoke about in John 15.

Leading others into a relationship with Christ, then, is a major challenge. It is much easier to contribute information to them than to bring them into Jesus' family. But, though many are able to establish a relationship on their own once they have heard the message, as a general principle *it takes a relationship to bring about a relationship.* This is why certain groups advocate *friendship evangelism,* a way of bringing people to Christ that involves the witness in first establishing a friendship relationship with potential converts.

I remember helping a young woman who had been seeing a Christian psychologist for some time. I had learned that the psychologist had gone way out of her way to help this young woman, going to be with her at all hours of the night, even driving some distance to rescue her when one of her personalities (she was a multiple personality suffering from Dissociative Identity Disorder) had taken her far from home. I asked the client what her relationship was with Jesus Christ. She replied that she probably didn't have one and went on to describe her deep disappointment at the way she had been treated in various churches.

Wondering what to do, I ventured the question, "Would you accept [your therapist's] Jesus?" Her face brightened as she said, "Yes, I'll accept *that* Jesus." And she did. Her relationship with the Christian therapist enabled this very damaged woman to experience genuine love. This experience, then, made it easy to lead her into a relationship with the Source of that love.

The following list summarizes my understanding of the allegiance/relationship dimension:

THE ALLEGIANCE DIMENSION (PRIMARY CONCERN: *RELATIONSHIP*)

1. This is the most important of the three dimensions.
2. It starts with conversion—a commitment to Christ—to establish a saving relationship with God through Jesus Christ.

3. The aim is to replace any other allegiance/relationship as primary—all other allegiances are to be secondary to this one.
4. It continues as growth in one's relationship with Christ and with others, expressed as loving God with one's whole heart and one's neighbor as oneself.
5. It includes all that the Bible teaches on subjects like love, faith/faithfulness, fellowship, the fruits of the Spirit, intimacy with Christ (e.g., John 15), forgiveness, repentance, reconciliation, obedience, etc.
6. True intimacy and relationship should not be confused with knowledge about intimacy and relationship.
7. All other allegiances are to be countered with commitment to Christ.
8. Under this dimension, the church is to be experienced as family.
9. Witness to one's personal experience is key to communicating this dimension.
10. Theology is experienced in worship and submission to God (Rom 12:2).

THE TRUTH/KNOWLEDGE/UNDERSTANDING DIMENSION

This is the dimension most familiar to us. Jesus spent a high proportion of His time and energy in the teaching of truth. He wanted people to understand as much as possible about His Father, Himself, and all that the relationships between God and humans and between humans and other humans should involve. He punctuated His teaching with regular power encounters and appeals for allegiance. He regularly *demonstrated*, not just talked about, both the allegiance/relational and the power/freedom dimensions as a part of His teaching of truth.

One of the crucial aspects of Jesus' method was to enfold His teaching of truth in a relational context—discipleship. He chose twelve men to teach by example in the context of the day-in, day-out activities of living together and ministering to people in love and power. He used His freedom-giving power to minister relational love to others within a discipling relationship with His closest followers (including many disciples other than the Twelve, plus several women). But He wrapped all of this in a truth-teaching context. His was a balanced approach to *doing* and *thinking about the doing*. He never allowed His ministry to become a merely *thinking about* ministry.

Unlike Jesus, we in our Bible schools, colleges, seminaries, and churches tend to focus strongly on *knowledge about* some aspect of Christian life rather than on actually experiencing that aspect. We hope, often in vain, that people who hear about repentance and converting to Christ will come to repent and convert. We hope that people who hear about faithfulness or intimacy or love or reconciliation or grace or any of the other relational aspects of Christian life will, through hearing about them, grow in their experience of them. We also hope that those who hear about the freedom we can receive and impart to others through the use of the authority and power Jesus has given us will go ahead and use that authority and power. Unfortunately, there is often little or no transfer from *knowledge about* to *experience of* in many of these areas because we don't have the holistic balance Jesus had.

Nevertheless, we continue to fill people's minds with information, knowledge, and truth to the point of intellectual indigestion, because our training techniques seldom include actually doing what we are talking about—with one notable exception. In Christian training institutions focused on producing pastors, there are usually courses designed to train people to preach in which the students actually have to produce and deliver sermons. Well and good. They actually learn how to do something by doing it. Yet what they learn is seldom more than how to present information about Christian topics. Many have overdosed on information. If they are to learn anything about how to interact with people relationally to bring about healthy relationships with God and humans, they have to learn these things elsewhere. And if they are to learn how to operate in God's power to bring the freedom their people crave, they have to learn this outside of the curricula of the schools supposedly established to train them to do pastoral work.

Ideally, then, we should be teaching truth as Jesus did—*relationally*—to combat ignorance and error. We should know, however, that whenever the Scripture speaks of knowledge and truth, it is referring to *experiential* knowledge and truth, not merely the *intellectual* byproducts of these factors. And we should be led in teaching truth by the Holy Spirit, who is also both the Producer of the relational fruits of the Spirit and the Giver of the power-oriented gifts of the Spirit. That is, He is in charge of all three of these crucial dimensions.

THE TRUTH DIMENSION (PRIMARY CONCERN: *UNDERSTANDING*)

1. This dimension involves teaching led by the Holy Spirit (John 16:13).
2. Scripturally, both truth and knowledge are experiential, not simply cognitive.
3. Truth provides antidotes for ignorance and error.
4. Though spiritual truth is pervasively relational and experiential (John 8:32), it is also cognitive and informational.
5. This dimension embodies truth and knowledge of all aspects of Christian experience.
6. We are to learn in this dimension about the contents of the other two dimensions.
7. We are expected to grow in this knowledge dimension as in all other dimensions of Christian experience.
8. Satanic and human lies are to be countered with God's truths.

9. Under this dimension, the church is to be experienced as a teaching place (discipleship, mentoring, classroom).
10. Theology is both cognitive and experiential.

THE POWER/FREEDOM DIMENSION

Jesus said He came to set captives free (Luke 4:18). In making such a statement, He implied both that there is one who has captured many people and that people need the freedom God offers. People need freedom so badly that He, Jesus, came to earth to offer this freedom. He then demonstrated throughout His ministry what He meant by this statement.

We read in Philippians 2:5–8 that Jesus laid aside His divinity and worked totally as a human being in the power of the Holy Spirit while He was on earth. He did nothing until after His baptism to indicate to the world—including the people of His hometown, Nazareth—that He was, in fact, God incarnate. Then, functioning wholly as a human being under the leading of the Father (John 5:19) and the power of the Holy Spirit (Luke 4:14), He began to set people free from captivity to the enemy, whom He blamed for sickness, lameness, blindness, demonization, and the like. Jesus worked in the authority and power given Him by the Father, *never once using His divinity while on earth.*

Jesus did all this to demonstrate God's love (a relational thing), to teach us what God and the Christian life are all about (knowledge/truth things), and to free people from Satan (a power thing). Thus He showed us how we should go about our lives as participants in the kingdom of God, which Jesus planted in the middle of Satan's kingdom. He gave to us the same Holy Spirit under whom He worked, saying that *whoever has faith in Him will do the same things He did, and more* (John 14:12). Since the enemy is doing power things today, as in Jesus' day, Jesus gave us His authority and power (Luke 9:1) to carry on the freedom-giving activities of kingdom builders.

When Jesus left, He gave us power in His name. We are therefore to operate in His authority to bring about the same ends He came to bring. We are to focus on bringing people into a relationship with God as Jesus did. But we are to recognize, as He did, that many are in captivity and therefore in need of freedom from the hold of the enemy. Only when they are freed will they be fully able to understand the gospel and, building on that understanding, to commit themselves to Christ.

This is the dimension that Western and westernized people understand the least. Many in the West fail to see either the extent of the satanic blinding (mentioned in 2 Cor 4:4) or the possibility of breaking through that blinding by working in the power

Jesus gave us. But if we are to imitate Jesus, our ministries should be filled with instances of healing and deliverance as well as authoritative praying and teaching. The evangelists of Argentina (see Kraft 2015 and Annacondia 2008) have been demonstrating to us the effectiveness of an approach to evangelism that starts with breaking the enemy's power over people before witness takes place.

According to the Western model, many are still captive to emotional hurts and demons even after witness and conversion. How different our churches would be if, like the early Christians, classes leading to church membership employed the power of God to heal and "clean up" the new converts before they joined the church! God's power is available both at the start and throughout a Christian's life to bring healing and deliverance.

Many Christian leaders ignore the fact that their followers remain captives, even after conversion. Then they consciously or unconsciously heap blame on their constituents by teaching that all hurts will be gone when we convert. Others attempt to rectify this situation by throwing knowledge about spiritual warfare at converts. But the power of Satan cannot be countered merely by knowledge and truth. Knowledge and truth are very important in their place, but *power can only be fought with power*. So those Christians still under the power of Satan—wielded through wounds of the past and demonization—will get little or no help from sound teaching on spiritual warfare if they do not experience the application of God's healing and delivering power to their specific problems.

THE POWER DIMENSION (PRIMARY CONCERN: *FREEDOM*)

1. The power in focus here is spiritual power (not political, personal, etc.)
2. This dimension recognizes that humans, even Christians, are held captive by Satan.
3. Jesus worked in the power of the Holy Spirit to set captives free (Luke 4:18,19). He did nothing under the power of His own divinity (Phil 2:5–8).
4. Jesus passed this power on to His followers (Luke 9:1; John 14:12; Acts 1:4–8).
5. Satanic power must be defeated with God's power. It cannot be defeated simply with truth or a correct allegiance, though these help.
6. Under this dimension, the church is experienced as both a hospital where wounds are healed, thus freeing people, and an army that attacks the enemy, defeating him both at ground level and at cosmic level.
7. Awareness of the power dimensions of Christianity needs to be taught both cognitively and, especially, experientially (as Jesus did).
8. Theology is experienced as victory in warfare resulting in freedom to relate and think.

WAYS IN WHICH THE DIMENSIONS FUNCTION TOGETHER

All three dimensions are present in every activity of God in the human sphere. If a given interaction with humans is from God, it will involve the power and love of the true God in operation. Any teaching of God's truth, furthermore, will involve the power of God with the aim of bringing about growth in relationship with God. In contrast, whenever the enemy's power is active, it is a counterfeit power rather than God's true power, and it is designed to lead people into a wrong allegiance.

I have spoken above of the frequent need for God's power to be in operation before people can understand enough to pledge allegiance to Jesus Christ. It is the power of God engaged through prayer, then, that enables us to grow stronger in our commitment to Christ and in our knowledge of His truth. Likewise, it is prayer-power that enables us to minister to others the truth that leads to Christian commitment.

As indicated above, I suggest a threefold approach to bringing people into church membership. What is usually done is simply to increase the potential member's knowledge and to make sure that he or she has experienced a conversion to Christ. This ought to happen, but much more needs to be done for most people if they are to experience freedom through the healing and delivering power of Christ and to grow in their relationship with Christ.

I have no statistics to prove it, but if my experience in ministering to hundreds of hurting Christians is any indication, I suspect that a high percentage of church members (and church leaders) are in great need of being healed from deep emotional hurts and freed from demons. The lack of freedom is crippling our churches. *An approach to these problems that focuses as much on spiritual freedom and relationship as it usually does on truth and knowledge could revolutionize Christian experience and expression.*

CONTEXTUALIZATION IN THREE DIMENSIONS

How does all of this relate to the contextualization of Christianity in which insiders practice Jesus' approach to intimacy and ministry? First of all, it should become clear to us that we are to deal with contextualization in three dimensions, not just one. It has been our habit to speak of the contextualization of theology for insider Christ-followers. How about the insiders' relationship with each other as a pattern for their relationship with God? Or the experience of spiritual power and the freedom that issues from the correct use of the correct power? These are subjects for encounters. They are also subjects for contextualization.

With regard to contextualization of relational experience, we should not be content with simply communicating *knowledge about* an experience with God. What should that experience look like in other cultural contexts? And how is it brought about (not simply how is it described)?

There have been some discussions of conversion in cross-cultural contexts. We have learned that in many societies, conversion needs to take place in people movements, rather than *one by one against the stream* (McGavran 1970). Well and good. These studies need to be included in discussions of contextualization. In addition to what we have done on conversion, however, we must pay more attention to the dynamics of relational growth and the attaining of spiritual and emotional freedom in various sociocultural contexts.

Jesus taught through discipleship. First of all, He demonstrated relationship by practicing it, both with His Father and with His disciples. In this context, then, He demonstrated how to work in authority and power to set people free. And He coupled His demonstrations with the teaching of truth, designed to explain experience and undergird further experience. We should contextualize incarnational relationship, ministry, and teaching. We make this difficult for ourselves by being attached to a school-based approach to teaching and an intellect-focused approach to theologizing.

Do we know how to contextualize all three of these dimensions? I doubt it. We will need more experimentation as we seek to contextualize our ministries in appropriate ways.

HOW DO WE CONTEXTUALIZE NON-COGNITIVE ELEMENTS OF BIBLICAL CHRISTIANITY?

It is clear that most of the current discussions of contextualization relate to how we contextualize in the cognitive dimension. On occasion we speak of contextualizing church structures. This gets us a bit away from the purely cognitive into the realm of thinking about *doing* certain of the necessary things. When we think about allegiance/relationship or power/freedom, likewise, we are getting a bit away from the purely intellectual aspects of theologizing. But we are still in our heads rather than into experiencing what Christianity is all about.

Turning to thinking about actually contextualizing in these other two dimensions, the question we need to ask is, what are biblically, culturally, and personally appropriate expressions or contextualizations of the allegiance/commitment-leading-to-relationship dimension?

It is likely that there will be culturally different ways of expressing allegiance and commitment. In many societies *loyalty,* a form of allegiance, is very important. Should not the ways in which loyalty is expressed in family, clan, tribe, or nation in each society be studied as possible models for the expression of commitment to God and His people?

Biblically, we know that we must teach the importance of Christians living out the fruit of the Spirit (Gal 5:22,23) in every society. But what are culturally appropriate ways of expressing love, joy, peace, patience, kindness, goodness, faithfulness, humility, and self-control? Surely there will be differences, perhaps great differences, in cultural behavior attached to these qualities. Cultural uniqueness in expressing these qualities, then, should be expected and encouraged in contextualized Christianity.

I have mentioned that some study has been done of people movement conversion. Undoubtedly, there are a variety of culturally appropriate ways of expressing such a major change. What are they, and how can people be encouraged to convert in their own ways and then develop culturally appropriate rituals to signify such change? In adopting baptism, for instance, the early church chose a culturally appropriate form that was in use in several religious contexts to signify the change in allegiance that we call conversion. It would seem appropriate that a truly contextualized church in one society would develop different initiation rituals than one in a different society. Likewise, it would be appropriate for the members of a church in one society to differ along cultural lines from those in another society in their conversion experience.

The way people in different societies experience growth in their relationships with God and with other believers will also differ. There will be differences in their forms of repentance, forgiveness, and reconciliation. For example, in some African societies forgiveness is expressed by spitting on or at the feet of the forgiven person. Differences will likewise be found in their forms of prayer, fellowship, and "familyness," and in the way people express their obedience and faithfulness to God and to their Christian brothers and sisters.

All of these issues and many more fit into the allegiance/relationship dimension. Cultural differences need to be discussed. But more than that, relational factors need to be *experienced*.

What, then, are biblically, culturally, and personally appropriate expressions or contextualizations of the spiritual-power-leading-to-freedom dimension?

It is likely that there will be culturally different ways of expressing spiritual power and also of experiencing freedom from demonic oppression. As important as this area is to the peoples of most societies, we can expect a variety of approaches. What are they, and can any of them be models for the expression of God's power?

We may expect appropriate cultural differences in approaches to power encounter (see chapter 15). In the beginnings of Christianity in the South Pacific, power encounters often involved the challenging of the traditional gods by their priests or chiefs who had converted to Christ. These were usually initiated by cultural insiders, the converted priests or chiefs, perhaps under the influence of the missionaries (Tippett 1971). The power encounter initiated by Elijah against the prophets of Baal resulted from a command by God to a cultural insider. In the case of Moses challenging Pharaoh, the encounter was commanded by God and was carried out by a partially inside advocate on behalf of cultural outsiders. In the temptations of Jesus, it was Satan who initiated the encounter. In most of Jesus' healings and casting out of demons, the Lord initiated the encounter at the request of the affected persons. What are the various kinds of culturally relevant approaches to power encounters in today's societies?

Many societies already have those who heal and deal with demons, with well-defined expectations concerning how they will go about bringing healing. In some societies, for example, a healer is expected, under the guidance of the spirit under which he or she works, to tell the client what is wrong without any input from the client. If the healer has to ask, he or she is considered a charlatan. What do this custom and others suggest about the ways a healing and deliverance ministry ought to be conducted in such societies?

And what about the personnel who operate in spiritual power? Most societies have well-defined expectations concerning the life and behavior of healers. In some societies the shamans and priests are expected to be virtual recluses or ascetics; in some they may be required to go into ecstasy or trance as they perform their rites of healing. What do such customs suggest concerning culturally appropriate contextualizations of spiritual power? The contextualizer will need to help people sort through such practices and perhaps help them to discard some of them while recommending others.

Bible translators have worked a bit on discovering the words and phrases to use concerning spiritual power. A major problem in many societies is that there are too many words for "spirit," all of them referring to capricious entities that are more likely to be harmful than helpful. A "holy" spirit is, therefore, an oxymoron to such people.

And what about culturally appropriate ways of dealing with the gifts of the Spirit? Are tongues intended by God to be the same for all peoples? What about prophecy, preaching, healing, encouragement, hospitality, words of knowledge and wisdom, etc.?

What varieties might there be in dealing with deep inner wounds? Given that many peoples are quite reluctant to share their deepest feelings and hurts, are there other, more culturally appropriate ways of seeking freedom by doing deep-level healing and deliverance?

How should the church as hospital function in culturally appropriate ways in various societies? And what about the church as army? Each of these truths concerning the nature of the church needs to be expressed in ways that are true to the Scriptures but also recognizable by the people as appropriate expressions of the scriptural injunctions. For example, we learn in Revelation 1–3 that local churches are to overcome the enemy. How is this best done in society after society?

A further consideration, related to the whole of our subject, is the question, how do the three encounters get contextualized?

QUESTIONS IN THREE DIMENSIONS

The consideration of contextualization in three dimensions leads us to a series of questions, some of which we seek to deal with in this volume, others of which will have to await future studies and applications. These are questions that can be used by researchers and practitioners who seek to broaden their approach to working toward appropriate Christianity.

The first series of questions to ask relates to the *allegiance/relationship dimension*.

1. With regard to allegiance, what would be appropriate expressions of allegiance in a given society? Who is to be approached when decisions such as those leading to change of religious allegiance are to be considered? Further, what are the decision-making patterns in this society? How in this society ought an allegiance encounter to take place?
2. With regard to relationship, how are human relationships expressed in this society, and what do those patterns suggest concerning how Christians in this society ought to relate to God and to other Christians?
3. With regard to growth, how are children socialized in this society, and what do such patterns suggest concerning the ways in which people should grow spiritually in this society?
4. With regard to the fruits of the Spirit, what are the ways in which the people in this society express the human counterparts of love, joy, peace, patience, kindness, goodness, faithfulness, humility, and self-control (Gal 5:22,23), and what do such expressions suggest concerning appropriate expressions of the Spirit-led manifestations of these attitudes?
5. With regard to such things as faithfulness, trust, forgiveness, reconciliation, and the like, how are these appropriately expressed in this society, and how should Christians adapt and "capture" such customs for Christ?

Another series of questions can be asked to uncover some of the areas not much dealt with in the *truth/understanding dimension*.

1. With regard to the introduction of knowledge, how is new knowledge appropriately introduced in a given society? Who should be approached with new knowledge? There are structures for the introduction of new knowledge in most societies, and the reputation of what is brought in often depends on how it is introduced and who introduces it.
2. With regard to dealing with truth, what would appropriate truth encounters look like in this society? Are distinctions made between absolute truths and relative truths? What about distinctions between truth and fact, truth and error, knowledge and ignorance?

3. With regard to ignorance and error, how are they treated traditionally, and what does this suggest for dealing with Christian truths and for establishing training structures?
4. With regard to training, what kind of training structures are appropriate? Are the people being misled by Western schooling, and if so, what can be done to make training of Christian leaders more appropriate?

Some of the following kinds of questions can be asked to pave the way toward appropriate dealing with the *spiritual power dimension*.

1. With regard to power encounters, what would appropriate power encounters look like in a given society? What kinds of things are recognized by the people as power encounters?
2. Who are the right power brokers to challenge? How much of such challenges should be done in secret and how much openly?
3. When those with spiritual power are challenged, how is it appropriately done? Should such confrontations be staged, or should we simply wait for them to happen?
4. What is assumed when one power defeats another? Will people assume they should follow the more powerful god? Or will they simply continue with their old allegiances?
5. When healing from God through prayer is offered, are there people of status who need to receive prayer before it is considered legitimate to help others?
6. Where are the places of power, and how can they be challenged appropriately? Can they be captured and used for the true God, or should they be destroyed?
7. What are the times of power, and how should they be appropriately challenged? Can these be captured?

These are some of the questions that flow from the above consideration of a three-dimensional approach to contextualization. In the chapters that follow we will attempt to show more of how this can be done.

CHAPTER 6
DON'T TAKE YOUR RELIGION, TAKE YOUR FAITH

One of the major areas of concern in contextualization and in any insider movement is the matter of how Christ-following should be compared with the religions of the world. When we talk of appropriate Christianity, are we talking about one religion among the many religions of the world? Or are we talking about something that by its very nature is of a different sort? That is, is biblical Christianity a religion or is it something else, something deeper? Or better, *was Christianity intended by God to be a religion in competition with the religions of the world?* Or was it intended to be something else? If so, what?

Whatever Christianity was intended to be, the fact remains that people have made a religion out of it. So, at one level, Christianity *is* a religion. This is necessary, since all human behavior will be expressed in cultural forms, and religion is an organization of cultural forms. My question, however, is this: does God intend Christianity to be *simply* a set of cultural forms that we can call a religion, or did He intend something more?

If ours is simply a religion, we can speak of *adaptation* when we take it to other peoples. We can see so-called "Christian" forms (i.e., the cultural forms used in the practice of Christianity in the home country) introduced into the cultures of the world with slight modifications to accommodate to the receiving culture. But we cannot speak of *contextualization*. For contextualization is *the expression of Christian meanings and commitment* in the cultural forms of the cultural insiders. Any major changes made by Christians in their culture, then, will be in the meanings conveyed and the commitment/ allegiance chosen rather than in the forms themselves.

We may picture a religion as a box that can be taken intact from one place to another, and although the corners may be rounded and perhaps other changes made to adapt it to the new setting, it is still easily recognizable as a structure that has come from another culture.

FIG. 6.1. Differing cultures and religions

A faith, on the other hand, is more like an arrow that is aimed at a particular society. The arrow is allowed to enter the culture and then pricks people at various points to elicit a response to God, not simply a response (i.e., acceptance or rejection) to a cultural structure (the religion box) that has its origin in another place, time, or culture.

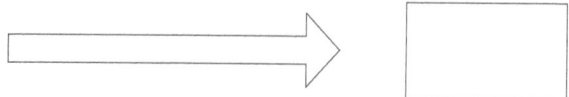

FIG. 6.2. A faith enters a culture

Jesus said He came to bring life (John 10:10). Does this mean He came to add one more religion to the list of the religions of the world? Or does it mean He was bringing something that differs from the religions and can therefore be conveyed even through traditional cultural forms, including those cultural forms that are identified with the former religion of the people who use them?

RELIGION DEFINED

If we are going to answer this question properly, we will need to define what we mean by "religion." For not everyone means the same thing when they use that term. Let's look at some definitions.

1. Some would define religion as the collection of basic assumptions in terms of which a people live their lives (i.e., what I would call "worldview") plus the rituals they use to express those assumptions. If that definition is accepted, the religion of most of the members of Western societies (including a large number of those who call themselves Christians) would be something called "secular humanism" or perhaps "scientism." This is a non- or even anti-supernaturalistic perspective that exalts humans and human thinking above anything claimed to be a revelation from a supernatural being. Such a perspective, then, would function within Western societies in a way very similar to how supernaturalistic beliefs and practices do within most non-Western societies.

If we choose to go in this direction, we can speak of scientists as the priests of Western religion and the various rituals of scientific and/or educational activity as the rituals of that religion. A university education, then, would be seen as a religious rite of passage for our youth. And the activities that most people would label religious activities would be seen as the concern of a subset of our population who happen to believe in God.

With this approach, then, we can justify the widespread competition between Western cultural perspectives and those of traditional peoples around the world as proper from a religious point of view. We could, like many of the early Western missionaries, choose as our motto, "Civilize (i.e., westernize) in order to evangelize." We who have given our lives to the cross-cultural communication of biblical Christianity could then dispense with the whole concept of contextualization and continue in the name of religion the conversion of the peoples of the world to Western ways.

2. Or, like many, we could see religion as the beliefs concerning supernatural beings and powers, and the behavior and rituals associated with those beliefs. This definition would nicely cover the beliefs and practices of most of the peoples of the world plus the minority of Westerners who take their relationship with God seriously. It would see religion as embodied in a culture, whether as the core of that culture or as something more peripheral, and as requiring the learning of some important aspects of the originating culture, if one converts to it.

As Christians, then, we would see our beliefs and practices as basically in competition with the beliefs and practices of non-Christians, whom we would seek to convert to the cultural forms of our religion on the assumption that these forms—our religion—are the best of the competing religious options available. This is in fact what has ordinarily been aimed at by Christian witnesses down through history. Christianity has been identifiable by the cultural forms in which it has been encapsulated, and it is those forms that are carried from society to society as the religion spreads. Taking the Christian religion to the peoples of other societies, then, involves taking our religious forms and adapting them to the culture of the receiving peoples.

3. A third approach is, however, the one that is basic to any consideration of contextualization. This approach is the one practiced by the Apostle Paul and approved at the Jerusalem Council in Acts 15, when James said that Gentiles were not required to be converted to Jewish custom in order to follow Jesus. Paul had learned this approach by watching God give the Holy Spirit to Gentile converts on the basis of their faith alone, in spite of the fact that they had made no attempt to convert to Jewish culture. Although the early Christians set out to win people on the basis of approach number two above, the Holy Spirit broke their rule and endorsed Gentile cultures as adequate vehicles for Gentile interaction with God. The culture in which Jesus met His followers was not to be the cultural norm for the expression of Christianity.

The focus, then, was to be on the relationship between the converts and God rather than on the cultural forms in terms of which that relationship was expressed. It became clear to those who agreed with Paul that what God wants is not a certain set of cultural forms but a faith response that can be expressed in a multiplicity of cultural forms. The battle for the Christians of the early centuries of our faith was to be over whether one worshiped Caesar, calling him Lord, or whether one worshiped Jesus as Lord—not over whether one practiced the religious forms followed by the Jewish Christians. It was okay to God for insiders to follow Christ without converting to another (Jewish) culture.

But down through the centuries, those who have come to Christ have tended to "domesticate" their Christianity. Just as the early Jewish Christians who disagreed with Paul required Gentiles to accept Christ in a Jewish cultural package, so too have Romans and Germans and Americans pressured those who convert to Christ to also convert to the culture of those who bring the message. Thus, our faith has come to be known as primarily a cultural thing, a religion wrapped in the cultural forms of the group in power. And from about the fourth century on it has been seen largely as a European cultural thing—captured by our European ancestors and domesticated in cultures very different from that in which the faith was originally planted. Converts to Christianity, then, are seen as those who have abandoned their own cultural religion and chosen to adopt the religious forms and, usually, many of the other forms of European culture. Often such converts are regarded as traitors to their own people and their ways.

If ours is simply a "form religion," as approach number two above assumes, it can be *adapted but not contextualized*; it can be *in competition with other forms of religion* but not flow through those forms, because by definition it seeks to replace those forms. But biblical Christianity, unlike culture Christianity, is not simply a set of cultural forms. And we get tangled up in our discussions because it is often not clear whether we are speaking of essential, biblical Christianity or of the traditional religion of Western societies that is also called Christianity. In *Christianity in Culture* (1979), I have attempted to make this distinction by spelling biblical Christianity with a capital *C* and culture christianity with a small *c*.

I would define religion as a cultural thing, a surface-level expression of deep-level (worldview) understandings of the beings or structures or ideas we deem worthy of honor and the rituals and beliefs developed to honor them. At the deep, worldview level, most of the peoples of the world assume the existence and activity of a large number of invisible spiritual beings and powers. Their responses to these beings and powers are what their religion is all about. And since much of their cultural life is spent in dealing with this area, we would say that they are a very religious people. In other societies (e.g., the West), many claim to not believe in supernatural beings or in other things considered religious. In their cultural lives, then, there is very little if any activity ordinarily labeled "religious," though their activities in other areas (e.g., science, sports, career) might rival—in function if not in form—the dedication of the most ardent religionists.

I would therefore call religion a form thing, the expression through cultural forms of deep-level (worldview) assumptions and meanings. Religious forms are culture-specific, and if the religion has been borrowed from another cultural context, it requires certain of the forms of that other culture to be borrowed. Islam, for example, requires certain forms of prayer, a specific pilgrimage, an untranslatable Arabic book, and even clothing styles; likewise Judaism, Hinduism, Buddhism, and culture christianity. These are all religions.

Essential biblical Christianity, however, requires none of the original cultural forms. That's how it can be "captured" by the West and considered Western even though its origin is not Western. *Essential Christianity is an allegiance, a relationship, from which flow a series of meanings that are intended to be expressed through the cultural forms of any culture.* These forms are to be chosen for their ability to convey proper biblical meanings in the receptors' cultural contexts.

I believe Christianity is intended to be "a faith," not a set of cultural forms. It is, therefore, different in essence from the religions. Religions, because they are cultural things, can be adapted to new cultures but not contextualized. Adaptation is an external thing resulting in smaller or larger changes in the forms of the religion. Contextualization, on the other hand, is a deep-level process in which the same meanings may be carried by quite different forms in various cultures.

Unfortunately, due to the interference of culture christianity, we have not seen all the variety that is possible. Like a religion, the usual form of initiation into Christianity is a first-century cultural form involving water, and the consolidation ceremony called Communion usually involves the original drink, wine (though many churches have contextualized this to grape juice), and bread (often contextualized to our kind of bread rather than unleavened Jewish bread). True contextualization for many peoples would employ a form of initiation similar to that of their tradition and staple items of their diet for the Communion service. It would also employ their methods of communication rather than culture christianity's preaching forms, and their forms of worship and music rather than Western forms, to express these important meanings.

RELIGION OR A FAITH?

A way that I have found very helpful to deal with this subject is to ask two questions: What characterizes a religion? and, What is the essence of biblical Christianity?

I believe the answer to be the distinction between religion—or rather *a religion*—and a faith. What I mean by "a faith" is a commitment to someone or something, supported by a set of deep, worldview-level assumptions. For most of the world, such a faith involves commitment to a God, gods, or spirits. In the West, the majority of people both outside and inside of the church seem to have opted for a commitment to human achievement, especially scientific, economic, or political achievement, supported by human scientific, economic, or political structures that serve as the real religion of Westerners, called "scientific humanism."

A religion, then, is a set of cultural forms in terms of which a faith is expressed. These cultural forms are at surface-level in any given cultural structuring, as opposed to the worldview-level forms of a faith, though they are designed to express the worldview-level understandings of the faith. The practicing of the religious forms, furthermore, may or may not involve a deep-level commitment to a God, gods, or spirits. The forms may be seen as valuable in and of themselves and, indeed, may be the object of a people's commitment. That is, a people may, in their religious life, in reality be pledging allegiance to the religious forms themselves rather than to any being or thing that exists beyond the forms.

Inherent in this analysis is the distinction between people and structures set forth in my book *Anthropology for Christian Witness* (1996). That analysis emphasized the fact that cultural structuring and human beings are quite different things. And even though human beings live by cultural patterns, we are not determined by them. One important implication of the consistent recognition of this distinction is to note that the thing that keeps us following cultural patterns is not the patterns themselves but the fact that we have, along with our learning of the patterns, developed *habits* of following them. The customs themselves have no power to keep us following them. What keeps us following the patterns or customs is something inside of us—human habit—not something inside of the customs themselves. So, in analyzing religious behavior, we need to look at both the cultural patterns and the human activity in relation to those patterns.

Another important implication of this analysis is to note that a major part of human activity in relation to culture is *commitment*. And commitment, like the learning of our customs and the habits of following them, is something we learn as we grow up. In childhood, we not only learn our customs and develop the habits that keep us following those customs but we also, mostly unconsciously, make a commitment to them. And we practice that commitment habitually as well.

Our commitment, then, is certainly to the culture itself, to the customs that distinguish us from others. But it also involves commitments to *beings*, both beings within our society, such as family members, and beings outside of the society, such as spirits and gods. Our commitment to the people we love is a different thing from our commitment to our customs. Likewise, if we commit ourselves to God, gods, or spirits, beings that are not culture-bound, these commitments will be of a different order than our commitment to the culture or to some of the people who share our culture with us.

People can, of course, commit themselves to ideas as well as to beings. In such a case, the commitment is to something inside the culture. It is not to beings such as family members, who are not in the culture but are a part of the society that uses the culture. Nor is it a commitment to someone outside the culture, such as God, a god, or a spirit.

The point is, we have in the world both religions and faiths or commitments. Religions are structure. Faiths are personal/group commitments. These are two very different things. A faith commitment is the first step, whereas the expression of that faith in cultural structures, called religion, is a second step. The most obvious part of this two-step process is, however, the cultural expression called religion. This fact confuses some people, especially if the term "religious faith" is used to distinguish the religious type of faith from, say, faith in a government, in an economic system, in a family, in oneself, or the like. To make the point that there is a difference between these two things, let's look again at the ten contrasts we discussed in chapter 3. The various points are discussed below.

RELIGION (STRUCTURAL)	A FAITH (PERSONAL)
Structural, Cultural/Worldview	Personal/Group/Social
Rituals, Rules	Relationship
Beliefs	Commitment/Allegiance
Perform	Obey
Adapt	Contextualize
Borrow/Accept/Imitate (e.g., worship forms of the source culture)	Create/Grow (e.g., cultural forms of the receiving culture)
"One size fits all"	Cultural varieties of expression
Like a tree, must be transplanted	Like a seed that gets planted
Like a loaf of bread that gets passed on	Like yeast that gets put into raw dough
An Institution	A Fellowship

TABLE 6.1. Religion vs. a faith

TEN CONTRASTS

These ten contrasts are crucial in distinguishing religion from a faith. The differences are as follows:

1. *Structural, Cultural/Worldview vs. Personal/Group/Social.* Religion, being a cultural thing, is structural. It involves religious beliefs and behavior grounded in a cultural worldview. A faith, however, is a personal thing, experienced by people, usually in groups, often as a whole society who make commitments to a being (e.g., God, a god, a spirit, an ancestor, a living human) or thing (e.g., an idol, an idea such as communism, or a structure). This difference is the basic one, opening the way for each of the others.

As discussed below, a faith, like every human commitment, is expressed culturally, but it is not the same as the cultural expression. And it is the cultural expression of a faith, not the faith itself, that I will use the label "religion" to designate, though popularly this distinction is often not made.

2. *Rituals, Rules vs. Relationship.* A religion revolves around a certain kind and number of rituals accompanied by rules and regulations for both ritual behavior and everyday behavior. A faith, on the other hand, revolves around a relationship, usually

with one or more supernatural beings, based on a person's commitment to that being or, alternatively, to an idea, an idol, a structure, or a living being. Though the relationship is primary, a faith is usually ritualized, even if it is just a commitment to an idea (e.g., communism, evolution).

Rituals conducted in worship of God, gods, or other beings with which people have established a relationship are well-known. There are, however, also academic, economic, and political rituals performed by those with a religion-like commitment to certain ideas and theories.

3. *Beliefs vs. Commitment/Allegiance.* A religion involves a set of intellectual beliefs. These are worldview-level assumptions on the basis of which the religion is practiced and lived. A faith, however, is a commitment, an allegiance to someone or something. There are beliefs underlying the allegiance, to be sure, and these assumptions are also worldview-level. But the allegiance itself is not simply an intellectual thing; it is a matter of people's will to commit themselves to that something or someone outside of themselves. Commitment, therefore, is a person thing, not a structure thing. It is the act of a person, not of cultural structure, in spite of the fact that it results in cultural behavior, as do all commitments.

At this point we need to reiterate that the thing committed to may be any part of the culture, including the religion itself, if not to supernatural beings—or even in addition to a commitment to supernatural beings. This fact may confuse some people if they fail to understand the distinction I am making between structural things such as religion and the personal thing called allegiance or commitment. Since people are entirely immersed in culture, however, they will automatically express whatever allegiances they have in cultural ways.

I have said "allegiances," in the plural. Up to this point I have been speaking of an allegiance or commitment as if people have only one. In reality, though, each person has many allegiances. And the allegiances that are directed toward supernatural beings or religious structures may not even be at the top of the list. For many of the peoples of the world—including the Jews of Jesus' day, for example—allegiance to family is their primary allegiance. All other commitments or loyalties are secondary to that one. What Jesus intends, however, is that our allegiance to Him be primary, with all other allegiances, including family, secondary to that (Matt 10:37).

4. *Perform vs. Obey.* The essence of a religion lies in the performance of the beliefs and behaviors in terms of which that religion is expected to be expressed. The essence of a faith, especially if it is to a personal being, is *obedience*. If we worship God or gods or spirits, the object is to obey Him/them according to the worldview guidelines that accompany that faith. If we worship a human, we are to obey that person. If our faith commitment is to an academic discipline or some other system of ideas, we are to obey those things specified by the underlying worldview assumptions of that system.

With worldview assumptions underlying both a religion and a faith, then, we cannot avoid the structural, cultural requirements for expressing either. But again, a religion and a faith need to be separated analytically if we are ever to fully understand contextualization.

5. *Adapt vs. Contextualize.* A religion, being a cultural thing, can be adapted to the receiving culture when taken from the originating people to the people of another society. The rituals, beliefs, and other customs of that religion can be moved. But since a religion is already a cultural system, when it is moved to another people, it will have to be adjusted to those people and their culture. *But such adjustment is not contextualization; it is adaptation.*

A faith, on the other hand, since it is rooted in personal devotion to beings or ideas, can be expressed in any cultural forms. It does not require as a precondition that the cultural forms in which it was first expressed be carried to another people. The personal relationship between God and Abraham, for example, could have been expressed in other cultural forms if Abraham had been immersed in some other culture. As it was, he responded to God in terms of the rituals and behaviors that characterized his life before he and God made their covenant. That same faith relationship between a human being and God, then, became the experience of many people within Western societies who express that faith quite differently than Abraham expressed it.

But this possibility was not in the minds of the majority of Jewish Christians in the early years of Christianity. For they saw our faith as a religion, encased in and wedded to Jewish cultural forms, perhaps allowing for some adaptation by Gentile converts but certainly not to be contextualized in Gentile culture. But God had other ideas. In the events recorded in Acts 10, God attempted to blast Peter out of his ethnocentric view of what Christianity was to be. In Acts 15, Paul and Barnabas reported on how God had broken the rules of the Jewish church and given the Holy Spirit to uncircumcised Gentiles on the basis of faith alone, without cultural conversion. *Thus God showed that He was in favor of contextualization, not simply adaptation.*

6. *Borrow/Accept/Imitate vs. Create/Grow.* With a religion, if one is to follow it properly, one accepts, imitates, and learns certain cultural forms brought in from the source culture. To become a Muslim, one has to learn to pray in a certain way and in a certain direction. To become a Buddhist, one has to learn to use incense and clap one's hands to awaken the spirits when going to a temple. But there is no cultural requirement for how Christians should pray, though certain Christians may prefer certain postures for prayer. Jewish Christians, for example, may prefer to stand. Others may prefer to kneel or sit. The crucial thing is not the posture (a cultural thing) but the attitude (a personal thing).

Thus, a faith can be expressed creatively in a variety of cultural forms, and people can grow in that faith whether or not they follow the cultural forms meaningful to someone else. Though one Christian may prefer a given posture for prayer and a given musical and communication style, another can be just as committed to God and prefer other postures and styles. One person, in fact, may prefer different styles in different settings because the important things for a faith are allegiance and meanings, not cultural forms.

7. *"One Size Fits All" vs. Cultural Varieties of Expression.* A religion typically is a single entity. Thus, one size, one set of forms, is to be carried wherever the religion is taken. A faith, however, is flexible and takes on the cultural form of the receiving people. Thus, if a faith is properly contextualized there will be endless variety in the ways in which it is expressed. *There should, I believe, be as much difference between the forms in which true Christianity is expressed as there are in the forms of the various cultures of the world.* The creativity discussed under point 6 is to be a major feature of properly contextualized Christianity.

8. *Tree vs. Seed.* A religion is like a tree that springs up in one place and then is taken, half-grown, to another. It has been nurtured where it was planted, with the water and nutrients available there, and needs a certain amount of such water and nutrients to continue to live in the new context. A seed, on the other hand, is planted where it is to grow and lives for the rest of its life on the water and nutrients of that place.

Unfortunately, though Christianity once came to our Gentile ancestors as a seed, it has often been transplanted as a European religion rather than planted like a seed. As a result, much of the world has gotten the wrong impression of our faith, thinking that they must accept a Western package, a Western transplant, if they are to be acceptable to God. But as Jesus said, our faith is intended to be a seed, even a very small seed, that sprouts in the soil of the receiving people, being nourished on their water and nutrients. It then is to grow tall and vital, becoming a refuge for the birds of the air (Luke 13:19).

9. *Loaf of Bread vs. Yeast in Dough.* Or, to refer to another picture that Jesus drew, our faith is to be like yeast, not like the loaf of bread that the yeast has permeated (Luke 13:21). A religion is like the loaf. It has already grown to its full size and may be taken from one place to another fully formed.

But yeast, like a faith, is small and may even go unnoticed. Someone inserts it into the dough of a culture and it grows there, spreading throughout the culture and influencing every part. This is what contextualization is all about.

10. *Institution vs. Fellowship.* A religion is soon institutionalized, leading to all kinds of problems for those who seek true Christianity. For the fellowship that the Christ Way is intended to be can easily be submerged in the concerns of an institution. Note, for example, what happens in the second, third, and following generations of a church or school as it becomes more and more an institution, with its primary concern becoming self-preservation. If looked at in terms of actual function rather than in terms of someone's ideal, many churches and especially training institutions now exist mainly to perpetuate themselves.

It is a very sad thing when the actual function of a training institution becomes to train a few people who will fill the teaching positions in that school or others like it, with or without much concern for serving the needs of the churches they are supposedly training people for. But this is what most of our seminaries and Bible colleges have become. People learn what they do. And what students in these institutions do is learn how to conduct classes, buying and selling information, often at the expense of the development of their faith.

Christian churches and training institutions are, however, intended by God to be centered in relationships with God and with others. Note Jesus' statement of the two greatest commandments (Matt 22:36–40). Fellowship rather than institutionalization should therefore be the primary concern of these entities if we are to be true to our calling. The tendency for a faith to become institutionalized is probably the reason why it seems necessary for each church or training institution to experience a faith-renewal movement every generation if the proper relationship with God is to be maintained.

RECOMBINATION THEORY

Years ago, an anthropologist named Homer Barnett wrote an excellent book on culture change entitled *Innovation: The Basis of Cultural Change* (1953). One of the concepts Barnett suggested is called "recombination theory." This concept is intended to assist us in understanding one of the things that may happen when people adopt another society's custom or when they seek to introduce a custom into another culture.

The theory says that when we seek to introduce a custom into another culture, we may divide that custom into its form and its function. We then do the same thing with the custom we would like to displace in another culture. With this done, we can assist the receiving people to combine "Form 1" in their culture with "Function 2" in the donor culture or vice versa.

The way this would work with a religion can be charted as follows:

RELIGION 1 OF CULTURE 1	RELIGION 2 OF CULTURE 2
Forms 1	Forms 2
Faith Commitment 1	Faith Commitment 2

TABLE 6.2. Religions divided into form and function

Note that each of the cultures has its "religion," consisting of forms plus faith commitment. If we look at Islam and Christianity, for example, we would see Muslim forms and Muslim faith in one column, with so-called Christian forms and Christian faith in the other column. If we sought to contextualize one of these "religions" in the opposite culture, we would seek to combine "Forms 1" with "Faith Commitment 2," or "Forms 2" with "Faith Commitment 1." If "Religion 1" is Islam and "Religion 2" is Christianity, our diagram would look like this:

ISLAM	CHRISTIANITY
1. Muslim Cultural Forms	2. "Christian" Cultural Forms
1. Muslim Faith Commitment	2. Christian Faith Commitment

TABLE 6.3. Islam and Christianity divided into form and function

If we wish to contextualize essential Christianity in Muslim cultural forms, then, the recombination would look like this:

CHRISTIANITY CONTEXTUALIZED IN MUSLIM CULTURAL FORMS
1. Muslim Cultural Forms
2. Christian Faith Commitment

TABLE 6.4. Christianity contextualized in Muslim cultural forms

Note that the opposite combination—Christian cultural forms and Muslim faith—cannot be done if one is to be an orthodox Muslim, since Islam, unlike essential Christianity, requires certain cultural forms to be brought over into the receiving culture. Many Western converts to Islam, however, are attempting to contextualize Islamic faith by committing themselves to the God (Allah) and religion of Islam without adopting the cultural practices required of the orthodox.

CULTURE CHRISTIANITY IS MERELY A RELIGION

In popular parlance, Christianity is regularly classified as a "religion." It has beliefs, a faith-allegiance to a supernatural being, rituals, places of worship, a holy book, a priesthood, and many other characteristics that parallel the characteristics of the religions of the world. We can find all of these things in Hinduism, Buddhism, Islam, animism, etc.

People have taken the teachings of the Bible and worked out a belief system that is supported by Christian leaders and taught to the adherents of the faith. That faith, then, is expressed in personal and group rituals in homes and churches. So are the world's other faiths. Each faith is based on worldview assumptions and personal and group commitments.

When looked at from this point of view, Christianity sure looks like a religion. But is this the way it ought to be seen? Contextualizers need to ask and answer this question. *For if ours is simply one of the religions of the world, our relationship with the other religions is a competitive relationship and our aim should be to replace those religions with ours.*

As mentioned previously, culturally naïve missionaries often saw Christianity in this light. They saw their task as introducing people to their "Christian" beliefs and practices in the hope that they would convert from their false beliefs and practices and embrace Christianity. And along with conversion to Christ (the faith commitment), the usual expectation was that the converts would embrace the Western cultural packaging in terms of which the missionaries expressed their Christianity. To ensure this, the missionaries set up Western schools to teach children how to live "Christian" (i.e., Western Christian) lives. There were additional, and better, reasons for the schools. But winning children to Christ and training them to live as Christians were often articulated as goals of the schools.

When the receiving people were impressed (or intimidated) by the culture of the missionaries, many would come to the schools and convert to both the faith of the missionaries and as much of their culture as possible. Thus, large numbers of the peoples of Korea, Africa, the South Pacific, Latin America, and other areas converted to Christ and to Western culture at the same time. In places like China, India, Japan, Thailand, and the Muslim world, however, if anything the missionaries brought was accepted, it was more likely to be the perceived benefits of the schools and the culture they taught rather than the missionaries' faith. It was easy for people to see that the schooling did not depend on the acceptance of the faith. They could take the one without having to take the other. It was not so easy in many parts of the world, though, for people to accept the faith without the cultural packaging. Literacy, for example, was often a requirement for baptism.

So, for many of the peoples of the world, Christianity is simply a religion, a cultural thing with or without the faith that is intended to be central to biblical Christianity.

A CHRISTIAN WORLDVIEW?

It is common for Western Christians, especially conservative evangelicals, to speak of *a* or *the* Christian worldview. They have learned that the term "worldview" is to be applied to the basic assumptions of a people and have come to label the basic assumptions of Christianity as "worldview assumptions." So far so good.

But what these people are generally referring to when they speak of a Christian worldview is a set of doctrinal assumptions that are important to Christianity—things taught in the Bible that Christians need to give assent to if they are to be truly Christian. These assumptions, then, are to contrast with humanistic assumptions or the underlying assumptions of non-Christian religions. And once again, Christianity is put in competition with the religions of the world.

The problem here is that the concept of worldview, as defined by anthropologists, those whose expertise is in dealing with culture and worldview, is much broader than this popular usage of the term. For anthropologists, a worldview is the deep level of culture (see Kraft 1996) and includes assumptions concerning time, space, and classification as well as persons and power. Though Christian assumptions deal a lot with these latter two aspects of worldview, a so-called "Christian" worldview has little to say about changes required by Christian faith in assumptions concerning time, space, and classification. What is apparent to Christian anthropologists, the experts on the subject of worldview, is that the relatively few worldview assumptions focused on by those who use the term "Christian worldview" should not be treated as if they are the whole of a person's worldview. For although these few things are truly significant, they do not come near comprising a total worldview.

Instead, such a focus gives the misimpression that Christianity offers a total worldview that is in competition with the cultural worldviews of the peoples of the world. This view, then, would assume that Christians are to be radically different from the non-Christians in their society in a much larger number of assumptions than is necessary. *This would be competition allowing only for adaptation, not contextualization.* Granted, we are to differ radically in a few crucial areas. But as mentioned above, the number of these areas is comparatively small. Most of a people's worldview assumptions require little if any change when they convert to Christianity. This is what allows for contextualization within a culture rather than replacement of it.

If Christianity is seen as a religion in competition with religions, ours is a worldview in competition with other worldviews. And our job is to convert people from their worldviews to ours. In such a case, there can be some adaptation but no real contextualization of our faith. I believe that there is a better way.

A MATTER OF MEANINGS

It is, I believe, crucial that we see the essence of true Christianity in the area of meaning and allegiance (both person things) rather than in the forms (cultural, structural things) through which meaning and allegiance are expressed. Our faith is a matter of relationship with a living God and a living Christ, and the rituals we perform can vary widely in form as long as the meanings are there. We can worship in a wide variety of ways and even on different days as long as our worship is "in spirit and in truth" (John 4:23,24). We can pray in any posture as long as our motivation is right. We can even interpret the meanings of various doctrines differently as long as our allegiance is to the one Christ.

As mentioned above, in the religions certain cultural forms are required, usually those that originated in the source culture or, as with Christianity, in the Western cultures that have become Christianity's primary home. Whether these cultural forms are a certain posture for prayer or a specific language or certain rituals or special artifacts, without them the religion cannot function properly. To practice a religion one has to learn what these forms are and how to use them properly. To practice Christianity appropriately, however, one has only to learn what the supracultural meanings of Scripture are and to set them to whatever cultural forms one feels are appropriate to convey those meanings.

For religion is a facet of culture. And just as the non-religious forms of a culture are available for the expression of Christian faith, so the religious forms of that culture can also be used—on condition that the satanic power in them is broken and the meanings are Christian. Almost any cultural forms can be captured for Christ.

The tragedy of requiring Western rather than traditional forms to be used in Christianity is twofold: that the foreign forms will not be assigned the proper meanings; and that Christianity will devolve into simply being seen as a religion. This misunderstanding, then, produces a pull back toward the meanings of the traditional religion. And Christianity devolves into merely a competing religion rather than a faith that is intended to capture the cultural forms once used to express that other faith.

CONCLUSION

It is my conclusion, then, that true biblical Christianity neither is nor was intended to be a religion in the sense of the cultural structuring that is ordinarily in view when people talk about the religions of the world. Rather, it is intended to be a faith, a commitment to God through Jesus Christ, which, though it must be expressed culturally, can be expressed through any cultural system. Therefore, unlike religions, Christianity can and should be contextualized—not simply adapted, as is required of cultural religions when they are taken from one society to another.

CHAPTER 7
WHY ISN'T CONTEXTUALIZATION IMPLEMENTED?

In his 1997 article "Contextualization: the Theory, the Gap, the Challenge," Darrell Whiteman raises the question as to why what we've been teaching for several decades is often not implemented even by those who know enough to do so. It is easy to assume that once missionaries and national church leaders know what to do, they will do it. Unfortunately, this is often not the case.

Though we have much to learn, and each attempt to construct an appropriate Christianity must still be seen as experimental, we have made considerable progress in theorizing what we believe ought to be done, at least in the theological area. In other areas, such as church governance by "national" rather than foreign leadership, church leaders and their missionary partners seem less able to implement culturally appropriate models. With regard to worship, in many places we find impressive experiments in contextualization, especially in the use of traditional music. But a survey of the history shows that much remains to be done, both in conceptualizing and in applying what we think we know.

Even with the progress that has been made, a major problem is the lack of application of the insights already arrived at. There are at least two sources of difficulty when those involved in planting and growing churches deal with contextualization. There are problems from the outsiders' point of view and problems that insiders face. We will look first at outsider problems, then at those of the insiders.

OUTSIDER PROBLEMS

What I'm calling "outsider problems" are those faced by cross-cultural workers who should be concerned about receptor-oriented approaches to the spread of biblical Christianity. As we see below, some of these workers are trained but not involved in contextualization. Others are not trained and don't know that they should be contextualizers.

1. A Broader Concept of Contextualization

The first hindrance to contextualization I'd like to mention is something we'd like to help rectify in this book: the lack of a broader approach to contextualization. We've always talked of contextualization of theology (read: contextualization of knowledge), but it is probable that most people, including most pastors, are not very interested in theological knowledge. Though from an academic point of view we can contend that theology covers all that needs to be done, it is unlikely that most people perceive it that way. They are more likely to be interested in things that are more easily seen to affect day-by-day behavior, such as relational things or spiritual power things or worship or patterns of communication—things that the average person, or even the average pastor, may not see as theological.

I am convinced that the primary questions in the minds of most of the people of the world who either have turned to Christ or are considering that possibility are not questions concerning knowledge. People are more practical, and their concerns more "down to earth," than to be interested in the usual theoretical presentations of theology. They want to learn how to deal with the practical problems of life—things like how to handle difficult relationships, how to heal or prevent sickness, or how to assure good fortune.

In fact, most of their questions relate to perceived needs for spiritual power. The fact that those who deal with the contextualization of Christianity don't ordinarily deal with this issue, then, dampens interest in discussions of how Christianity can be expressed in culturally appropriate ways. One reaction to this deficiency is seen in the fact that many of the breakaway movements from Western Christianity make spiritual power issues central. They see such power exemplified in Scripture but not in the churches. So they break away in order to be more appropriate to Scripture as well as to the concerns of their people.

In addition to people's concern for power is their major concern for relationships. Though we who attempt to communicate Christianity frequently talk about commitment to Christ, love, faithfulness, fellowship, the fruits of the Spirit, intimacy with Christ (e.g., John 15), forgiveness, repentance, reconciliation, obedience, and other components of the relationship dimension of Christianity, often very little attention is given to how these are to be expressed and experienced in culturally appropriate ways. Treatment of these issues tends, following the lead of the West, to be reduced to rules rather than adapted to the sociocultural life of the people into whose context these values have been introduced. This often leaves people to continue their traditional relational patterns with little or no biblical Christian influence.

Behind such a deficiency lies the intellectualized Western Christianity and its disdain for focusing on experience rather than on doctrine. The intellectualization of evangelical Christianity has been pitted against the experiencing of Christian truth, to the detriment of an emphasis on the latter. We tend to act as if it were sufficient for people claiming to follow Christ to have one experience—conversion—but from then on to focus on intellectual knowledge of the doctrines of the faith. It is recommended that they express their faith in culturally appropriate ways, but we can rarely offer them much assistance in this area.

Contextualization that is appropriate to the Bible and to culture should, I believe, focus as much or more on relationship and spiritual power as it does on knowledge. Most of the non-Western peoples to whom the gospel has been taken are highly relational and deeply concerned with spiritual power. It is very important, then, if we claim to be biblically and culturally appropriate, to strongly emphasize these areas so prominent in the Bible and in their cultures.

2. Lack of Implementation

The second problem, one mentioned by Whiteman, is how to get what we think we know academically across to field missionaries, to entrenched church leaders, and to the administrators of missionary-sending organizations. The place where most research breaks down is at the point of implementation. Many of the things we missiologists teach and write have been known for decades, but they are either unknown to or ignored by one or more of the above groups.

National church leaders have often been trained well in Western ways and have a considerable emotional investment in keeping their present positions. They therefore have no interest in changing, even if they privately admit that the new way suggested might be better. I remember discussions with the Nigerian church leaders I worked with in which they were quick to admit that the church needed to change in the direction of contextualization. The discussions, however, tended to come to naught when these leaders admitted that they were not willing to risk their leadership positions (and salaries) to advocate changes that they felt would turn the church against them. As it turned out, some of these leaders did make changes but then had to look for different employment. One of them worked his way up into a significant position of leadership from which he could make some changes, but even then he found that the majority of church leaders would not implement the changes.

Field missionaries, for their part, often have neither read the studies nor understood the issues behind the calls for contextualization. They often see themselves as simply encouragers of the nationals as they carry on with what they have always done. Or, on the other hand, they may feel they need to take over situations they don't fully understand because things don't seem to be going as they do at home. It can be a scary thing for missionaries who have learned to lead churches in their home countries to be asked to put aside what they have learned and to learn new, culturally appropriate approaches to church and ministry. Change can be especially scary for missionaries if they don't have the cultural understandings concerning how churches should relate to the cultural context in which they operate. Not understanding what's going on around us makes us feel ignorant in spite of all the schooling we may have had.

It is the custom in America for missionaries to have completed college or Bible school as a precondition for being accepted by a mission board. But it is unlikely that in those schools they would have learned much about culture in relation to Christian faith and biblical interpretation. And if they have learned anything in this area, it is unlikely that they have dealt more than superficially with the extent to which contextualization occurred in the Bible and therefore should be advocated in today's cultural contexts. The fact that missionaries have attended advanced educational institutions, however, often misleads them into thinking that they understand cultural things better than they do. Thus, they may feel more certain than they ought to about their decisions with regard to the interactions between culture and Christianity.

Furthermore, the administrators of missionary sending organizations are often negative to what seem to them to be new ideas. Often those in charge of mission boards have had very little or no cross-cultural experience themselves. They have been appointed from the ranks of the sending churches for their administrative abilities or their denominational loyalties, with precious little cultural insight. Their concern for the realities of administration, then, often hinders any desire to expand their vision of what ought to be done. In addition, as in Whiteman's illustration, many mission administrators are accountable to denominations and boards for whom denominational expansion is more important than the inculturation of Christianity.

On the other hand, some administrators have spent considerable time expanding their understandings of what Christian mission ought to be. Thus, they find themselves ahead of their field workers theoretically. But often they find it difficult to make the kind of changes enlightened theory demands because of the conservatism of field missionaries or, more typically, of the national leaders of the churches. These national leaders have usually been practicing non-contextual forms of Christianity for some time and are not about to change.

Back in the late 1960s and early '70s, we at Fuller's School of World Mission conducted several church growth seminars in various places for people in positions to implement change in missionary organizations. These seminars seemed to have a positive effect on the thinking of many of those who attended, though they tended to attract more field missionaries than administrators. Unfortunately, though strong on the need for church planting, the seminars were less strong on the cultural implications of planting truly contextualized churches. I believe we would do well to institute contextualization seminars both at home and abroad for church leaders, missionaries, and administrators, if we are to get this message across.

3. Knowing but Not Doing

A third issue is how to solve the problem of missionaries who know enough to work in culturally sensitive ways but do not do it. Many who go out as cross-cultural witnesses have read and received good instruction in the theory and practice of contextualization, but they nevertheless tend to dominate and to impose foreign patterns on their converts.

A major reason for this is insecurity. Many who volunteer for missionary work are personally insecure. In standing for Christ in their schools and even in their churches and then in volunteering for missionary service, they may have felt unaccepted by others and not quite sure of who they were and whether they had committed themselves to the right thing. The insecurities arising from such experience frequently lead missionaries to "lord it over" those they work with in an effort to convince themselves that they are capable of doing what they are assigned to do. Perhaps without realizing it, and without noting the difference between what they are doing and what they believe ought to be done, such missionaries dominate their people and impose their ideas in very destructive ways.

Often the people with whom such cross-cultural witnesses are working are quite compliant, not wanting to be impolite to the foreigners. Thus, they may be quite willing to go along with the domination of an insecure missionary. In addition, since a typical attitude is that Christianity is a foreign thing anyway, the receiving people may not even be aware that there might be a better way than the way they are being taught.

Another type of insecurity plagues missionaries who would like to contextualize but feel threatened by those over them who might not agree with what they are doing. Many a missionary who agrees with what we at Fuller are teaching has "knuckled under" to senior missionaries who do not believe in working with rather than against the culture. I can speak from experience on this issue, having confronted our mission leaders over certain cultural issues and having been forced to leave missionary work and seek another career. Many junior missionaries, knowing that this kind of thing has happened to others, are fearful lest it happen to them and therefore do not push for changes they believe to be for the better.

Whether or not they are insecure, missionaries, especially if they are new, may simply fall into the familiar Western patterns and fail to work to improve the situation. They may lack seniority or feel they have no right to suggest new ideas in a context dominated by senior missionaries and/or senior national leaders. If there is to be change, some feel, let the senior people suggest it and bring it about. For the program is theirs, not mine. "Maybe, if I get to be a senior missionary," they say, "then I can suggest changes."

I suspect that for many the primary culprit is culture stress (often incorrectly referred to as "culture shock"). It can be observed that people under the stress of working cross-culturally tend to revert to familiar patterns, even if they know better. The disequilibrium of working in another cultural context, in another language, can create a high degree of insecurity and fear, even among those who were quite secure in their home context.

In defense of inaction, some point out that the missionized people want things to be foreign since the foreignness gives them more prestige. In many parts of the world there are churches that have been started without foreign support (e.g., African Independent Churches) that have little prestige compared to the ones started by mission agencies. So the nationals resist efforts to contextualize, in some cases committing themselves to Western patterns to a greater extent than even the missionaries had. But even if prestige is not the main motivation, many resist contextualization simply because they have never experienced or observed any approach to Christianity other than a Western one and think that's the way things ought to be. They may not be able to even imagine another approach.

A more acceptable attitude that hinders contextualization is the feeling that if we as outside advocates seek to introduce new ideas, we are likely to come across as manipulating and dominating or at least interfering in something that belongs to the people, not to us. Many missionaries feel that the people have been pushed around quite a lot in the past, so they are reluctant to repeat the past and become pushy, even in an attempt to introduce better ideas. Whether for this reason or for some other reason, many missionaries allow themselves to be isolated in Bible school teaching positions, teaching the Bible in Western academic ways. In such positions they are often unable to really get close to the people to find out what their life is all about. Indeed, many in such teaching positions are so totally unprepared to study the cultural situation that they wouldn't be able to find out much even if they did spend time with the people.

Or the problem may simply be laziness, an unwillingness to step out simply because it will be too much work. Or there may be the feeling that it's too late for things to be changed.

Whatever the reason, this is a major problem and has been for some time. Perhaps the kind of seminars suggested above would provide a way of tackling this problem as well.

4. Lack of Training

A fourth outsider hindrance to the implementation of appropriate contextualization is the fact that most missionaries and national church leaders have had no training at all to help them in dealing with the cultural aspects of their task. The feeling in many of the sending churches, both in North America and in the Two-Thirds World (e.g., Korea, Nigeria) is that commitment to Christ and enthusiasm are enough to qualify people for missionary service, whether or not the missionaries have much understanding of their task. In North America it has often been felt that working in other societies doesn't require the same level of expertise that working as pastors in the home churches does. I'm afraid this attitude is prominent in non-Western sending churches as well.

Though most mission agencies in the West ordinarily require university-level or at least Bible school training for those they send out, that training usually involves very little that prepares people to work in another society. In fact, traditional college and Bible school curricula have often been counterproductive in assisting people in understanding and working in other cultural contexts. Typically, Bible schools and Christian colleges have been strong on preparing their students in biblical understanding, at least from a Western perspective. This is commendable, though it tends to lock students into absolutized Western interpretations that obscure in the students' minds the possibility that other, more culturally relevant interpretations are possible. Little or no attention is given in Christian institutions to the need for cultural relevance, much less how to go about working toward it.

In the non-Christian (often anti-Christian) institutions attended by some missionary candidates, a politically correct valuing of and tolerating other people's ways of life has become extreme. In these places, openness to other people's ways has devolved into an absolutizing of relativism and tolerance. We are taught to believe that people of other societies are okay no matter what they believe and do and we are wrong if we criticize or try to change anything in their way of life. Caught between such teaching and the dogmatism of conservative Christian interpretations of Scripture, many young missionaries find themselves hard put to figure out what a balanced approach might be.

Behind the lack-of-training problem, at least in the West, is the fact that when Western missions started there was virtually no training available in cultural issues. The tradition of mission boards sending out people without cultural training, once established, was pretty well "set in cement" before modern training institutions came into existence. Pastors, likewise, have often been ignorant concerning the need for those they advise and send out to engage in cultural studies. There usually were no such studies in the institutions in which the pastors trained, even though many of these institutions claimed to be training missionaries as well as pastors. So the pastors and teachers often fail to properly advise missionary candidates in this area.

Though things may have changed for the better in many contexts, I look back on my own quest to find the proper kind of training for pioneer missionary work and marvel at how close I came to following poor advice given by those who sincerely wanted to help me. I remember being advised at the Christian college I attended to major in Bible or history or even Greek—subjects designed to help the missionary's understandings of the message we are to take rather than subjects designed to help us understand the people we are to go to. It seemed like a chance conversation, then, with a prospective missionary that led me to go into anthropology. Fortunately, unlike most Christian institutions to this day, the college I attended had a (struggling) anthropology department.

In my four-decade teaching experience in an institution committed to providing top-notch training for missionaries and Two-Thirds World church leaders, I have noticed another major problem. Many who take our classes just don't seem to "get it." This may be because they come before they have had enough life experience for the material we present to "connect" with and bring about change in long-held attitudes and presuppositions. Or it may be because of the persistence of biases toward certain interpretations of Scripture and/or Christian witness. I have had students, for example, who strongly resisted my claim that we need cultural and communicational insight to go along with a high level of commitment to the guiding activity of the Holy Spirit. They believe that the Holy Spirit is all we need, and that the fact that many missionaries have done a poor job of presenting the gospel in cross-cultural contexts is to be explained by a lack of listening to the Holy Spirit. These students just don't accept my contention that if we learn to do a better job of communicating, the Holy Spirit will be able to do His job more effectively.

5. Non-Contextual Churches Often Seem More Successful

A fifth reason why contextualization is not as widely implemented as we could wish is the fact that there are many non-contextualized, very Western-looking churches that are large and growing. As we look at the churches of the world, it becomes clear that many of the largest, apparently most "successful" churches (e.g., in Korea, the Philippines, Singapore, Nigeria) are poorly contextualized. This fact discourages would-be church planters who might plant contextualized churches if it were obvious that churches that grow contextually grow bigger and are healthiest. Instead, they tend to imitate what is working without regard to whether or not the churches they plant are culturally appropriate.

Or, to look at this factor another way, perhaps churches that look non-contextual are in reality contextualized, but to a westernizing segment of the population rather than to the traditional majority. In Korea, for example, though we rejoice that about a quarter of the population has turned to Christ, they have largely turned to Western-style churches probably at least partly for cultural reasons. There is nothing wrong with churches that are culturally appropriate to westernizing people, as long as people aren't given the impression that Western expressions of Christian faith are the only ones acceptable to God. Unfortunately, that is the impression that many come away with.

Such a situation raises several questions for me, one of which is, if Korean Christianity was more culturally Korean, would more of the traditional populace be attracted? I'm afraid that a major part of the Christian message as perceived by Koreans is that one must express Christian allegiance in Western ways. They may believe that traditional Korean ways of expression are not acceptable to the Christian God.

That impression might be overcome if there were, in addition to the Western-style churches, approaches that are culturally appropriate for traditional peoples. Might it be, for example, that the majority of the population of Korea that is now rejecting Christianity would be more open to the gospel if their traditional cultural ways were in evidence in some of the churches? Given the fact that part of the society is quite westernized, there is still a part that is quite traditional. Shouldn't there, then, be at least two kinds of churches—one kind that is culturally appropriate to westernizing people but another that is culturally appropriate to traditional people? In many parts of Africa, the African Independent Church movement has provided just such churches as an alternative to the Western-style churches brought by the missionaries.

To turn to another possible reason for non-contextualization, could it be that there are factors in Christian experience that override cultural fit? That is, are there things in non-contextual churches that are seen by their adherents as more important than cultural appropriateness? I suspect there are. Among them would be the desire on the part of many to identify with the West. Those who have attended Western schools, for example, are often proud of their westernized ways. Many of these find their ways to the cities of Asia and Africa where a semi-Western way of life is in vogue, or at least considered prestigious. If a church is a part of the life of these semi-westernized people, then, it is more likely to be one that assists them in their quest to be seen as westernized.

Another quality of many successful non-contextual churches is an emphasis on healing and deliverance. Probably the majority of the large non-contextual churches are Pentecostal or Charismatic, with issues of spiritual power in focus both in Sunday worship and in their small group activity. Since a concern for spiritual power is high on the list of most people's felt needs, the cultural relevance of such a focus would seem to outweigh in people's minds the cultural irrelevance of much of the rest of what goes on in these churches.

However great may be our commitment to cultural appropriateness, we dare not simply ignore the "success" of non-contextualized churches. For the success of non-contextualized churches diminishes motivation to plant churches that are more appropriate to the culture of the people. This is especially true if such churches do offer something that meets a felt need, such as the prestige of Western forms or an emphasis on spiritual power.

INSIDER PROBLEMS

In addition to the considerable number of problems faced by cross-cultural witnesses coming from outside the societies they work in, there are a number of problems faced by insiders who seek to contextualize.

1. Expectations and Reputation

Whether we like it or not, Christianity has a long-standing reputation of being Western and even of requiring a Western cultural orientation. This is regrettable both for historical reasons and because it hinders present appropriateness. For historically, the origin of Christianity was not Western but Middle Eastern.

This perception partners with another perception to hinder serious attempts at developing culturally appropriate forms different from those of the Western source countries. That second perception is that Christianity is a religion and, as a religion, belongs to a particular culture, major elements of that culture being required if the religion is to be practiced correctly.

It is not widely understood outside or even inside of Christianity that our faith is intended to be different from the religions in its relationship to the culture of the people who practice it. Whereas religions such as Islam, Buddhism, and Hinduism require a sizeable chunk of the culture in which they were developed, Christianity rightly understood does not. Jesus came to bring life (John 10:10), not a religion. It is people who have reduced our faith to a religion and exported it as if it were simply a competitor with the religions. And so, those receiving our message tend to interpret Christianity as if it were simply another religion—a culturally encapsulated religion—rather than a faith that can be expressed in terms of any culture.

But Christianity correctly understood is commitment- and meaning-based, not form-based. A commitment to Jesus Christ and the meanings associated with that commitment can therefore be practiced in a wide variety of cultural forms. This is what contextualization is all about. And this is an important feature of Christianity that is often misunderstood by advocates as well as potential receptors.

Still another part of the reputation of Christianity worldwide is that it is more a matter of thinking than of practicality. For many, our faith has little to do with the issues of real life, such as how to gain protection from evil spirits, how to gain and keep physical health, and how to maintain good family relationships. Instead, Christianity is often seen as a breaker-up of families. And when the issue is a need for spiritual power and protection, even Christians feel they need to keep on good terms with a shaman, priest, or medicine man/woman since, in spite of biblical promises, Christian pastors can only recommend secular approaches to healing and protection.

A Christianity that is appropriate both to the Bible and to the receiving culture will confront these misperceptions and, hopefully, get them changed.

2. Traditions Die Hard

Any discussion of this topic needs to take into account the fact that the situations most cross-cultural workers are working in nowadays are seldom pioneer situations. Thus, we who teach contextualization are dealing primarily with those whose major concern will have to be how to bring about change in already existing situations rather than how to plant culturally appropriate churches.

Typically, then, those who learn what contextualization is all about find themselves working with churches that are quite committed to their Western approach to Christianity. This has become their tradition, and they are not open to changing it.

The leaders of many such churches may never have seen culturally appropriate Christianity and probably lack the ability to imagine it. And even if they can imagine such an approach, they are unlikely to want to risk what they are familiar with in hopes of gaining greater cultural appropriateness. For many, the risk of losing their position may be very real since their colleagues, committed to preserving the "sacred" tradition, may turn against them and oust them from their parishes.

We therefore need to learn not only the principles of cultural appropriateness, but also the principles of effective communication. And this needs to be coupled with patience and prayer plus a readiness to make the right kind of suggestions if asked.

3. Fear of Syncretism

A major hindrance for many, especially those who have received theological instruction, is the fear that they might open the door to an aberrant form of Christianity. They see Latin American "Christo-paganism" and shy away from what is called Christian but is not really. Fearing that if they deviate from the Western Christianity they have received they are in danger of people carrying things too far, they fall back on the familiar and do nothing to change it, no matter how much misunderstanding there might be in the community of unbelievers concerning the real meanings of Christianity.

There are, however, at least two roads to syncretism: an approach that is too nativistic and an approach that is too dominated by foreignness. With respect to the latter, it is easy to miss the fact that Western Christianity is quite syncretistic when it is very intellectualized, organized according to foreign patterns, weak on the Holy Spirit and spiritual power, strong on Western forms of communication (e.g., preaching) and Western worship patterns, and imposed on non-Western peoples as if it were scriptural. It is often easier to conclude that a form of Christian expression is syncretistic when it looks too much like the receiving culture than it when it looks "normal" to Westerners and the westernized.

But Western patterns are often farther from the Bible than non-Western patterns. And the amount of miscommunication of what the gospel really is can be enormous when people get the impression that ours is a religion rather than a faith (see chapter 6) and that foreign forms are therefore a requirement. To give that impression is surely syncretistic and heretical. I call this "communicational heresy."

But what about the concept of syncretism? Is this something that can be avoided, or is it a factor of human limitations and sinfulness? I vote for the latter and suggest that there is no way to avoid it. Wherever there are imperfect understandings made by imperfect people, there will be syncretism. That syncretism exists in all churches is not the problem. Helping people to move from where they are to more ideal expressions of Christian faith is what we need to address ourselves to.

As long as we fear something that is inevitable, we are in bondage. I remember the words of one field missionary who was studying with us: "Until I stopped worrying about syncretism, I could not properly think about contextualization." Our advice to national leaders (and to missionaries), then, is to stop fearing syncretism. Deal with it in its various forms as a starting point, whether it has come from the receiving society or from the source society, and help people to move toward more ideal expressions of their faith. And trust the Holy Spirit to lead people out of syncretistic understandings and practices.

4. Insecurity

I have spoken above about the insecurity factor in missionaries. Nationals can feel at least as insecure as missionaries. They may be in positions that can easily be taken away from them if they don't conform to the expectations of those in authority over them. So, if they experiment with approaches that their superiors consider threatening, they may have to look for new employment, just as some of us former missionaries have had to.

I came to a new understanding on this issue one day while discussing with a prominent Nigerian leader the change I believed we ought to make with regard to baptizing believing polygamists. He had been cured of leprosy, but the disease had taken parts of his fingers and left him with hands that could no longer wield a hoe for farming. At one point in the discussion, he looked at me and said, "I would gladly baptize believing polygamists. But if I did, what could I do with these hands?"

His meaning was clear to me: if he did what I recommended, he would lose his position as a pastor and would have to go back to farming. But his hands were so damaged that they would not let him succeed at farming, and his family would suffer because of the stand he took. He was insecure because a new stand might cost him his job. So he retreated for fear of the consequences from a position that was easy for me as an outsider to recommend, even though it was a position that he believed in. This same leader had earlier backed off on approving of church-sponsored square dancing out of the same fear.

When I challenged the mission leaders on these issues, I was fired, but I was able to find other employment. The Nigerian leader may not have been able to find other employment if he had followed my lead and lost his job.

5. Believing That All Converts Have to "Pay the Price"

One group of nationals that is most against contextualization is made up of people who have paid a high social price in becoming Christians. In parts of the world where Islam or Hinduism is the majority religion, those who come to Christ are often banished from their families and lose all of their social privileges. Their lives may even be in danger, and if they are unmarried they may have difficulty attracting or arranging for a spouse.

When such people are asked to allow others to become Christians without going through the hardships they have had to endure, they often object strenuously. They look on contextualized Christianity as an easy and invalid way of coming into the church and, if they are in power, will often fight against any changes in that direction. They assume that a contextualized church has lowered the standards. "Everyone who comes to Christ must pay the price as we have," they contend. They are therefore unwilling to consider contextualization if it means that people can become Christians without some or all of the social rejection they themselves have experienced.

CONCLUSION

In spite of the fact that missiologists have been speaking and writing about contextualization for decades, there seems to be little real implementation of the concept. There are, however, encouraging examples of contextualized churches. We can point to the house churches of northeast Thailand, planted by missionaries supported by the Evangelical Covenant Church, as a shining example. Or the movement of Muslims to Christ, mosque by mosque, in Bangladesh. Or many of the thousands of African Independent Churches.

Beyond these and a few other instances, though, non-contextualization seems to be more the norm than the exception in worldwide Christianity. We can thank God for all that He is doing in the body of Christ, even while lamenting that westernization is all too often a part of the Christian message as perceived by the followers of Christ. But it is my prayer that these chapters will help some to overcome their reticence to attempt to truly incarnate the gospel in whatever society they may be working.

TYPOLOGY AND DYNAMICS

CHAPTER 8
A TYPOLOGY OF APPROACHES TO CONTEXTUALIZATION

One of the problems faced by those of us in the contextualization movement is the assumption that whatever approach a given society takes with regard to contextualization, there can be only one approach to doing church. In other words, people should choose the forms they prefer and everyone should get on board.

It is easy to fall into this fallacy and the assumption behind it: that the people of this society all respond to the same thing and in the same way. We think that because the people we work with are not Western, they will not be well served by a Western church. So we recommend a church that is culturally "like them" rather than like Western churches, as if "they" are culturally homogeneous and will be well served by a single set of cultural forms.

Unlike Islam and Buddhism, where certain cultural forms are prescribed, there is no single set of cultural forms required by Christianity. Proper contextualization means the expression of faith in cultural forms appropriate to the people. But in any sizeable population, there will be variation. Not everyone will be well served by a single approach. Therefore, not all churches should look alike. The cultural thing we call "religion" should differ from society to society. Churches should look as different from society to society as the cultures of the people do. Faith comes first; religious forms developed as appropriate cultural expressions of that faith come later.

With contemporary culture contact, there are many varieties of culture in any given society. Each society has westernizing and traditional segments—often several varieties of each. There are schooled westernizing, non-schooled westernizing, city traditional, rural traditional, and various subcategories of each of these.

God wants to reach each group in appropriate ways. For some, a Western church is just right. For others, a Western church gives a wrong impression. For traditionalists (whatever tradition we refer to), there are some who need a very traditional approach. There are others who want a modified traditional experience.

Any given society may have many different kinds of Christian faith expression. In 1998, John Travis developed a typology to describe groups of believers in Muslim contexts based on their cultural expression of faith. He called these varieties "C1–C6," *C* standing for "Christ-centered community" (Travis 1998). Although these categories reflect realities in Muslim societies, we find it more broadly applicable. (See *Appropriate Christianity* for two chapters explaining and illustrating this scheme among Muslims and Buddhists.) I use Travis' typology here as the basis for discussing some of the widely occurring dynamics of faith experience in relation to the cultural preferences of a given people who follow Jesus. It is helpful here to revisit the original C-Spectrum descriptions to understand how similar phenomena are at work in non-Muslim settings.

> *C1: Traditional Church Using Outsider Language.* May be Orthodox, Catholic, or Protestant. Some predate Islam. Thousands of C1 churches are found in Muslim lands today. Many reflect Western culture. A huge cultural chasm often exists between the church and the surrounding Muslim community. Some Muslim background believers may be found in C1 churches. C1 believers call themselves "Christians."
>
> *C2: Traditional Church Using Insider Language.* Essentially the same as C1 except for language. Though insider language is used, religious vocabulary is probably non-Islamic (distinctively "Christian"). The cultural gap between Muslims and C2 is still large. Often more Muslim background believers are found in C2 than C1. The majority of churches located in the Muslim world today are C1 or C2. C2 believers call themselves "Christians."
>
> *C3: Contextualized Christ-Centered Communities Using Insider Language and Religiously Neutral Insider Cultural Forms.* Religiously neutral forms may include folk music, ethnic dress, artwork, etc. Islamic elements (where present) are "filtered out" so as to use purely "cultural" forms. The aim is to reduce foreignness of the gospel and the church by contextualizing to biblically permissible cultural forms. . . . C3 believers call themselves "Christians."
>
> *C4: Contextualized Christ-Centered Communities Using Insider Language and Biblically Permissible Cultural and Islamic Forms.* Similar to C3, however, biblically permissible Islamic forms and practices are also utilized. . . . C4 believers, though highly contextualized, are usually not seen as Muslim by the Muslim community. C4 believers identify themselves as "followers of Isa the Messiah" (or something similar).

C5: Christ-Centered Communities of "Messianic Muslims" Who Have Accepted Jesus as Lord and Savior. C5 believers remain legally and socially within the community of Islam. . . . C5 believers meet regularly with other C5 believers and share their faith with unsaved Muslims. Unsaved Muslims may see C5 believers as theologically deviant and may eventually expel them from the community of Islam. Where entire villages accept Christ, C5 may result in "Messianic mosques." C5 believers are viewed as Muslims by the Muslim community and refer to themselves as Muslims who follow Isa the Messiah.

C6: Small Christ-Centered Communities of Secret/Underground Believers. Similar to persecuted believers suffering under totalitarian regimes. Due to fear, isolation, or threat of extreme governmental/community legal action or retaliation (including capital punishment), C6 believers worship Christ secretly (individually or perhaps infrequently in small clusters). . . . C6 believers are perceived by the Muslim community and identify themselves as Muslims. (Travis 1998)

DYNAMICS IN RELATION TO C1–C6

Although non-Muslim contexts are obviously different, we can loosely adapt these categories for use in other religious settings, because the basis for each description is the fellowship's degree of "foreignness" or appropriateness in relation to the local culture. Large numbers of believers fit into each of these categories, but the situation is not static. Due to the fact that missionary advocacy has favored C1 and C2 types, however, greater cultural prestige has usually accompanied these more foreign expressions. It is C1 and C2 Christianity that provides the schools and hospitals that carry great prestige. This sets up a dynamic that often results in believers of types C3–C5 seeking to identify with these less culturally appropriate forms of Christianity. If C4 or C5 believers become aware of the greater amenities (e.g., schools, travel) and prestige accompanying the more foreign churches, there is a powerful pull in the direction of these forms of Christianity. Though the pull is away from biblical meaningfulness, the quest for prestige and advantage may be too hard to resist.

For example, when members of Lao-speaking congregations in northeast Thailand who might correspond to C5 on the Spectrum move to Bangkok and attend C1 and C2 churches there, they find that there are opportunities for cultural advancement in relation to the dominant Thai society. There may be such things as schools for their children, assistance with material needs, contact with people of prestige who call themselves "Christians," and a feeling of connection with the outside world that they did not experience back at home. These advantages provide powerful motivation for movement into a less culturally appropriate form of Christianity.

But a movement away from appropriateness and relevance may occur even in small towns and rural areas such as the one in northeast Nigeria where my wife and I served. Though in the early days of the Christian movement among the Kamwe, our churches were known for their "capturing" of indigenous musical expression, the pressure to have hymnbooks with songs in the trade language—Hausa—was just too great for many of the congregations, even though a majority of the people could not read. And the church leaders often succumbed to the pressure to use the prestigious Hausa language rather than Kamwe in preaching and the conducting of church services as well—especially those who wished to show off their fluency in that language.

Thus C4 and C3 Christians get "weaned" from appropriate and relevant forms of Christian expression and move into C2 or C1 expressions, considering these to be more prestigious and even more orthodox. They miss the point that Christian faith is intended to be contextualized in relevant indigenous cultural forms and instead settle for some adaptation of foreign forms, thus learning to express their Christian faith with a foreign accent.

Yet, in other places, some who have been practicing C1 or C2 Christianity may develop a deepening understanding of God's desire to reach them in their own familiar cultural context. They may sense that God meant Christianity to be truly theirs and gravitate toward more culturally appropriate forms of Christian expression, moving from C1 or C2 into a C3 type of Christianity. For instance, there is a vital movement among American Indians that is attempting to do just that. Several generations of "Amerindian" Christians have only had Anglo forms of Christianity available to them, and many of the older leaders in these churches are so entrenched in these foreign patterns, and have been so thoroughly taught that no native Indian cultural forms are acceptable to God, that they are dead set against any use of Indian cultural practices in Christian expression. But a younger generation of leaders is helping a growing number of Amerindian Christians to recapture traditional cultural forms for Christ.

As I point out in chapter 10, often such movements are a feature of third- or fourth-generation Christianity. Whereas the first and second generations of Christians could not imagine that God would want to use traditional cultural forms, from the third generation on there is often a movement within the society as a whole—including the Christian segment—that seeks to recapture traditional forms. Pride in a people's ancestry often develops, moving Christians to reevaluate cultural forms long since condemned and to experiment with more contextual expressions of their faith.

One of the important dynamics of Christian expression is therefore the instability of at least certain types of Christian expression with regard to the cultural forms used by the members of those groups to express their Christian faith. Christ-centered communities that are introduced to the faith in one of the C1–C6 types may, either within any given generation or between generations, move to another type—moving either toward or away from what we would consider greater cultural appropriateness and relevance.

REEVALUATE IN EACH GENERATION

In chapter 10, I write of the need for the Christian community in each generation to reevaluate and adjust their relationship to the culture. The dynamic of such reevaluation and adjustment can be an important factor in keeping the pressure on for change, especially if the guiding principle is that the community experience growth toward maturity.

The process of looking at the forms in use and asking questions about their relevance at least every generation is an enlivening and motivation-building process. The changes that are made during and after such a process can result in greater attractiveness of Christianity to the non-Christian population, and a corresponding influx of new converts. Such evangelistic success would be a great encouragement to the Christian community and could stimulate them to spiritual growth as they enfold and teach the new converts.

Having said this, it is unfortunate that we have to note that churches ordinarily do not reevaluate each generation and therefore do not take advantage of this dynamic. Christians seem, rather, to largely carry on from generation to generation whatever practices were developed in the earliest generations without asking whether these practices are appropriate to the present generation. In so doing, the Christian community tends to move into nominalism and spiritual deadness.

Worse yet, if the first generation simply imitated the cultural forms of the advocates who brought them the gospel, it is these uncontextual forms that get carried down from generation to generation. And a nationalistic reaction, usually by the third generation, against both the forms and the meanings of what is experienced as a foreign Christianity often results in a serious decline in both the membership of the churches and their vitality.

CHAPTER 9
DYNAMICS OF CONTEXTUALIZATION

In 1979, I published a book on contextualization titled *Christianity in Culture* (revised 2005). One of the concepts I discussed in that book was the importance of the pressure a community of believers puts on the process of cultural transformation. Specifically, once a person or group makes a commitment to Christ, they are expected to embark on a process of change in the direction of greater Christlikeness. That process is not an easy one. It ordinarily requires guidance so that people will know what the goal is and how to get there, and pressure to keep them working in the right direction against their natural tendency to resist change.

It is from this perspective that I want to discuss the dynamics of contextualization. It is well and good that we discuss, as we have done, the nature of appropriate Christianity and its various facets. But an important question is, how do we get there? Does movement toward local expressions of Christianity just happen without any effort? If people are left alone with nothing but the Bible to guide them, are they likely to develop culturally and biblically appropriate forms of Christian expression?

Unfortunately, the answer to these last two questions is no. The answer to the first—How do we get there?—is more complex. And it is to the various facets of the answer to that question that I wish to direct our attention in this chapter.

THE GOAL

It is not necessarily obvious to people who are newly Christian what the goal of their new faith commitment is. Oftentimes neither the individuals who come to Christ nor the groups of believers who form the churches seem to understand that the ideal for a church is that they be

> a group of believers who live out their life, including their socialized Christian activity, in the patterns of the local society, and for whom any transformation of that society comes out of their felt needs under the guidance of the Holy Spirit and the Scriptures. . . . An [appropriate] church is precisely one in which the changes which take place under the

> guidance of the Holy Spirit meet the needs and fulfill the meanings of that society and not of any outside group. (Smalley 1958, 55–56)

Nor do they see that it is only

> when the indigenous people of a community think of the Lord as their own, not a foreign Christ; when they do things as unto the Lord meeting the cultural needs around them, worshipping in patterns they understand; when their congregations function in participation in a body, which is structurally indigenous; then you have an [appropriate] Church. (Tippett 1973, 158)

Though we may seek for "an expression of Christianity that is both culturally authentic and genuinely Christian" (Stott and Coote 1980, 214), the goal in the minds of many may be nothing more than achieving new and more powerful friends, or the benefits of schooling, or the chance to perhaps travel overseas. For others, it may be some other personal or social attraction. But even if the motivation for coming to Christ is more or less pure, converts may be puzzled as to what comes next.

As we know, the Christian community may be living far below any ideal for the Christian life that we find in Scripture. And new converts may not even know they are supposed to live up to scriptural ideals, especially if they, like 70 percent of the world, cannot read. Christians may not be more moral, more honest, or more admirable than non-Christians, and they may not know they are supposed to be. In addition, they may be more westernized, which might be a plus or a minus for those considering turning to Christianity.

Such characteristics, however, may not be entirely the fault of the Christians themselves. The local Christians might simply be ignorant of the need for change that is so prominent in Scripture, for they might know little of what the Scriptures teach. They may be illiterate or not functionally literate in an area where the missionaries focused on reading the Bible rather than hearing it (e.g., via cassettes). The missionaries may have conducted literacy campaigns but been unaware of the fact that most literacy campaigns fail to bring people to a position in which they are able to get new information from reading.

Furthermore, what they have learned concerning the need for change may have focused more on changes of custom in the direction of certain Western practices than on learning to express scriptural ideals in their own cultural context. They may have been presented with Christianity as religion, or from their own perspective interpreted the new message that way rather than learning that it is a faith relationship with God that can be expressed in their own way. They then assumed that all they needed to do was to adopt and adapt a new set of religious customs.

If the confusion is to be overcome, then, we must be clear about what a Christian in any society should be aiming for. What is the goal toward which Christians are to move? We have stated the goal of cultural appropriateness above. This is an appropriateness in *meaning* and *commitment*. No cultural forms in use for Christian purposes are appropriate if people attribute to them the wrong meanings or fail to get into the right relationship with God. See chapter 6 on whether or not Christianity is a religion and chapter 3 on meaning equivalence Christianity for more on this subject.

Appropriateness to the Scriptures means appropriate scriptural meanings in the receptors' minds, with appropriate responses to those meanings. The ideals presented in Scripture are, therefore, important goals for a people to understand and to express in life. Things like righteousness, truthfulness, kindness, compassion, humility, love, and the rest of the fruits of the Spirit (Gal 5:22,23) immediately come to mind—all expressed in ways appropriate to the culture. I would add ministering in the love and power of Jesus. Most of these are manifested in observable behavior. However, other, less easily observable things should be included too. Among these are closeness to Jesus, prayerfulness, the ability to resist temptation, and a God-approved thought life. All of these add up to being like Jesus, the perfect example of what humankind was intended to be—again, expressed in culturally appropriate ways.

The ideals seem clear in the abstract. But questions arise when we recognize that Christianity is meant to be contextualized and when we ask how these ideals should look in a culture quite different from that of the persons who brought the message. For each society has its own definitions of righteousness, love, and the rest of the visible behaviors. And there may be differences between peoples when it comes to some of the invisible behaviors as well.

A start toward an appropriate goal may, however, be made by *attempting to imagine what Jesus' behavior might look like in any given society*. How would He show righteousness, love, compassion, etc., in culturally appropriate ways in society *X*? How would He express prayerfulness and closeness to the Father in that society? And how would Jesus avoid the trap that both missionaries and nationals ordinarily fall into of borrowing behavioral patterns from a foreign culture?

The goal, then, is clear. But the implementation is a challenge in terms of our aim to see produced a contextually appropriate Christianity.

THE UNIQUENESS OF CHRISTIANITY

As discussed in chapter 6, biblical Christian faith is unique, especially when compared with the religions of the world. For, as mentioned above, it is *a matter of meanings*, not of cultural forms. Religions are locked into certain cultural forms. They come in cultural containers. If one is to be an orthodox Muslim, for example, certain ways of worship, modes of dress, and memorization of the Quran in Arabic are required—

all of which are parts of the culture of origin of Islam. Likewise with Hinduism, Judaism, Buddhism, Shinto, and the rest.

Animism, the faith of probably three-quarters of the peoples of the world—including most of the adherents of the above-named religions—may be an exception to the rule. The reason is that animism is Satan's cleverest counterfeit of Christianity and is therefore adaptable to—contextualized in—any culture, just as Christianity is supposed to be.

Biblical Christianity (as opposed to the religion called Christianity) is not intended to be merely a religion. Jesus said, "I am come that they might have *life*" (John 10:10). And this life, according to the Apostle Paul, is to be expressed in Jewish culture by Jews and in Gentile culture by Gentiles (1 Cor 9:19–21). The intended cultural container for Christianity, then, is not that in which our faith was born but that in which those who receive it live. Ours is a "receptor-oriented" faith, made up of meanings and life-expressions that are intended to be detached from its cultural source when embraced by those from societies other than the Jewish society in which it was born.

For this reason we talk about contextualization rather than adaptation. Religions can be adapted to a certain extent to the receptors' culture. But, in addition to the adapted forms, the religions of the world (except for animism) always require cultural forms that originated in the source culture. Christianity, however, is made up of commitments and meanings that can and should be expressed in cultural forms that bear no such stigma of foreignness. The fact that many cultural expressions of Christianity have failed in this regard is unfortunate. But it produces an agenda for Christian leaders who understand that if Christianity is to be appropriate in any given society, it should be expressed in cultural forms as different from those of another cultural expression of Christianity as the overall forms of those two cultures differ.

Some may object to this characterization of the uniqueness of Christianity vis-à-vis the culture in which it is expressed. They might contend that such elements of Christianity as worship, church, and the sacraments are givens that need to be expressed in all cultures as they were in the New Testament. I would contend in response that each of these things, and all else in Christianity, is to be planted in every society as *meanings*, not as forms. That is, our faith is to involve us in worship, but how worship of the true God is appropriately expressed in any given society can and should be quite distinct. It should be easily identifiable by cultural insiders as worship.

We can point to Japanese Christianity as an example of the ignoring of this principle. One traditional form of worship in Japan (perhaps not the only one) is to go to a shrine to honor the god (*kami*) of that shrine by pouring water over a stone representation of that god (plus perhaps doing additional things) and asking it for a blessing. Unlike Western Christians who worship only at set times, Japanese are accustomed to performing such rites to seek spiritual power at shrines at any time of day, and well into the night. (The shrines I observed closed from about 11:00 p.m. to about 7:00

a.m.) A culturally appropriate form of Christian worship—one that would be easily interpretable by non-Christian Japanese as meaning worship—would involve the use of places and rituals similar to the shrine places and practices. We would not, of course, bathe idols. But establishing places that look to Japanese like they are places where one can meet God (the word *kami* is used for the Christian God as well as for pagan spirits) would go a long way toward communicating to Japanese that God wants to enter their culture rather than simply to convert them to American cultural worship forms.

As with worship, so also with church. The groupings called church in the New Testament were appropriate to each of the cultures in which they functioned: synagogue-type churches in Jewish culture; house churches in Gentile cultures. American churches are often quite different in many ways from NT churches, as they should be. The structuring of the church in other societies should, like worship and all the other structuring involved in Christian expression, also be easily understood by the receptors (non-Christians as well as Christians) as serving the biblical function intended by God. These functions should be culturally appropriate and therefore enable the receptors to readily attach the proper meanings to them without the need to learn what these things signify in the culture of the foreigners who brought the Christian message.

With regard to the sacraments, I would contend (contrary to some opinions) that for Christianity to be appropriate in a culture in which rice and *sake* are the typical food and drink for special occasions, these should be used in communion services. And the way initiation is regularly done in any given society should provide the model for the initiation into Christianity that we call baptism. If people want to borrow the traditional baptismal and communion forms in order to demonstrate their solidarity with the worldwide Christian community, so be it. But this is not required and may mark Christian faith in that society as foreign, especially if the foreign elements make up a large part of the ceremony. If used, then, these "historically Christian forms" should be practiced as parts of larger traditional events, so that people understand the significance and importance of the ceremonies and that they are not magic.

In many societies initiation ceremonies are quite elaborate. Thus, if entrance into Christianity is to be seen as important, the initiation ceremony needs to be elaborate. An elaborate ceremony opens up the possibility of performing most of the ceremony in a culturally appropriate way but including the foreign baptismal custom as a small part of that ritual. A people could do something very much like their own cultural tradition for initiation and fellowship that is both understandable and meaningful to cultural insiders, with the forms of worldwide Christian tradition added. When the percentage of foreign elements in a mostly traditional ceremony is small, the people of a given society would ordinarily have little problem recognizing the whole ceremony as theirs. That would be appropriate Christian ritual.

The point is that *Christian expression is to be translated culturally as well as linguistically.* Just as we expect the words of a good Bible translation to be easily interpretable by the receptors, so the other forms—the cultural forms—in terms of which our faith is expressed should be such that the receptors assign the correct meanings to them. This is the Apostle Paul's intent when he uses Jewish cultural forms to appeal to Jews with a message that is intended to convey God's meanings through their familiar forms. It is also his intent when he uses Gentile cultural forms to express that message in ways that enable Gentiles to correctly interpret God's meanings (1 Cor 9:19–22).

THE PROCESS

In *Christianity in Culture* I presented a number of models to help us think through the various aspects of theologizing in relation to culture. One of those models is what I have called "point plus process." This model simply labels the fact that God starts with people where they are and then seeks to partner with them to move them toward Christlikeness. Once again, though, it is culturally appropriate Christlikeness that we seek.

In working with people who have recently chosen Christ, it is important to help them understand that although God accepts them as they are, He has no intention of leaving them that way. Though it is not Jesus' intent to take them out of their familiar cultural life, *they are to be changed within that cultural context.* Change is built into true Christianity with the goal of Christlikeness firmly in view.

God has no problem accepting a selfish person who, even perhaps from selfish motivation, comes to Him through Jesus. But it is God's intent to work with that person toward selflessness. Likewise, God will accept people deep in habitual sin. But it is His intent to work with and empower such people to gain victory over both the sin and the habits. He regularly partners with unloving people to make them loving, with proud people to make them humble, with liars to make them truthful, with uncompassionate people to develop compassion in them—and none of this with the added requirement that they adopt the customs of another people.

Likewise, God has no problem with accepting people who, at the start, are not loving toward other people groups. An important part of the movement toward maturity for such people (probably all of us), however, is learning that God loves all of us, even our enemies, and that we are to love everyone too. We are taught in Scripture to love even our enemies (Luke 6:27–36). This is the ideal toward which we all are to work. But there are very few who are already practicing such love when they come to Christ.

A basic principle of God's interaction with humans has been codified in what has been termed the "homogeneous unit principle." This principle, simply stated, is that God accepts people groups as they are, with all of their idiosyncrasies and sub-Christian practices when they turn to Him in faith. Where God starts with a people is not, however, where He intends to end. At the start, He accepts and endorses their homogeneity, their "groupness," ignoring for the time being their exclusiveness and even animosity toward other people groups. But an important part of their growth in Christianity is the recognition that even enemies who belong to Jesus are their brothers and sisters, and are therefore to be accepted as "us" rather than "them."

So when we talk of people growing in their Christian experience, we are talking about the process of change that God expects of them. Where He starts is not where He intends to end. The start is merely the beginning point of a process during which a convert moves toward Christian maturity.

MOTIVATION TO CHANGE

A problem in all of this is the fact that people tend to be culturally conservative and unwilling to expend the energy required to change habits and customs. Consequently, they are usually not seeking to change, unless it is obvious that there is some major benefit to be gained. The economic principle of gain minus cost is often key in the thinking of those considering change. That is, if they count the cost of the change (e.g., the possibility that their family might turn against them), and subtract that from the anticipated benefit (e.g., eternity with God in heaven), and decide that the gain is more valuable than the cost, then they may be willing to make the change—if they are willing to expend the necessary energy.

Since it is habits that keep people following their customs, habits are what have to be changed. And changing habits is hard work, even if a person or group is highly motivated. Such change is even more difficult if the goals are not clear. If people are highly motivated to make the recommended changes, there can be great success. If, however, their motivation is not high and/or the goals are not clear, the process of change may not go very far.

A place where agents of change often fail is in the setting of clear goals. Many American converts, for example, are welcomed into the kingdom when they first decide to follow Christ, but they are not realistically informed as to what awaits them in their journey with Christ in the years to come. They may be taught that there is something called "Christian maturity" toward which they should strive. But just what that amounts to may be quite vague. In cross-cultural situations, then, the closest thing to defining the goals toward which people are to strive may be the impression people receive that they should imitate Westerners. Such external things as learning to read, having only one wife, earning a salary, and living like Euro-Americans may (whether consciously or unconsciously) be considered requirements for spiritual growth.

The challenge for contextualizers, then, is to discover what the goals should be in any given society and to make them clear to the Christian populace. For the marks of spiritual maturity in one society should not be automatically considered normative for another society. And in any event, the focus needs to be where Jesus put it—

on internal motivation rather than simply on external behavior, though the latter should be in view as well.

If in the process of change we can assume that the goals are clear, great attention needs to be given to developing and increasing the motivation so that the process will go the full distance. Something as difficult as changing habits needs strong motivation to see it through. Perhaps the two major factors in increasing the motivation necessary for permanent change are what might be termed things that "push" and things that "pull."

People can be motivated toward or away from change through group pressure. Such pressure is a kind of external push factor when it is used to bring about change. Another external push factor for many is the presence of rules and/or laws. People can also be motivated toward or away from change by internal push factors, such as the fear of failing to live up to the rules or of not remaining in good standing with the society.

Push factors that come from outside a society are likely to be less effective than those coming from within a society. Or, if outside pressure is effective, it often results in a negative reaction and a reversal of whatever change has been made once the outside force leaves. That is, outside push factors such as missionary rules may bring about fairly quick change that gets reversed once the missionaries are no longer in control. In the area of northern Nigeria where we served, teachers in mission schools were required by the mission to be monogamous. Several of them took additional wives, however, after the government took over the schools.

In addition to push factors, there are things that pull or entice people to change. The desire to become like some admired person would be a pull factor. So would the desire of a group to become like another group. Unlike push factors, pull factors coming from outside the society can remain powerful even after those who introduced them have left.

Dissatisfaction with what already exists provides what is possibly the greatest push factor. When things aren't working, people often develop high motivation for change, if they know of or can imagine a better approach. When needs, especially needs considered basic, are not being met by a person or group's present cultural involvement in a given area, such persons or groups are often (though not always) more open to possible change than otherwise. We are told that when the early missionaries arrived in Hawaii, they entered a situation in which the traditional gods were felt to have died. This resulted in a cultural void that provided the local people with a push toward consideration of the new faith.

That kind of push, when combined with the pull of something that appears to be a good way out of a problem, produces a strong impetus toward change. The Hawaiians were wide open to the message of the missionaries to make that initial change into Christianity, with both a motivational push and a pull toward change.

As I have written in other chapters, a major area of pull in most societies is the promise of greater spiritual power. Perhaps the greatest quest for the majority of the world's peoples is the quest for enough spiritual power to make the living of life more bearable. Thus, the introduction of a Christianity that demonstrates more power and better power (i.e., without the negative consequences of traditional options) can provide a strong pull in a Christward direction. For many people their traditional understandings of and approaches to spiritual power are felt to be oppressive. This opens up for Christians the opportunity to point people to the power wrapped in love that Jesus demonstrated and commissions His followers to provide.

The possibility of being in relationship to the members of an attractive group can also be highly motivating, bringing with it the desire to change to fit into that group. Such a pull is a horizontal relational pull. A desire to be pleasing to God provides a kind of vertical relational pull. Such a pull may center on gratefulness for what God has done for us, motivating us to obey His commands not out of obligation but out of love and a strong desire to please the One who has done so much for us. When the horizontal pull of an attractive group is combined with the vertical pull of gratefulness to God, the impact on motivation is great.

A major pull for Christians is to be like Jesus or like someone who follows Jesus closely. The Apostle Paul recognized his own responsibility in this area by inviting people to follow him as he followed Jesus (1 Cor 11:1). For those deeply committed to Jesus, the pull of Christlikeness can be a powerful motivating factor. We are instructed in Romans 12:1,2 to work with God to transform our whole lives into a long-term act of worship. Such a commitment makes the pull of Christlikeness effective. There may, however, be challenges if the person being imitated is of a different culture than those seeking to imitate him or her. Cross-cultural witnesses need to be aware of this fact and continually use as their model how Jesus and they themselves would live if they were part of the receiving society.

The greatest challenges in this area come from the attempts to motivate groups who have just begun to change to continue to press on toward Christian maturity. The temptations to quit once the hard work begins are many. While highly motivated individuals usually succeed, the task of keeping the press and pull in the direction of Christlikeness on whole churches is fraught with difficulties, and the danger that groups of new converts will be drawn back into their pre-Christian understandings and behavior is a real threat. For worldview assumptions can have what might be called a "bungee cord" influence on people who may be moving in the right direction but have not completely replaced their previous assumptions. As with Gideon in the Old Testament (Judg 7–9) and the people of Judah every time a wicked king succeeded a good king, people who at one time decide for Christ may at a later time revert to their previous worldview if the pressure to keep moving in the right direction is relaxed.

The church is God's instrument to keep the right kind of pressure for change on those who convert. It is often the case, however, that any given church body is not itself pulled or pushed enough in the right direction to provide the proper motivation for its members. We see in Latin American Christianity the results of a movement toward Christianity that did not involve the right kind and amount of motivation to move people into orthodoxy.

In this case, it is a fact that the Christianity that came from Spain and Portugal had already been "paganized" before it was brought to the New World. That is, such things as worship of Mary and the saints were already a part of the version of Christianity introduced in Latin America. This syncretized form of Christianity was accepted by the people as little more than an overlay on their pre-Christian worldview and loyalties. The result is what we call "Christo-paganism"—a system of loyalties and practices that have "Christian" names (e.g., the names of European saints) and employ certain Christian symbols (e.g., the crucifix) but perpetuate most of the pagan beliefs and practices they were intended to replace. (For example, the names of the saints and of God and Mary really represent pre-Christian deities.) Though there were changes on the part of the converts, there has not been the push or the pull to move them into true Christianity.

THE NEED FOR PRESSURE

The conservatism of people contemplating change leads to the need for something to apply pressure for change. As mentioned above, high motivation toward seeking to become Christlike is probably the best form of pressure, since motivation-induced pressure comes from within. It is important, then, to seek ways to nurture and increase such motivation. This is to be a major function of the church.

Jesus admonished us to seek first His kingdom and righteousness (Matt 6:33). The church, the Christian community, should apply pressure on its members to aim at that goal, a relational goal. Jesus also indicated that it is in the keeping of His commandments that we show love toward Him (John 14:21). This too is relational. The Christian community is the vehicle, established by God, that is charged with both informing us of what those commandments are and pressuring us to keep them. Our growth, however, is to be in the relationship with the Command Giver, not merely in the impersonal keeping of the rules, as if it were the rules and not the relationship that were central.

When the activity of the church, then, devolves to merely providing a weekly lecture (sermon), the amount of pressure for relational growth is usually not enough to bring about the appropriate kind, amount, and speed of change. As communication experts tell us, lectures are seldom effective in bringing about change in people unless the people are already highly motivated to change. And when, as is common around the world, the lectures are more likely to revolve around intellectual issues than the kinds of things that could motivate people to grow in their relationship, their ineffectiveness is magnified.

Jesus lectured from time to time. It is instructive to note, though, that He spoke pictorially rather than intellectually, and almost always with a relationship to God and/or people in focus. His use of stories that can be pictured corresponds with insights underlined in research into how our memories work (see Schacter 1996). This research shows that our ability to remember pictures and stories is much greater than our ability to remember statements, doctrines, and intellectual propositions.

Although Jesus used the best way to communicate verbally, His primary communication was relational and experiential, primarily with the disciples but also with others with whom He interacted. What He said was much less important in His ministry than what He demonstrated of God, what He demonstrated concerning how humans ought to live and behave, and His relational way of teaching His followers. He pressured His followers to change by leading them relationally, setting an example for them to follow, and then empowering them with the Holy Spirit and leaving the kingdom in their hands.

An additional important aspect of the press and pull Jesus was able to exert was the fact that He offered the thing most people were most attracted to: spiritual power. The essence of His ministry and the thing He focused on concerning God the Father was, of course, love—a relational thing. However, He used His power to show His love, combining an emphasis on relationship with a use of spiritual power. Spiritual power provided a motivational draw for the people of Jesus' day. It does the same for the people of our day. Relationship, then, together with the example He set for His followers, provided powerful motivation for those with Him to become like their Master. These facts should reinforce our interest in the contextualization of relationship and spiritual power in addition to our emphasis on contextualizing knowledge/truth.

As pointed out in chapter 5, the relational dimension of the church pictures the church as a family. A healthy family grows together, each person encouraging and helping the others to become all they are meant to become. The spiritual power dimension of the church, then, pictures the church first as a hospital, bringing healing to people, and second as an army, fighting the enemy and taking "territory" from him. Working with Jesus in power motivates both by bringing healing and by the renewing power of experiencing great results when we work with Jesus to set captives free. Each of these dimensions, then, can play an important part in helping to keep the pressure on for change.

The place and practices of leaders are crucial if pressure is to be applied for change. Unfortunately, leaders tend to support the status quo, lest they be relieved of their responsibilities. If, however, those leaders who are more committed to God than to their positions can be helped to see that God wants growth and change to meet changing conditions, there may be hope. Such leaders need to recognize that Christianity is intended to be dynamic, not static, and that their concern should be for moving forward, not simply maintaining the present structures and practices.

To equip leaders for dynamic leadership, an apprenticeship model is much more effective than a classroom model. I believe that Jesus was not simply being relevant to His sociocultural context by choosing to train His followers through discipleship, but that He was using a cross-culturally valid, dynamic form of training that enables the trainees to learn by doing and thus to participate in the process of the Christian witness and growth that live Christianity aims at. A concern for keeping the pressure on for change should therefore provide as much of such dynamic teaching as possible, avoiding the static nature of non-experiential, classroom, information-based teaching.

WAYS OF KEEPING THE PRESSURE ON

There are various ways in which the Christian community can keep the pressure for growth on themselves. Scripture study and memorization should be a major concern, since it is Scripture that provides the clearest goals and guidelines. An interesting confirmation of this fact is that research concerning African Independent Churches that split off from mission churches showed a significant difference between the orthodoxy of those churches that centered their life and ministries on the Bible and those that did not (see Barrett 1968). Those that made the Bible central moved toward greater orthodoxy. Those that did not make the Bible central moved away from orthodoxy.

Bible study in small groups is, of course, more effective in this regard than simply listening to sermons. When the church is made up largely of nonliterate or minimally literate people, the use of taped reading or dramatization of Scripture is an important method. Whether the people are literate or nonliterate, singing Scripture and scriptural themes can be perhaps the most effective way of getting Scripture into the hearts of people.

In taking the gospel to the Behinimo people of Papua New Guinea, Wycliffe translators Wayne and Sally Dye developed a contextualized approach that served well to keep the pressure on. Having learned the language and started Bible translation, they carefully chose for translation those portions they deemed to be most relevant to their people. As they translated these portions, the Dyes presented them to the tribal leaders for discussion among the leaders in village gatherings on Sunday mornings. These discussions became the Behinimo church services. Though at first the leaders had made no profession of faith in Christ, the aim of the discussions was to determine how these words from God would be applied to their lives and the lives of their followers. In this way, the pressure was generated by sincere people with the encouragement of the missionaries for personal and cultural change.

In all situations, prayer should be a major part of the process. Invoking the help of the Holy Spirit to keep the pressure on for change should be rule number one. All discussion, all use of Scripture, all singing and worship, even all lecturing, should be bathed in prayer and openness for God to show the group what changes need to be made and when. Every Christian ministry should have people with the gift of intercession active in supporting that ministry in intercessory prayer.

CONCLUSION

The aim of this chapter has been to alert us to at least some of the dynamics of contextualization. Christianity is not meant by God to be a static thing. It is to be dynamic, living. God expects change, growth, and movement toward spiritual maturity. Our goal is to be as like Jesus as possible, individually and corporately. He is our Alpha and our Omega, our Source and our Goal.

A key function of the church, then, is to keep the pressure on its members toward growth. The greatest source of this pressure is the motivation that we internalize as Christians who sincerely want to please our Lord by becoming more like Him. For most of us, though, it helps if there are incentives such as satisfactory relationships with God and other Christians plus benefits such as healing for ourselves and the privilege of working with Jesus to bring about change and growth in others.

CHAPTER 10
CONTEXTUALIZATION AND TIME
Generational Appropriateness

When we discuss contextualization, we usually ignore the time factor. I have only seen one brief mention of the differences between first- and second-generation approaches to contextualization in the various studies I have surveyed (Shaw 1995, 159). We act as if any group that needs to consider whether or not its Christian expressions are appropriate will need to deal with the same things as any other group might. However, situations differ. And one of the major ways in which contextualization situations differ is in the generation in which the people in focus find themselves with respect to their acceptance of Christianity. It is important for us to know where a given people group is in their Christian experience before we can speak knowledgeably about the kinds of things that would be appropriate for them.

We often assume we are working with the first generation of Christians in any given society. But most people are no longer in that generation. So, if we are to be relevant to those who are helping people in the contextualization process, we need to address ourselves to the challenges that face Christ-followers at whatever point they are.

In the first generation of a people's Christian commitment, when everything is new and they are just coming out of their pre-Christian allegiance, the major issues in their minds may not be concerns about relevance and adaptation to their culture. First-generation Christians are more likely to be concerned about issues of *separation* and *contrast*. Their attention is most often focused on assuring that they are safe from the revenge of the spiritual powers they have renounced. Furthermore, they want to discover which customs they are supposed to reject in order to demonstrate their new faith in contrast to the lives of those around them who have not converted.

True, it is important that the newly chosen faith be experienced as relevant to at least parts of the lives of the converts. But it is probably too much to expect new converts to develop the energy and insight needed to work out the multitude of details involved in changing their way of life, and especially their worldview, to fit their new faith. And the converts should not be criticized if they adopt what may eventually look like too much foreignness in the first generation. There will be much adaptation, to be sure, but we should not be surprised if it is quite incomplete at this point, since imitating the outsiders who brought the good news may be the only way they can imagine of expressing their faith.

As we see in Acts 15, even those Jewish Christians who had known Christ for some time had difficulty imagining that Christian faith could be appropriately expressed in Gentile cultural forms. How much more is it likely that those who come to Christ where the gospel is new have the same difficulty of imagining their own cultural forms as vehicles of the new faith? They are therefore usually inclined to simply imitate the cultural forms of the outside witnesses on the assumption (often shared by the outsiders) that those forms are God-ordained.

A major problem, however, is the fact that practices that get started in the first generation tend to get "set in cement" and may not be modified or replaced in succeeding generations with more culturally appropriate practices. It seems to be a well-nigh universal tendency for people to regard as absolute, even sacred, most or all of the cultural forms the missionaries brought to them. They see to it, therefore, that the church members carefully imitate and scrupulously pass on these "sacred" traditions to newcomers and new generations.

This first-generation problem is quite different for those who have entered Christianity through a people movement. When large groups come in with their pre-Christian cultural ways largely intact, they may change their behavior and worldview less than they should. They may simply continue practices that honor their previous gods or that are incongruent with Christian moral standards without even knowing that they should change them. It is more likely to be those who convert one by one, or who choose in small groups to go against their previous allegiance, who accommodate to the outsiders and change their behavior more than they should.

Either way, there is much contextualizing to be done in succeeding generations. Because of the likelihood of incomplete, inappropriate, or otherwise inadequate contextualization, perhaps we should be looking more to the second, third, or following generations for most of what we seek in the development of appropriate cultural expressions of biblical faith.

PERCEIVING RELEVANCE

From an evangelical point of view, the essence of contextualization (inculturation, localization, or dynamic equivalence) is the implementation of biblical Christianity in culturally appropriate ways. This is ideally to be done by the insiders of any given society who perceive the gospel to be relevant and work out ways to express their new faith in appropriate cultural forms. This process is facilitated by the relevant communication of biblical messages to those insiders. But perceptions of relevance differ from generation to generation. What is considered very relevant in one generation may be looked at in quite a different way in a later generation. Likewise, structures and other forms of expression of the faith that have been worked out as quite appropriate in one generation may be seen as quite inappropriate at a later time.

Given, say, three generations of Christian witness and experience with Christianity, we can assume that there are reasons why the early converts turned to Christ. We can also assume that there are reasons why those of the second and third generations have continued to follow Christ and conversions from the non-Christian populace have continued to happen. But the reasons for each succeeding generation will be different.

I think we can safely assume that what is appropriate thinking and structuring in the first generation will at best be only partially appropriate for the second, and at worst be totally inappropriate. In addition, whether or not the first Christians did a good job at contextualizing for their time and cultural circumstances, succeeding generations will always have more work to do to "complete" the task. This is true for at least two reasons: (1) the first generation would not have been able to complete the job even for their own generation's needs; and (2) culture change will have raised some new issues to deal with.

I advocate, therefore, that there be built into the principles on which any group of Christians operate the concept of *continuous contextualization*. What this would involve would be continuous, generation-by-generation re-evaluation of church customs, and consciously experimenting in one generation with approaches that might well be abandoned in another. This is necessary because the issues are different for each generation, especially in view of the rapid pace of culture change throughout the world. Even if the contextualization was done appropriately in the first generation (and usually it is not), there will be different issues to deal with in the following generations. We must therefore ask how what might be labeled a "spirit of openness to continual adjustment and change" can be instilled in converts, lest they simply pass on from generation to generation patterns that are culturally and personally dysfunctional.

DEALING WITH FORMS, MEANINGS, AND EMPOWERMENT

As anthropologists we have learned to use the label *cultural forms* to designate all of the parts of culture, including customs, material objects, and cultural patterns such as words, grammatical patterns, rituals, and all of the other elements of culture in terms of which people conduct their daily lives. All of culture, whether surface-level and visible or deep-level (worldview) and invisible, is made up of what we call cultural forms.

People, as they use and think about these cultural forms, assign meanings to them, usually according to what they have been taught by their parents, peers, and teachers. Though the forms are parts of culture, the meanings belong to the people. They are not inherent in the forms themselves. They are attached to the forms on the basis of group agreements. That is, the people of a society, largely because they have been taught by their elders, agree that certain forms will have certain meanings and therefore will be used for certain purposes. When outsiders enter a society, they have great difficulty understanding what's going on because they do not know the agreements of the insiders.

But cultural forms can also be empowered with spiritual power. Such things as material objects, buildings, and rituals can be dedicated and thus convey the power of God (if dedicated to Him) or of Satan (if dedicated to him). In dedications, blessing, and cursing, words are used to convey that power. These words are empowered as they are used in obedience to either God or Satan. When cultural forms are thus empowered, they *convey* (not *contain*) spiritual power.

In the Scriptures we see God empowering such things as the Ark of the Covenant (Josh 3:14–17), Paul's handkerchiefs and aprons (Acts 19:12), Jesus' gown (Luke 8:42–48), and anointing oil (Jas 5:15,16). But Satan can also empower cultural forms. One passage among many in which it is clear that God recognizes the dangers of satanic empowerment of objects and places is Joshua 7:11,12. There He commands Joshua to cancel that power by destroying captured objects, tearing down altars to pagan gods, and consecrating the land.

Missionary Christianity has been delinquent in dealing with empowerment issues, probably because missionaries didn't know what to do about spiritual power. The fact is, however, that satanic power is usually easy to deal with if it is recognized and handled with understanding and the power of Christ. Material objects that have been dedicated to pagan gods can usually be "cleansed" simply by asserting the authority of Christ to break the power in them. If, however, the object has no other purpose than a religious or occult one, I recommend that it be destroyed as well. Land and buildings can also usually be disempowered relatively easily. All that is necessary is for those in authority over them to assert that authority in the name of Christ, thus breaking the power that has been bestowed upon the elements in the past and in the present.

There are objects and places that need to be *disempowered* before Christian activity can take place unhindered. One of several biblical examples of this principle occurred when King Josiah *purified* the temple from all the abominations of the worshipers of Baal (2 Kgs 23:4–24). Clearly Josiah disempowered the objects and the temple from all evil power. Then, by re-consecrating the objects and the place to the Lord, he restored God's empowerment to them.

On several occasions I have been consulted about or heard of mission stations, homes, or churches that have been built on land that turned out to be infested with evil spirits. One such story comes from Sierra Leone, where about a century ago the village leaders deliberately gave the missionaries rights to a plot called "spirit hill" because they knew it was inhabited by spirits. Missionary after missionary who lived in the homes built on that land was forced to leave the field by such things as illness, marriage problems, accidents, problems with children, and the like, until fairly recently, when someone who understood how to handle satanic empowerment helped them break that power. Breaking the power was relatively easy because of the much greater power of Jesus. It was discovering the problem that was the hard part, due to the missionaries' ignorance concerning spiritual power. Because of this ignorance, family after family of dedicated missionaries experienced satanic attacks that could have been prevented.

In addition to places that need to be disempowered, power needs to be broken over any objects that have been dedicated to gods and spirits. Not infrequently, missionaries and national church leaders are given or buy art objects or work implements that have been dedicated or cursed. In many societies, such dedication is routinely done by the maker when the object is made. And sometimes a curse is deliberately put on the object by those who wish to thwart God's work. As long as such objects are in homes or churches, there will be enemy interference. Again, such empowerment is usually not difficult to break for those who know what they are doing.

The meaning problem is, however, much more difficult to deal with. For, as pointed out above, meanings exist in people and are attached by people to cultural forms according to group agreements (see Kraft 1991). The introduction of Christianity into a society will, of course, involve both the introduction of new cultural forms and the use of certain traditional forms in new ways. With regard to the latter, there will need to be changes in the meanings attached to them. Converts in the first generation will have to decide what changes to require in the meanings they attach to the traditional forms they retain. They will also have to decide the approved meanings of the new forms.

Advocates of the new faith (such as missionaries), since they are outsiders, will not be able to guide all of the choices made by the converts, making it probable that the latter will misunderstand at least certain of the meanings intended by the advocates. These misunderstood meanings, then, will likely be passed on to the next generation of Christians, creating a problem (whether or not it is recognized) for the second generation.

Since first-generation converts usually have a primary concern to dissimilate from their unconverted neighbors, they often borrow too many of the cultural forms of the missionaries on the assumption that those forms are a sacred and necessary part of Christian faith. Such borrowed forms are almost certain to have mistaken meanings attached to them, especially by the non-Christians who have little or no contact with the missionaries or other advocates of the new faith.

Since people in groups change slowly, even highly motivated Christians may not, at least in the first generation, change the meanings of traditional forms sufficiently to assure that the biblical message is being properly communicated. Attempts to "cleanse" words, rituals, and other cultural forms of their pagan meanings often take a long time, even under great pressure. And often there is not enough pressure put on such forms to bring about the necessary changes. An example mentioned in an earlier chapter is the use of the word *kami* for God by several generations of Japanese Christians. This word is still far from adequate, however, since it is simply the general word for *spirit* to most people, even to many Christians. Though for many Christians the pressure for change of meaning has been reasonably effective, there has not been nearly enough pressure to measurably affect the meaning in the minds of non-Christians and even of many Christians, especially new converts.

Recognizing the fact that it is a very slow process for people to change the meanings of traditional forms, many outside advocates have simply introduced foreign words and rituals. As mentioned previously, after nearly five hundred years of exposure to Christianity, in Latin America the meanings of many (perhaps most) of the words and rituals introduced by Roman Catholic missionaries are still quite pagan. A case in point is the Spanish word *Dios*, which often does not have the same meaning for ordinary people that it had for the Europeans who introduced it. Even after this length of time, *Dios* is usually understood, even by those who call themselves Christians, to be the sun god, with the name of the Virgin Mary used to label the moon and the names of Catholic saints attached to lesser traditional gods and ancestors. There has not been nearly enough pressure for change coming from inside or outside of the community of those who call themselves Catholics.

What is usually not built into the first-generation concept of Christianity is the need for understandings of Christian things to be continually in process. This process of meaning change needs to be calibrated to the growth of the Jesus community in their understandings of Scripture and their experiencing the presence and power of Jesus Christ. Whenever the expectation of such growth and change is not engendered in the first generation, there will be serious hindrances to increasing the inculturation of the gospel in subsequent generations.

Ideally, the new converts need to learn that whatever cultural forms are adopted, adapted, and created in the first generation should be seen as experimental, subject to revision in succeeding generations. Those in the second and succeeding generations, then, should understand that it is incumbent on them to evaluate the first-generation choices in the light of their scriptural understandings and experiences, and to make whatever changes and adjustments seem appropriate for the present.

Since this ideal is seldom realized, Christians of the second and succeeding generations need to be helped to understand the need for them to evaluate and, if necessary, adjust the cultural forms initiated by the first generation. Even in the occasional cases where the first-generation Christians contextualized well, subsequent generations will need to adjust their Christian forms and meanings to *their* reality, a reality that will always differ to some extent from that of their predecessors.

CONTEXTUALIZATION AND COMMUNICATION

The process of appropriate contextualization is enhanced by communication of biblical messages that receptors perceive as relevant to the realities of their life. Receptors have felt needs. Christianity rightly perceived relates very well to many of the felt needs of a people.

But receptors attach their own meanings to the messages communicated and therefore choose how to use Christian messages in relation to their own felt needs. Consequently, we who witness cross-culturally do not have as much control as we would like over what our receptors understand and how they use what we present.

Some people are well-adjusted in their cultural system; others are not. The former are unlikely to want to change their allegiance when the missionary comes to them with the message of the gospel. Unless there is good reason, such as economic gain or political prestige, the well-adjusted members of a society are not likely to embrace the new faith.

Those who are not making it in a society, however, often jump at the chance to adopt an alternative approach to life, or some part of it. Thus, when foreign ideas are introduced, these people convert, hoping to achieve the prestige and status in the new system that eluded them in the traditional one. They have learned to move "up" in the world by moving out of their traditions.

There are other, more legitimate felt needs, though people are not often as aware of these as they might be of the desire to escape from their traditional structures. The need for love, the need for meaningfulness, and the need for forgiveness fall into this category. The need for more spiritual power is usually also present—and generally at a more conscious level.

Historically, Christian witnesses have often given or allowed the impression that the satisfaction of these deeper needs comes only at the cost of ancestral traditions. In other words, people perceive that only if they leave their own traditions and become like the foreigners in many ways will they be eligible for such benefits.

Moving away from at least some of a people's traditions may well be required at some point for true Christian commitment, and a primary concern of the first generation is dissimilation. What is unfortunate, though, is that people have usually felt they have to dissimilate more by adopting new surface-level cultural forms, usually from Western sources, than by learning to express their deep-level commitments within their own traditional way of life.

When this happens, it is because something of the essence of Christianity has not been communicated. Converts miss—usually at least partially because the advocates have not emphasized it—that Christianity is a *process*, requiring continual reevaluation and adjustment as we grow in Christ.

Unfortunately, converts often understand their conversion as induction into a fairly well-defined and permanent state in which all the rules are set and simply adopted without question, even if the result involves a good bit of poorly understood foreign thinking and behaving.

So while the messages transmitted may have been relevant, they did not deal adequately with the biblical process of growth, and the impression the converts came away with was that the cultural forms associated with the first generation are to be followed forever. These forms are often regarded as sacred, unchangeable, delivered once and for all from heaven to the missionaries and through them to the receiving people. Furthermore, these "Christian" forms (including rituals) are often seen as *magical*, containing supernatural power made available to those who practice them exactly.

There is an important communication principle involved here. *When cultural (including language) forms that deal with the supernatural are not understood, they will often be perceived as sacred.* People will therefore often hold firmly (even fanatically) to these forms as if the *forms* themselves, as opposed to the *meanings* they convey, were God-given. They will assume that these forms are *magical*, containing power in and of themselves. And people are loath to abandon or change them, lest they lose the blessing or power that these forms supposedly contain.

Missionaries down through the centuries have seldom been aware enough of the dangers inherent in such an adoption of their foreign ways to take steps to prevent it. Indeed, like their converts, many missionaries have assumed that the foreign ways of worship, organization, buildings, education, and theological thinking are God-ordained and thus worthy of adoption by the converts. Only recently have the small percentage of missionaries who receive training for cross-cultural ministry begun to recognize the need to help people to resist such (often unconscious) cultural imperialism. They have begun to see the unscriptural nature of the implicit requirement that cultural conversion accompany spiritual conversion.

The adoption of such "sacred" foreign cultural forms is dangerous because it misleads converts into the unbiblical posture of seeing the essence of Christianity in the *forms*, including the rituals, rather than in the *meanings*. And since the foreign forms/rituals are regarded as magical, invested with power, they are felt to be efficacious only if they, like magic, are carried out exactly.

Resistance to change of such adopted customs is, therefore, based on spiritual misinterpretation as well as on such things as ignorance of the meanings of Christianity and respect for the advocates and their ways. As Darrell Whiteman (1997, 6) points out, this spiritually motivated attachment to Western church customs is probably a greater problem for the first generation than even the common understanding that Christianity requires such customs.

Often, neither the converts nor the missionaries have grasped one of the essential concepts underlying Christianity: that it is the Christian *meanings* (the faith) that are sacred, not the cultural *forms* (the religion) used to convey them. Our primary concern, therefore, whether in initial witness or in the continuing practice of the faith, should be that the forms employed be interpreted as conveying the proper meanings. With this in mind, Eugene Nida perceptively contrasts the Islamic concern that Muslims everywhere adopt a large number of "Islamic forms" with the Christian advocacy of what he terms "dynamic obedience" within each cultural context. Nida says,

> While the Koran attempts to fix for all times the behavior of Muslims, the Bible clearly establishes the principle of relative relativism, which permits growth, adaptation and freedom under the Lordship of Jesus Christ. . . . The Christian position is not one of static conformance to dead rules, but of dynamic obedience to a living God. (1954, 52)

DIFFERENCES OF CONCERN

To illustrate the different concerns of first- and second-generation Christians, let us take the issue of *baptism*. Though the first generation of believers in New Testament times baptized converts as adults, what were they to do in the second and succeeding generations, when children were brought up in Christian homes?

Children brought up by Christian parents are in quite a different situation than people who are being converted "out of the world." Adult converts typically have to turn from their un-Christian ways and adopt a new way of life. But children of Christian parents, if they accept their parents' faith, simply affirm the same way of life they were taught as children and continue in it. So, as children of Christian parents, they could be seen as children of the covenant their parents had made with God.

Soon after the beginnings of Christianity, it occurred to the believers that it would be appropriate to develop an initiation ceremony that would function like Jewish circumcision, to label each newborn child as participating in the commitment his or her parents had made with God. Hence, rightly or wrongly, the church began to practice infant baptism as a contextualization of Christian initiation for those born into Christian families.

In contemporary contexts, we note the concern of the first-generation converts to demonstrate their differences from the society around them. But at least by the third generation, we frequently find the Christian community sharing a concern of the non-Christians—to "discover their traditional roots." Such sentiments provide fertile ground for discussions of cultural appropriateness, though resistance to change on the part of entrenched leaders often keeps the discussions from accomplishing much in real life.

Separation

In the first generation of Christianity, when the gospel is new, converts are usually more concerned with breaking from their old ways in order to establish their new identity, so their tendency is to imitate the advocates' ways. Thus leadership and worship patterns, organizational structuring, biblical and theological training and understandings, and the like tend to be patterned after foreign models, whether or not the missionaries were recommending them. The result is *differentiation from* rather than *contextualization in* the surrounding culture.

Thus converts in many places have adopted the kind of clothing used by Westerners and a myriad of other surface-level customs, ranging from housing and eating to courtship and marriage patterns, in their attempts to show supposed differences between themselves as Christians and their non-Christian neighbors.

Breaking the Power

Many first-generation Christians rightly see the need to break from and reject practices that have traditionally served as vehicles of satanic power. Missionaries, especially those from the West, recognizing that there is a problem but not knowing what to do about it, usually push people to reject such customs completely. The concern is right, but the way it is typically handled tends to result in what Tippett (1987, 200) has called a "cultural void"—a situation in which the local customs are condemned but no viable alternative is suggested.

The void leaves most churches planted by foreign (usually Western or westernized) missionaries with an enormous problem. Since no substitute for pre-Christian spiritual power has been provided, large numbers of Christians continue to make use of their traditional power sources. Their commitment to Christ may be quite sincere. But when they need such things as healing, blessing, guidance, and fertility—things local shamans, priests, and diviners traditionally provide—they feel free to continue their pre-Christian practice of appealing to these traditional practitioners and to the spirits that provide their power.

Several of the problems related to this practice may be illustrated from an experience our Christian community had while I was in Nigeria. The wife of the village shaman had died quite suddenly. The funeral would, according to custom, last three days, with a great deal of crying followed by dancing and singing. On the second day, the headmaster of our Christian school put the school drum under his arm and led about ninety students to participate in the funeral. This gesture of concern and love from the Christians so impressed the shaman that he started to come to church. He found, however, that the church was filled with his clients—people who, in spite of their commitment to Christ, came to him when they needed blessing or healing. Since, then, he found no power in Christianity, he soon stopped attending church.

Imitate the Powerful

Few things would be more natural for a receiving group than to imitate those who come with greater power, especially if, as is often the case, power is their primary concern. Historically, in most missionary situations, the outsiders came with an impressive array of technologically superior machines and implements. Observing such technology and interpreting it to be the result of spiritual power rather naturally led the receiving groups to assume that the rest of the missionaries' culture was also superior to their own. So those who converted to Christianity gladly accepted the customs, the cultural forms, recommended by the advocates.

Korean and Japanese Christianity are good examples of this, as are many mission-planted churches in Africa, India, the Philippines, and elsewhere. Koreans have developed the art of imitation to such a degree that visitors worshiping in a church in Seoul could easily imagine themselves in America, except for the language. These would correspond to C2 churches, to borrow categories from the Muslim context again.

Another example comes from the early days of missionary work in Kenya. We are told (Oliver 1952) that the Kenyans, greatly impressed by the technology of the Europeans, sought to discover the secret behind it, and focused on reading. They reasoned, perhaps not inaccurately, that if they could learn to read they would have access to the Europeans' power. The only flaw in the Kenyans' reasoning was that they assumed the power they would obtain would be spiritual power. Though that part of their analysis was wrong, this quest for spiritual power became the motivating factor behind the Kenyans' ready acceptance of Western schools.

PERSEVERANCE OF FIRST-GENERATION CHOICES

Such first-generation choices would not be a big problem if people understood the importance of making different choices in the second generation. In most parts of the world, however, there is a pattern of the cultural forms adopted in the first generation persevering into the following generations, whether or not these forms are culturally appropriate. Whatever choices have been made in the first generation tend to determine the forms in which Christianity will be expressed forever after. Thus, if the early converts adopt a Western form of Christianity, the form tends to get "set in cement," with the foreign practices seeming to be sacred, even magical, especially because they are foreign and not well understood by the receptors.

A major problem arises for second- and third-generation Christians who learn that God wants to interact with them in terms of their own cultural forms. When they attempt to make changes in the direction of appropriate contextualization, they find themselves at odds with older leaders who insist on preserving the foreign forms adopted by the early converts. They often feel that these forms are both right, since the early missionaries were the ones who introduced them, and even sacred and magical. The first generation of Christians tends to assume that the missionaries knew what they were doing when they introduced these forms. I encountered this kind of attitude early in my own ministry. Some Nigerian church leaders and many of the missionaries felt that I, a young, inexperienced missionary, had no right to question the validity of the recommendations made by the pioneer missionaries, who had sacrificed so much to bring the gospel to Nigeria.

The assumption of the early missionaries (as articulated to me by one of my contemporaries) was, "We have had two thousand years of experience with Christianity; we know how things ought to be run." This assumption was so unquestioningly accepted by the first-generation believers that it never occurred to them to attempt to think things through on their own. So they never expected to be able to interpret the Scriptures from their own points of view, or to use their own music and musical instruments in worship, or to develop their own requirements for church membership or their own ways of training leaders, or to finance their Christian activities in their own ways, or to do anything else that would signal that Christ and His ways were rooted in their soil rather than imported wholesale from abroad. They thought Christianity was *supposed* to look foreign.

The leaders I worked with had more or less willingly given themselves to what they perceived to be a totally foreign system. But when some of them learned that they could question and adapt the foreign system and, furthermore, that they could adopt customs and perspectives that came from their own cultural roots, I, as their missionary, was accused by some of my missionary colleagues of undermining what the mission was advocating. And a major piece of evidence against me was the fact that our churches were growing so rapidly! When we left, the mission leaders assigned a missionary loyal to the organization (the same missionary who had made the "two thousand years of experience" comment) to bring the Nigerian leaders back into line with the westernized system of the mission. He failed in his mission, however, because these leaders had tasted the freedom that comes with experiencing Christianity in their own way.

Baptism can again be used as an illustration. Since the Greek word *baptizo* was transliterated rather than translated into English, its meaning can be argued over forever and the significance of the form exaggerated. Likewise with verbal expressions such as "the blood of Christ" and even "in Jesus' name" or "born again." Such expressions and the form of baptism used, since they are so poorly understood, seem sacred and magical and are used as such by many Western Christians, especially the more conservative ones.

The Bible, too, is for many Westerners a magical thing, invested with power of its own, especially if the language is antique and/or academic and sounds theologically sophisticated. Hence the attachment of many to Bible versions they cannot fully understand, which gives the impression that God uses a more sacred form of the language than that spoken by people every day. Such an attachment fosters the extreme resistance of many to Bible translations in contemporary language. This attitude on the part of missionaries often meets with the willingness of non-Western converts acquainted with sacred books of their traditional religion, which are preserved in antique, "sacred" language (e.g., the Quran, the Bhagavad Gita, the Vedas), to settle for minimal intelligibility. They thus miss the point that most of the Bible was written in highly communicative, even slangy vernacular language, and is therefore best represented in translation into that type of language.

In this way "anticontextual" decisions may be made by first-generation Christians and, often, carried on into the second and following generations, even though they are misleading in the practice and communication of Christianity.

CONCERNS OF SECOND AND FOLLOWING GENERATIONS

Though situations will differ from society to society, there are a number of common concerns in the second and following generations—some valid, some to be questioned. Legitimate concerns of these generations relate to any lack of appropriateness either to culture or to Scripture that has been passed down to them from the first generation.

Ideally, the second and following generations will give themselves to re-evaluating the cultural forms employed by first generation converts and making whatever changes might be deemed necessary to bring about more effective understandings of what God wants to do among them in the present. This habit of re-evaluation, and the accompanying process of experimenting with new approaches, could result in the capturing of more and more of a people's way of life for Christ. Sadly, very few inheritors of first-generation Christianity understand the need for and the biblical validity of such adjustments, preferring to perpetuate both the strengths and the weaknesses of whatever the first generation of converts developed in their approach to Christianity in their culture.

Leadership

Perhaps the most important of the questionable concerns are those that relate to the transfer of leadership positions to the younger leaders. The motivations of those not yet in power are often somewhat less than biblical. Often those preparing to be the next wave of leaders have spent more time in schools than their seniors and, in the process, have developed criticisms of how the first-generation leaders have been performing. In addition, the younger lot are often impatient to gain for themselves the power the older leaders have been wielding.

Although second-generation leaders may be critical of the excessive use of foreign cultural forms by the older leaders, often the training the younger leaders have received is designed more to enable them to work within the foreign system than to critique it. When this is the case, the opportunity to move the cultural expression of Christianity in the direction of greater appropriateness is lost.

However, when the training institutions include discussion of the biblically exemplified relationships of Christianity to culture, there is more hope for change. For example, by studying the ways in which the qualities of leaders listed in 1 and 2 Timothy and Titus relate to their cultural setting, younger leaders can gain insight into the ways in which their cultural leadership ideals can be both incorporated and challenged. Tragically, in many societies the use of schools to train leaders leads to the appointment of fairly young men to pastoral positions at culturally inappropriate ages, which communicates that God is not interested in older men or in working in culturally appropriate ways. Such mistakes can be rectified if training programs seek ways for older and younger leaders to work together so that the latter are mentored by their more experienced seniors when they pastor, either alone or in tandem. In many cultural contexts it would be appropriate for every pastorate to involve both an older man, who may be without academic qualifications but who has prestige in the community, and a younger one who has training and may actually do most of the work.

Thus, leaders from the second and subsequent generations, if they develop better cultural and biblical understandings, have a golden opportunity to move things in the right direction.

Relational Aspects of Christianity

Often, though the need for an initial commitment to Christ is communicated quite well, a focus on the need for growth and developing maturity in the relationship with Christ is neglected. We have usually exported the Western custom of leading a person to Christ and assuming that from then on growth in knowledge will automatically be accompanied by growth in intimacy with Christ and closeness to other Christians. Thus, in a family-oriented society such as Japan, Christianity has come to be known as primarily a classroom, knowledge-oriented faith.

Christians of the second and following generations would do well to study both the relational aspects of Christianity presented in Scripture (e.g., John 15) and the relational models available in their societies. Having studied these, attention should then be given to developing practices that produce growth in these areas. What, for example, are appropriate expressions of love in any given society? What are the culturally appropriate models of family, friendship, fellowship, recreation, intimacy, and the like, that can be adopted and adapted for use in the churches? And what aspects of social life in any given society need to be critiqued and abandoned for scriptural reasons? These issues, often neglected in the first generation, can and must be worked on by succeeding generations.

Music

Worship music passed down from the first generation is often inappropriate. Frequently, the tunes have been imported and put to words translated by missionaries and/or first-generation Christians who, in their attempts to dissimilate from their pre-Christian cultural forms, simply adopted foreign musical forms. Perhaps no one taught them that God could use their music and that *there is nothing sacred about Western musical forms*. Second-generation Christians ought to be very concerned about such inappropriateness (though they often are not), given the important part music plays in most societies.

Over 50 percent of the world's societies speak tone languages, and there are many more whose music employs a five-note scale rather than a Western seven-note scale. The use of Western music in these contexts does great disservice to the cause of Christ, because both unconsciously and consciously, the message of foreignness is driven home with more force through music than perhaps through any other vehicle.

Second-generation Christians would do well to recognize this and to develop a new and appropriate hymnody. As my colleague and former student Roberta King has discovered in teaching African music in Kenya, young Africans, though usually resistant at first to the use of traditional forms of music in worship, can be freed to appreciate and produce truly African worship music. Year after year, students have entered her course asking, "Why should we bother with traditional music?" But by the end the course, their attitude usually changes so much that they feel that this was one of the most valuable courses they have ever taken. They discover both the desire of God to reach their people in terms of their own cultural forms and the relevance and usefulness of traditional music in fulfilling this desire of God Himself.

Dependence on Literacy

Similarly damaging are the ways in which missionary Christianity has been taught in the first generation in the vast number of societies that had no tradition of literacy. It was natural for Westerners to introduce such culturally specific forms of education as schools and other educational techniques that are highly dependent on literacy. And there are obvious benefits for those who learn how to read. However, the fact that Christian advocates have largely ignored the rich variety of oral communication forms available in most of the world has again given the wrong impression that God's ways are limited to Western ways. The second and subsequent generations have the opportunity to correct this misimpression by developing the use of oral channels of communication while not ignoring the use and development of literacy.

The United Bible Societies, Wycliffe Bible Translators, and other organizations that have seen the need to go beyond literacy have recently started to develop creative approaches to the oral communication of Scripture. One of the discoveries coming out of such experimentation is the fact that oral, non-literacy-based communication is often more appropriate in so-called literate societies as well as in those without a long literary tradition. The second and following generations can greatly benefit the cause of Christ by freeing themselves from the captivity to literacy that has characterized much of first-generation Christianity, especially since memory specialists claim that thinking in pictures is our "native language." Literacy is an add-on, teaching us to think linearly rather than pictorially.

Spiritual Power

Though the first generation may have dealt with some power issues, there is usually much left for the next generations to deal with. This is especially true in the many places where missionary Christianity has largely ignored spiritual power issues and/or simply tried to wean Christians from traditional practices by condemning them. There are numerous instances of mission compounds and churches that have been built on land that was infested with satanic power. Those who have lived or worked in these places have experienced various kinds of maladies, from disease to accident to a high level of interpersonal dissension, often without a clue as to where the problems were coming from. Taking the land spiritually is therefore an important second-generation concern in many parts of the world.

This concern often needs to be brought to the attention of church leaders since, under the influence of Western advocates of Christianity, they have usually become desensitized in this area, at least on the surface. These leaders, like the first generation, would normally have been concerned about issues of spiritual power, as would be true of their non-Christian contemporaries. But the fact that their Western mentors did not deal with such issues—and, in fact, dealt in secular ways with health and emotional problems—led the first converts to either ignore spiritual power or deal with it underground. I recall vividly a discussion with a pastor serving under a strongly mission-controlled church who, when he found that I was open to and knowledgeable about demonization, finally confessed that he had a secret ministry of deliverance. Most of his colleagues would have either avoided such ministry, as the missionaries usually did, or kept what they were doing secret from church leaders and outsiders to perpetuate the fiction that demonic problems don't exist in their societies anymore.

A major issue is the problem of dealing effectively with demonization among church members. Following Western custom, the churches in most parts of the world have simply required a testimony of conversion plus some biblical and denominational teaching as entrance requirements. The fact that most, perhaps all, of the people coming out of paganism into Christianity are carrying demons has not been in focus.

Thus, our churches (both overseas and in America) are full of demonized people, and the demons have ample opportunity to work from within the churches. Of special concern should be the "cleaning up" of those coming out of non-Christian religions and secret societies. Often, in our ignorance of how demonization works, we assume that conversion gets rid of the demons. I wish that were the case, but it isn't. Christians of the second and following generations need to give major attention to this problem.

Fortunately, some understandings of these issues are coming into training programs both in the sending and the receiving countries. Unfortunately, in many places receiving peoples have developed their own ways to deal with these issues. I am appalled to hear stories both from Korea and from African countries of Christians attempting to free people from demons by beating them. Some demonized people have even died during such attempts at deliverance. These practices, and many others that create damage while attempting to free people, need to be taught against, and those who practice them should be shown better ways of dealing with demonization. I invite the reader to consult some of my books on this subject (e.g., Kraft 2015).

Other Concerns

Issues such as the cultural appropriateness of church government, how the faith is propagated, how the work of Christ is financed, and in many places, even what language should be used in worship all ought to be re-examined in the second generation, especially if they have not been handled appropriately in the first. In many situations, there has been some contextualization of these concerns in the first generation but more needs to be done.

Often, the way Christianity was presented and structured in the first generation remains fairly appropriate to one segment of any given population: the westernizing and generally more urban segment. More traditional (and usually more rural) segments of the society, however, often find very little that is culturally appropriate to their traditional way of life in the Western way that Christianity is practiced. A challenge that needs to be faced by the second and subsequent generations, then, is to plant churches that are contextualized within traditional and/or rural culture and therefore differ significantly from the more Western and/or urban varieties.

I wonder how many more Koreans or Japanese or Thai or Nigerians or American Indians might come to Christ if they could participate in churches that are more culturally appropriate to their traditional ways than the ones that represent Him in these places today. Not that the churches that are more or less appropriate to the culture of the westernizing segment are to be abandoned, but in every society there must be churches of other kinds, differing in their cultural orientation and aimed at attracting traditional and rural people.

It is likely that biblical standards that require changes in the culture will need to be addressed more fully in the second generation than they were in the first.

The application of these standards can have at least two types of thrust: the stiffening of standards that were not strongly applied in the first generation, and the relaxing of standards that were too strongly applied or applied in too Western a manner. In many contexts, for example, careful attention should be given to discovering and applying moral standards that are both culturally and biblically appropriate. Often the cultural disruption brought about by westernization (which was largely beyond the control of the advocates of Christianity) has resulted in major moral problems. On the other hand, if Christianity is to be appropriately scriptural, culturally insensitive rules against such things as polygamy, non-church weddings, dancing, social drinking of alcoholic beverages, and the like, will need to be re-examined in the second generation and, often, modified. When such re-examination and change does not happen, an overwhelmingly negative reaction against Christianity lies in store for later generations.

THIRD AND SUBSEQUENT GENERATIONS

The issues mentioned above usually continue to be issues in the third and following generations. As the years go by, however, things not dealt with become more and more entrenched—and usually more difficult to deal with. This is especially true in the many situations where biblical understandings of the relationship of Christianity to culture is minimal. For example, where Christianity is treated as merely a religion even by its adherents rather than as a relationship as it is portrayed in Scripture, a deadening nominalism easily takes over by the third generation, if not sooner.

The disease of nominalism speaks of the need for renewal. Renewal is often stimulated by new information and new approaches to old problems. Thus, the kind of cultural sensitivity advocated here, when properly linked to Scripture, can become a source of renewal. So can greater experiences of God's power. The latter is transforming Christian experience in Argentina (see Wagner and Deiros 1998). Third-generation Christians could well be advised to seek new emphases while praying that these will lead to renewal.

By the third generation, many peoples are expressing nationalistic concerns, especially if they feel they have been held down by colonial political and religious structures. Often, in reaction to Western domination in government, church, economics, and most other dimensions of life, the intellectuals begin to influence their followers in glamorizing traditional ways of life they have never really known. Contextualizing in these generations, then, needs to take into account nationalism and beware the tendency of people to use Christianity to serve concerns that are more cultural than biblical. Down through the ages, groups that have migrated out of their home areas—groups such as Armenians, Eastern Orthodox, Koreans, and Irish Catholics in America, and Japanese and Koreans in Brazil—have used their Christianity to enhance their ethnic identity. Certain brands of "America first" Christianity fall into this category as well.

Nominalism and nationalism, then, are crucial problems that third-generation Christians must deal with. There are usually also many of the earlier problems that have not been resolved. It is important at this stage for believers to not give up on the need to work toward greater biblical and cultural appropriateness.

CONCLUSION

The concern is for what *meanings* are getting across to the receptors. The question is how to inculturate Christianity in such a way that people attribute scriptural meanings to the cultural forms employed. First-generation Christians usually do some things right in this regard but frequently leave much to be done—and create much that ought to be redone—by later generations.

In this chapter, I have tried to focus on some of the issues that I believe are important, and to point to the responsibility of the second and following generations to deal with the omissions and commissions of the first generation. Though it is easy to criticize many decisions made by the first-generation converts and by the outsiders who often misled them, we should be sympathetic to the position they were in. They did not know how to do what needed to be done. We can therefore give them the benefit of the doubt and ask those from the second, third, and succeeding generations to rectify things.

The sad thing is that these later generations seldom attain much more understanding of the relationship of Christianity to culture than their predecessors had. Consequently, they simply perpetuate the mistakes of the past and even add to them their own mistakes, causing those around them to continue to misunderstand what Christianity is all about.

I wonder, for example, what might happen in Korea or Japan if a truly culturally appropriate Christianity is developed. Many Koreans have turned to Christ, of course, but they adhere to a largely Euro-American Christianity. But there are still about 70 percent of Koreans who have not come to Christ. Would the 70 percent respond positively to a truly Koreanized Christianity? And what about Japan? Though it will probably be necessary to break through the satanic power that Japan is committed to before anything major can happen there, what kind of Christianity will attract Japanese if that power is broken?

On the other hand, look at what has happened in China. After several generations of missionary contact followed by a generation or two without outside help, and under very uncongenial circumstances, millions of Chinese seem to have discovered great meaningfulness in Christianity. And though there are still traces of Western influence, they seem to have, at least to some extent, made the gospel their own culturally as well as spiritually.

I have sought in this chapter to alert us to some dimensions of the continuing quest toward more appropriateness that needs to be a part of the way Christianity is presented and experienced. Within any given culture, all decisions made in one generation concerning the practice of Christianity need to be regarded as tentative and experimental, open to re-evaluation and possible change by the next generation. And an even greater challenge than theorizing this necessity is getting the leaders of younger (or older) churches to act on the theory.

RELATIONAL ASPECTS

CHAPTER 11
APPROPRIATE RELATIONSHIPS

We have said that contextualization must involve asking questions concerning the appropriateness of any given custom both to Scripture and to the culture of the receiving people. The approach I want to take here is to start with scriptural ideals in the extremely important relational area and to ask how these may be expressed in any given society.

Preliminary to our main discussion, it is important that we focus on a series of considerations that underlie whatever is recommended. These considerations are as follows:

1. We need to recognize the difference, often a sizeable one, between scriptural ideals and the place where we and God must start in the process of helping people grow in their Christian experience. I have mentioned in chapter 9 the "point plus process" model that I introduced in *Christianity in Culture*. That model notes from Scripture that God is willing to start with sub-ideal customs and concepts when He begins working with a people. He then engages the people in a process in which He works with them to move them toward greater and greater approximation to His ideals.

Keeping that model in mind will help us recognize that any introduction of relational concepts and/or customs presupposes that there will be a process from that starting point in the direction of the scriptural ideal. The main problem, as I have pointed out in chapter 9, is how to see to it that there is enough press and pull to keep people moving in the right direction.

2. We must also consider that the culturally ideal form of many customs and concepts of a receiving people may already be quite close to scriptural ideals. Small-scale societies, especially, are often very relational, thus raising the possibility that a given custom or concept may be fairly acceptable to God as it is.

Often the cultural ideal of the custom may be quite close to Scripture, but the way that custom is practiced is wide of the mark. For example, a custom that involves parents arranging marriages is intended to ensure that the most experienced people in a society make this important decision on behalf of the inexperienced youth. This is the ideal. Yet greedy parents often arrange marriages primarily for economic reasons rather than for the good of their children.

The ideal is clear and makes sense when measured by Scripture, but the actual practice needs transformation by Christian families to come close to scriptural ideals. Note, however, that the necessary transformation involves a change in the concept of what must be done, not in the custom itself. Christian families, motivated by their desire to please Jesus, can practice this custom in its ideal form, providing for their youth the security that such a custom is intended to bring.

3. Some customs and/or concepts in the relational area, though they may be acceptable to God as starting points, may need radical change as people move closer to Christlikeness. The different treatment shown to the ingroup as opposed to outgroups in most societies is a case in point. We see in Scripture that God accepts the Jews as His people, His ingroup. He thus identifies with this ingroup. He frequently reminds them, however, that they should treat strangers well, for they were once themselves strangers in a foreign land (Deut 24:17,18). The fact that the Jews become cliquish, disobeying God frequently in this relational area, is cause for a good bit of anguish on God's part.

The point is, God is willing to start with the exclusiveness of a group such as the Jews, but He is not willing to endorse such cliquishness as His ideal. Rather, we are to be neighborly and loving even to those we consider enemies (Luke 10:30–37).

4. The form-meaning principle must also be kept in mind. It is the meanings attached by people to the customs they practice that should be the primary concern of contextualizers. A relational custom that sees ancestors as a part of the living community, for example, may have a different meaning to the people who practice it than it does to outsiders. And similar customs relating to ancestors may mean one thing in one part of the world and another in a different place.

Though any custom that regards ancestors as still functioning in the society of the living is a candidate for eventual change, what should guide the actions of the Christian community at the start of the transformation process is whether the attitude of the people is worship or simply honor. In Africa, where most of the peoples believe in a High God, the meaning of what a people do in relation to their ancestors may be more like honor than worship. In Asia, however, where any concept of a High God may be weak at best, the meaning is more likely to be worship.

Whether it is ancestor customs that are in focus, marriage customs, funeral customs, or ingroup-outgroup relationships, it is the meanings in the minds of the people, not the customs themselves, that must be the primary concern. The same is true of customs introduced from outside. For example, a lot of damage has been done to the perception of Christianity by the advocating of individualistic conversion concepts. In group-oriented societies where major decisions are group matters, one-by-one conversions, especially of young people, convey the wrong meanings about God. So too may prohibitions of relational customs such as polygamy, dancing, and drinking beer.

GOD'S MAJOR CONCERN

The Bible is quite clear concerning how people are expected to treat one another. Two major principles are stated and identified as summing up the Law and the Prophets. Mark's version of these principles is:

1. Love the Lord your God with all your heart, all your soul, all your mind, and all your strength (12:30); and
2. Love your neighbor as yourself (12:31).

The supreme relational principle is love—love as defined by the receptors, the insiders. And this love is to be the measure of both our vertical relationship with God and our horizontal relationship with other human beings. Indeed, we are told that "the whole Law of Moses and the teachings of the prophets depend on these two commandments" (Matt 22:40).

Given the confusion in many people's minds concerning what love is all about, it is good to look at the meaning of the Greek word used for love in this and most other passages in the New Testament. The word is *agape*, and it signifies a conscious choice to value and do good to the person loved, no matter what it costs the one who has chosen to love. This love involves a commitment, a deliberate choice on the part of the one doing the loving to be favorable toward the person loved. This love is in no way contingent on the qualities of the person loved, except that it involves a valuing of the *being*, not simply the *doing*, of that person.

We are exhorted, then, to make a conscious choice to highly value God and our relationship with Him, and on that basis to commit ourselves to Him with all our heart, soul, mind, and strength (see below). Similarly, we are to choose to love others as we love ourselves.

Contextualization problems arise, however, in the fact that not every people expresses love in the same way. What may be a perfectly understandable act of love to insiders in their cultural context may be interpreted as quite something else in another context. In our mission situation in Nigeria, for example, a major way we sought to express our love to the Nigerians was through hospitals and out-clinics. And some of the people got the point. But many, probably most, did not. Because our mission charged fees for medicine and medical procedures, these people saw money and not love as the primary reason for the medical facilities. Although some of this misinterpretation was probably inevitable, the situation could have been helped considerably if we had made an effort to explain our medical practices in relation to their traditional medical practices. The fact that we never took their medicine seriously predisposed them to draw their own conclusions concerning ours.

In addition, since their medical customs almost always related sickness and healing to the spirit world, it would have helped enormously if we had been able to perform and interpret our practices so as to connect with their understandings. As it was, our approach was almost entirely secular and therefore never really connected with their understandings. Our doctors had prayer before surgery and usually went out of their way to develop personal contact with their patients (though often the doctor did not speak the language well). This helped the patients to experience a measure of love. But the lack of a pervasive spiritual dimension in our Western medical practices, plus the largely impersonal style of dealing with medical problems, often hindered the communication of human love and totally obstructed any perception on the part of the receivers that there was a spiritual dimension to the healing that occurred. Thus, the Nigerians missed understanding God's love through their all-encompassing spiritual grid. *The language of the medical procedures may have left them impressed and physically healed but not relationally satisfied through experiencing what they perceived as love.*

Quite different was the ministry of a doctor from another mission who spent half-days out with the people, studying their medical practices and attempting to connect what he did in the hospital with where they were culturally. Though he may not have fully understood the spiritual dimensions of their healing procedures, his witness was powerful in terms of human relationships. The people may not have understood the secular nature of his medicine, or they may have understood it in more spiritual terms than the doctor did, but they knew he loved them because he spent time with them and took their customs seriously.

CONTEXTUALIZING A RELATIONSHIP WITH GOD

The principles discussed above for relating to human beings apply also to our relating to God. A small amount of time with God, especially if the time is spent in ritual rather than in very personal interaction, yields a poor and superficial relationship with God. The general principle is the same as with human beings: the more time with God, the better the relationship—depending, of course, on the nature of the interaction that takes place during that time. If, as with humans, the time is spent attempting to manipulate God to do our will, the value of the relationship is diminished. But if the time is spent both speaking and sincerely listening, there will be exciting growth in the relationship.

Prayer is the name we ordinarily give to the time spent speaking to God. For many, however, prayer time is like one end of a telephone conversation—we talk, talk, talk, talk, and then hang up. If God wants to say anything back to us, all He hears is the dial tone! Learning to listen as well as to talk is something that a lot of us miss. But again, this takes time.

Cross-culturally, we may face other problems. The receptors may be used to spending time in their interactions with the spirit world, but they may see such time as primarily to be spent in rather impersonal, mechanistic rituals. The scriptural ideal of close, person-to-person interaction with God, speaking to Him as friend to Friend, may be beyond a people's imagination.

The Israelites faced this problem. They believed that if God got close, they would die. Listen to the lament of Isaiah when he says, "There is no hope for me! I am doomed . . . [because] I have seen the King, the Lord Almighty" (Isa 6:5). Thus, one important aspect of Jesus' contextualizing of what our relationship with God should look like was proving to His disciples and to the world that *when God gets close, it is good news rather than bad news.*

Many of the peoples of the world have this same "bad news fear" of God. They don't want Him close. They have been deluded into treating Him mechanistically, assuming that if they do the right rituals they may be able to get Him to do their will. So they spend time, perhaps lots of it, performing rituals, usually designed to fend off dangerous spirits but sometimes aimed at seeking favor from God. They often see their primary vertical relationship as with capricious and dangerous spirits rather than with God. Though they may believe that God exists, they tend to ignore Him and seek to deal with the spirits on their own.

Whatever the specific understandings in this area, it is usually a challenge for contextualizers to guide the Christian community into a more intimate and personal relationship with God than their traditions allow them to experience. Probably most non-Western peoples need more ritual than most Westerners. The challenge, however, is to help them move from mechanistic manipulation of spirit beings through ritual toward intimate submission to God alone in meaningful ritual. When Abraham began his relationship with God, it was a very personal thing. But a major part of the continuing of that relationship involved Abraham learning to use for the true God the rituals and customs that he and his father Terah had used in relationship to counterfeit gods. God did not give Abraham new customs. He simply led him to redirect the customs he already had, even reintroducing the custom of circumcision that had apparently been allowed to lapse in Abraham's tribe.

Prayer is intended by God to be a relational thing. So is worship. As Jesus said, we are to abide in Him, in close relationship with Him, obeying Him, asking Him for things, bearing fruit with and for Him, loving Him and experiencing His love, experiencing the joy of close relationship, being known as His friends (John 15:1–17). How this is to be experienced and expressed in any given society is a major challenge for contextualizers. But this is perhaps the most important area we must deal with if converts are to really grow in Christ.

We are told in Romans 12:1,2 that our whole lives are to be acts of worship. The intent is that our worship be more than simply ritual. But worship at special times and in special places, including culturally appropriate ritual, is certainly to be in view as well. Contextualizers need to discover what worship is in their target society and aim at capturing traditional worship for Christ. In the Old Testament, pagan insider worship was captured for the true God. When Israel was being faithful, the places of pagan worship (usually high places) were taken over for God. Pagan rituals, including blood sacrifices, were captured for God. Planting and harvest rituals were captured. Circumcision was reintroduced and, as their history unfolded, new times of worship were introduced to commemorate the Exodus and the rescue of the Jews under Queen Esther.

Great attention needs to be given to the development of appropriate acts of prayer and worship. These are the ways we are to express our love toward God.

WITH HEART, SOUL, MIND, AND STRENGTH

We are admonished to love God with all our heart, soul, mind, and strength. The aim is total commitment and obedience—an all-consuming relationship that starts, as it did with Abraham, with a covenant, a binding agreement, and develops into a lifelong and life-giving intimacy. There may be rules for the relationship (e.g., the Law), but the rules are always intended to follow, not precede, to support, not eclipse, the covenant. The combination of heart, soul, mind, and strength is obviously to indicate a totality of this commitment. But what is each of these parts of a human being intended to contribute to the whole?

The term *heart* stands first in the list. This term is used in the Scriptures to focus on the totality of a person's internal being, including emotion, thought, and will. I suspect that here its focus is to be on the will. Jesus' intent is, of course, that we should love God with the totality of our being. This is the basic relationship for which we were created, and there will be no complete satisfaction in life without this total commitment.

How this total commitment is to be expressed, however, is likely to differ from society to society. Implied in the word is that a person is to *will* this kind of relationship. Without pressure to love 100 percent, people in many societies will settle for fearing God or even ignoring Him. In animistic societies, the assumption that since God is good He can be ignored will have to be confronted with the ideal of a much more active and positive approach to relating to God. And in most non-Western societies, appropriate expression of relationship will tend to be more often a group thing than an individual thing.

For a ritual-oriented people, a major part of this active relating may take the form of group rituals. Care must be taken, however, to ensure that the meaning of the rituals is *relationship*, not *magic*. There seems to be a human tendency to move toward magical understandings of activities that are repeated over and over—understandings that assume that if the ritual is done correctly, it will automatically bring the favor of

God. Even in Western societies, worship ritual plays an important part in the expression of this "total-being" relationship (with the same danger of it being regarded as magical). We must be aware, though, that the exporting of what is termed "contemporary worship" from Western societies may not engage the hearts of non-Western peoples as meaningfully as it does the hearts of Westerners, or to the same extent that such worship rendered in their own musical idiom would.

The term translated *soul*, though often used with a significance close to that of *heart*, may in this context refer more to the emotions than to the will. It is important to engage the emotions in our relationship with God. Gratefulness, though primarily an act of the will, should have an important emotional component as well. People who are expressing gratefulness need to feel it as well as to will it.

Appropriate expression of emotion will, however, differ from society to society. Emotional expression in Africa is likely to involve the whole body. In Korea, the movement is likely to be more restrained, with even greater restraint of movement in Japan. Contrary to popular stereotypes, though, I have observed both Koreans and Japanese expressing great emotion in worship. For many whose emotions have been constricted through cultural conditioning, including many Westerners, it is important that we learn to engage our emotions in worship. I myself, though one of those with dampened emotions through cultural conditioning, have been learning to *feel* in my relationship with God as that relationship deepens (see Kraft 2015).

Mind or *perspective* in this context probably refers to understanding, an important ingredient in any form of worship or other expression of relational commitment to God. As is usually the case in Scripture, the mind or perspective is seen as foundational to the ways in which we are to relate to God. We are not to simply express ourselves without understanding what we are doing.

The understanding dimension provides a special challenge to those who seek to help new converts in their relationship with God, for in animistic societies the primary relationships tend to be with the intermediate spirits rather than with the High God. Thus, sacrifice and worship ritual directed toward spirits needs to be either replaced or captured and invested with new meaning. Though capturing such ritual is not impossible, helping people to understand the changes is extremely important, especially in combating the tendency to view such ritual as a means of controlling the spirit being to which it is directed, in this case God.

I myself was misled in this area in my early ministry when I saw people sacrificing animals. I assumed that the sacrifices were to the true God until a Nigerian leader alerted me to the fact that the sacrifices I was observing were directed to spirits, not to the true God. If those sacrifices are to be used in contextualized worship, redirecting their aim must be carefully taught.

The term translated *strength* probably refers again to God's desire that we pour our whole selves, including our bodies, into this love relationship with Him. Those of us who have worked in Africa have no difficulty imagining such bodily involvement, as we have seen the total abandon with which Africans express themselves in dancing. Unrestricted worship, African style, is a total thing, at least at the time of worship. On the other hand, it would be difficult in most societies to imitate the level of total commitment of Japanese Christians as they give their money, time, and much else in expressing their allegiance and gratefulness to God. Though they may not do much with their bodies, the level of their commitment enables many very small churches to support their pastors and their various activities in impressive ways.

Our relationship with God naturally has both private (or personal) and public dimensions. Public worship and ritual needs to differ greatly from society to society if it is to be appropriate and maximally meaningful to the worshipers and the non-Christian audience looking on. Tragically, there has been so much copying of Western worship styles that culturally appropriate ways of expression that would really carry the intended meanings have been stifled. The work of Christian ethnomusicologists in Africa is a huge step forward in assisting African Christians to publicly express their relationship with God in ways that are meaningful to them and even to their non-Christian neighbors.

Personal and small group worship is another matter. Those Japanese who have learned to give time and money sacrificially may have learned what loving God with their whole being is all about, unless their loyalty is simply duty. Those who learn to express their devotion to God daily, in appropriate ways both in church and outside of it, have learned what Romans 12:1 is recommending. Praying without ceasing, with the lines of communication between humans and God always open and in operation, is always appropriate to Scripture. How this relational praying is to be appropriately implemented in any given society needs to be studied. Western customs of "personal devotions," centered on the reading of Scripture, may not be appropriate for the large number of nonliterate people in the world. Instead, for them the sharing of Bible stories in family groups, and individual memorization of biblical stories and texts, can greatly enhance relationships with God and with each other.

We need a lot more research as to what total commitment to God means and how it is appropriately expressed in the world's societies. I suspect that if such research were done, we in the West would discover that a good deal of creative expression is already going on outside of our limited understandings of how a relationship with God should be expressed.

LOVING OUR NEIGHBORS AS OURSELVES

In addition to loving God completely, we are to love our neighbors as we love ourselves. In Luke's version of that command (10:27), Jesus tells one of His most famous parables to illustrate what loving our neighbors is all about.

The parable of the Good Samaritan (Luke 10:30–37) is in response to the question, "Who is my neighbor?" In answering this question, Jesus does two startling things. First, He uses an outcast as His hero. Samaritans were looked down on and hated by the Jews, so a Samaritan was a very unlikely person to be the one to express love toward a Jew. Apparently, though, it is God's ideal that even a hated Samaritan be capable of treating with love a member of a group that hates him. But then Jesus changes the question. His story focuses not on who the neighbor is but on who is acting in a neighborly fashion. The question He wants us to ask is not, "Who is my neighbor?" Even a Samaritan could answer that question. Instead, Jesus teaches that we are to constantly ask, *Are we treating even enemies as neighbors?* We are to love even enemies as we love ourselves.

Given the innumerable ethnic divisions in the world, each with its own hatreds, the command to love people from other groups as we love ourselves is for many peoples of the world a major challenge. Yet, for many, their commitment to Christ enables them to break through this barrier. The Nigerian church leaders I worked with shared with me the fact that they could no longer obey a command of their tribal leaders to go to war with a neighboring tribe. The reason? They had eaten with members of that tribe. Eating or sharing the Lord's Supper with them meant that they could never again be enemies.

Breaking down such barriers and symbolically representing their removal, however, must be done in culturally appropriate ways. Simply forcing people of different ethnic groups to function as members of a single denomination, as our mission did, will not do the job. Indeed, it may even increase the animosity between groups or, worse, enable the enemies to be more effective in fighting each other. It may simply bring the existing competitiveness and animosity into a new context, the church context, where vying for power in church politics is added to the variety of ways in which their enmity has traditionally been expressed.

Don Richardson's account of the Peace Child custom among the Sawi and other peoples of Irian Jaya is a good example of a culturally appropriate way of symbolizing reconciliation between former enemies (Richardson 1974).

Although the starting point for God's working with people must always be the fact that they accept one another in their traditional groupings (i.e., the so-called homogeneous unit principle), it is not God's intent for His people to continue as cliques. We are to grow in our acceptance of believers from other groups, groups that are often radically different from our own.

As Jesus commanded in Luke 6:31, we are to treat others, even strangers and aliens, as we would like to be treated ourselves—as if they were members of our ingroup. Cross-culturally, however, this "Golden Rule" means that it is the receptor group that defines the treatment, not we ourselves. That is, we are to treat others as we would like to be treated *if we were members of their group*, not as if we were members of our own group. It is *their* definition of love that is to determine our behavior, not our own. Though it is always difficult to hold ourselves to the standards of others, Jesus wants us to do no less than He would as we reach out to those we seek to win for Him.

If the people we go to measure love by the amount of unstructured time we spend with them, then that must be our standard. If they measure love by their standard of kindness, of patience, of never speaking angrily, of always sharing, of always showing hospitality even to the point of sacrifice, or whatever it may be, then this must be our standard among them.

1 CORINTHIANS 13 IS CROSS-CULTURALLY VALID

The amazingly precise definition of *agape* love in 1 Corinthians 13:4–7 can provide guidelines for the kind of horizontal relationships God desires His people to practice. While each of the statements about love needs to be looked at in terms of the sociocultural definition of the terms, it is likely that most societies will have ideals close to those articulated here, at least in their behavior toward members of the ingroup. The goal of practicing love toward outgroups, however, must always be held out as part of the Christian ideal.

Godly love is patient and kind, we are told. It is likely, then, that the cultural ideals of patience and kindness will provide a good starting point for the Christians of that society in their quest to become more Christlike. So also is there likely to be a negative attitude toward jealousy, conceit, pride, unmannerliness, selfishness, and irritability. But again, this may only apply to the ingroup. And though the cultural ideal might be negative toward these things, the actual behavior of the people might demonstrate one or more of these characteristics. And then there are societies that seem to foster such characteristics as conceit and pride even though these attitudes are destroyers of good relationships.

When it comes to the kind of love that does not keep a record of wrongs, many of the world's peoples fall far short. Family feuds commonly go on for generations because people do keep such records. On one occasion I was ministering to a citizen of one of the South Pacific islands who became very violent as he fought against both a demon and what he had been taught was his own responsibility to retaliate for the murder of his father. His struggle against the demon was much less difficult than his struggle against his own conditioning, supported by the expectations of his extended family, that he would someday murder a member of the family of his father's killer. He finally gave in to what he knew Jesus expected of him, but it was not easy. For Christians in cultures such as his, it can be very difficult to trade in the society's ideal of revenge for Jesus' ideal of turning the other cheek (Matt 5:39).

Love, then, "is not happy with evil, but is happy with the truth." Again, though the ideals of a society may agree that people should be true to others and not wish or inflict evil on them, the actual behavior may fall short of such ideals. And the definitions of what is considered evil and what is considered truth can vary widely. In relationships, evil toward outgroups may be allowed or even encouraged, and keeping commitments to outgroup members may not be a high priority.

Ingroup-outgroup issues also emerge when we get to the final characteristic of love: the fact that one who loves never gives up but always exhibits faith, hope, and patience in relationships. These are likely to be considered ingroup ideals, but they may seldom be found in relationships with outgroups. People may also fall short of such an ideal between the sexes. Men often show little inclination to encourage their wives or even their children.

The Scriptures set high standards for Christian behavior in our relationship with others as well as in our relationship with God. Approaching these standards in culturally appropriate ways, then, needs to be a major concern for contextualizers.

PERSONAL CONCERN

There is a level of human-beingness that is deeper than our cultural differences. Love needs to be shown and experienced at that level. In many ways the life experiences of all peoples, no matter what their cultures, develop in very similar ways. Everyone experiences birth, childhood, physical and emotional maturing, adult relationships and responsibilities, difficulties of various kinds, and death. Although different cultures define these universal processes in slightly different ways, at base we are all human beings and respond to certain things in very similar ways.

One of the things to which people respond in similar ways is personal concern. If we are to relate well across cultural boundaries, then we must develop culturally understandable ways of showing personal concern.

Sometimes the occasion for showing personal concern arises when tragedy strikes. To return to an example mentioned above, I remember well what the shaman of our village in Nigeria said when the headmaster and about ninety students from our mission school visited him on the second day of his wife's three-day funeral. The headmaster and schoolchildren participated in the drum-beating and dancing that were appropriate in that situation. This so moved the shaman that he broke the taboo against coming out of isolation during this part of the ceremony and said to the headmaster, "I never knew you Christians cared about us traditional people."

Showing personal concern may not be as easy as it sounds, however. What is done needs to be interpreted by the receptors as concern, not as something else. If there is not already a trust relationship, it is unlikely that our actions will be properly interpreted. Some of our missionaries learned this when they went to a native dance in native dress and were interpreted as ridiculing the local people.

To avoid such misinterpretation, it is important for cross-cultural witnesses to develop a group of close friends to whom they will give themselves. These friends will learn to trust the outsider and will interpret him or her to the people who are not as close. This was a major function served by Jesus' disciples. They got to know Him intimately and then provided communication about Him to the wider populace. They also heard from the people what they were thinking about Jesus.

I remember two occasions, one in Nigeria and the other while working with junior high youth here in the United States, on which the closeness I had developed with some members of the group paid off in this way. In Nigeria, we were meeting with the leaders of a certain village. I was speaking, and the leaders seemed to me to be listening intently. The friends who had accompanied me, however, discerned that the leaders really weren't paying attention, so they stopped me and questioned the leaders about their relationship with me. This conversation turned the whole situation around. Having learned to trust me and take me seriously, my associates were able to gain for me the trust and attention of the village leaders. I had acquired a status that we might call "white man but different."

A similar thing happened with a junior high church group in the US. This age group is notoriously difficult to manage, and on the occasion I have in mind, some newcomers in the group were starting to crack up while I was trying to speak seriously to them. At that point, a couple of the youth who knew me well interrupted my talk to let the newcomers know that I wasn't like other adults, with little to contribute to their lives, but rather one who had something to say that they needed to hear. The newcomers straightened up right away. I had achieved a status with the young people that we might label "adult but worth listening to."

These stories illustrate the importance of having a group of associates or trusting friends who also have good contact with the receiving group; they can have significant influence on relationships, mediating personal concern. Any outsider attempting to reach people on the other side of a cultural boundary needs insider friends who will perform this function.

SPENDING TIME WITH PEOPLE

People of any society respond to personal interest. This usually involves spending time with them, an area in which two difficulties arise for those of us from the West. The first is that most of the world's peoples require more time to develop personal relationships than we Westerners do. Our view of friendship often appears superficial to those from more people-oriented societies. We think nothing of calling someone a friend whom we have met only two or three times. Other peoples would call such a person a mere acquaintance, reserving the label "friend" for those they see regularly over a long period of time.

The second problem facing Westerners is that we often see ourselves more as "doers" than as "be-ers." As someone has said, we tend to see ourselves as "human doings" rather than as human beings. I found in Nigeria that even though I attempted to spend what I thought was a lot of time with the people, they didn't consider it to be enough. In addition, I had difficulty spending time with them unless we were scheduled to do something together. And when they came to spend time with me without a specific reason, I tended to get impatient with them. My idea of spending time together was to spend it doing something, not just sitting around chatting. Though my insider friends told me I did better than most other missionaries, I don't believe I did very well at contextualizing the relating dimension of appropriate Christianity.

I think my example was only slightly better than that of one of my missionary colleagues of whom the Nigerians said, "The only things we see him doing are fixing his car or going to a meeting." And we soon learned how these leaders felt about another missionary. Although he greeted visitors properly when they came to his door, the next words out of his mouth would be, "Why have you come?" or "What do you want?" These were perhaps the most impolite things he could have said in this culture, where politeness (and love) demands that one wait for the visitor to state his reason for coming.

Beneath the cultural differences is the basic human need for spending time together to establish and maintain relationships, but the amount and kind of time expected differs from society to society. In reality, however, many in the West are starved for more relational time. This probably means that we Westerners are not dealing adequately with an important facet of human nature. For example, many of the relational problems that surface in counseling Western adults stem from the lack of time their parents, especially their fathers, spent with them. Spending more time in relating, then, is both contextually and humanly appropriate.

THE FRUIT OF THE SPIRIT

The fruit of the Holy Spirit listed in Galatians 5:22,23 provides another insight into how God wants people to relate to each other. The first fruit listed is, of course, love. Indeed, some would interpret these verses as speaking *only* of love but breaking love down into its many facets. That is, they would interpret the verses as saying that the fruit of the Spirit is LOVE expressed in joy, peace, patience, gentleness, goodness, faith (faithfulness), meekness, and self-control. Since each of these characteristics may be seen as a facet of love, according to these interpreters the list should be seen as an elaboration of the one quality rather than as a delineation of several parallel qualities.

Whether or not one agrees with this interpretation, it is helpful to see each as important in Christian relationships. But again, we must note that each of these characteristics is capable of differing cultural definitions. So we need to ask, how should joy be expressed in such and such a society? And what would it take for an outsider to be seen as patient, gentle, or good in such and such a society? And what about meekness and self-control? Faithfulness might be easier to define in horizontal relationships, but there is also an important vertical relationship to make explicit in this category as well (more on this below).

What is it in life that brings joy? Though joy may be thought of as primarily an individual, internal thing, I suspect the primary source of joy for most of the peoples of the world lies in the quality of their relationships with each other. What a blessing it can be for contextualizers to be able to help people experience the joy of Christian love in these relationships. The joy of learning to love and to be loved in a marriage relationship, the joy of bringing children into the world, the joy of watching them learn and develop through the various stages into adulthood—these would probably figure high on any people's list of potential joys. How these relationships are to be expressed among Christians in ways that are appropriate to both culture and Scripture should be of great concern to contextualizers. And feeling and expressing in culturally appropriate ways the joy of being in a proper relationship with the Creator and Sustainer of all the good things of life should be of equal concern.

Peacefulness too has an inner and an outer dimension. Contextualizers need to find culturally appropriate ways of enabling people to relate properly to themselves in the freedom Jesus brings through inner healing (see Kraft 1994). Each people needs to experience what it is to bring their heavy burdens, whether internal or external, to Him (Matt 11:28). How this is done appropriately in each cultural context must be discovered. And for many of the world's societies, dealing with internal burdens rather than simply suppressing them may be a completely new experience. How to make peace with enemies may be a more familiar concept than seeking inner peace to most people, but getting them to actually do it may prove difficult. And it may be naïve to assume that merely getting people of different groups to worship together will automatically bring peace in their relationships. Cultural appropriateness might require some sort of formal ritual and covenant to signify the ending of long-held hostility. How might things have been different in Rwanda if there had been some such ritual? And might some sort of ritual be appropriate at conversion to signify the termination of hostilities between each convert and God Himself?

I have mentioned the Peace Child ritual previously. In our area of northeastern Nigeria, several of the tribal groups had the custom of signifying the desire to end hostilities between individuals by chewing and spitting out guinea corn. In some tribes, when a person wants to forgive another person, he chews some guinea corn and spits it on the ground at the person's feet. In other groups, the person spits it *on* the other person! Perhaps this ritual could be adapted to signify reconciliation between former enemy groups who now choose to covenant together to follow Christ and to relate to each other as brothers and sisters rather than as enemies. Some such ritual could also become a meaningful part of the initiation ceremony of individuals into Christianity to signify their new relationship with God.

Patience is probably considered a virtue in all societies. But again, how patience is expressed may differ. Likewise gentleness. Jesus was known for His gentleness, and considering the difficulties He experienced with His disciples, His patience was equally exemplary. The challenge, then, is for the people of God to discover how Jesus would have expressed His patience and gentleness in their cultural context. In many societies, their ideal in these areas may already be close to Jesus' behavior. The most difficult thing for contextualizers in such cases might be to ensure that the motivation is Christian, not simply a matter of conformity to traditional custom.

When we come to goodness, we face perhaps the greatest challenge. Jesus said that only God is good (Luke 18:19). Learning to be good would again be a matter of imitating God's attitude and behavior within any given society. This would, of course, involve both personal righteousness and treating people as God treats people. God's people need to be seen as good by the members of their societies. Their behavior must be easily interpretable by their people if it is to truly represent the good God. This should put the contextualization of goodness, both personal and relational, high on the list of concerns for those who would be effective in relational contextualization.

Second only to love as a relational aspect of Christianity would be faith, although the usual meaning of the term in Scripture, both in Hebrew and in Greek, is "faithfulness"—the characteristic of faithful response to the one related to. We are told in Hebrews 11:6 that without faith (faithfulness) it is impossible to please God. Consequently, the contextualization of relationship requires that we help people discover how to express faithfulness to God within their cultural life.

Humility may be a challenge for many peoples since it is so likely to be interpreted as weakness. But it is a quality supremely modeled by Jesus, who turned His back on the honor He could have demanded, given His credentials. He thus endorsed meekness and humility as Christian virtues, cutting across the grain in His own society and challenging all who follow Him to motivation and behavior that surpasses that of their non-Christian contemporaries.

Self-control, the last virtue listed, also has both personal and group ramifications. Those who truly love will exercise self-control in their relationships with others. As Christians, the love expressed through self-control must be exercised both toward the ingroup and toward the members of outgroups. Again, though, a major focus in contextualizing this virtue needs to be the motivation behind the characteristic. Self-control simply as a custom is quite different from self-control motivated by love.

In these and many other ways, Jesus wants His love to be expressed in culturally appropriate motivation and behavior. The challenge for those involved in the contextualization of relationships, then, is to discover and press toward biblically and culturally appropriate expressions of these characteristics.

RELATIONSHIPS THROUGH INSTITUTIONS?

As a final item in this discussion of relational contextualization, let's look at what has to be a significant problem for those who take this area seriously. Since much of missionary effort has become institutionalized, is it possible to speak of contextualizing the relationships between those who operate the institutions and those who are ministered to through them? Some would give up, suggesting that such institutions as schools, hospitals, and even churches are too foreign in many societies to allow something as close to the heart of the local people as relationships.

I choose not to give up, though the challenge is great, especially among peoples in what have been called "person-to-person" or "face-to-face" societies. Culturally sensitive people working in institutions can surely find ways to spend time as learners with people outside of the institutions. I know of a single woman missionary who went to Nigeria as a teacher but spent many weekends living with the families of her students away from the school compound. She became greatly loved by both the students and their parents and was very effective in her witness to these families.

I have already mentioned the doctor who used his afternoons to conduct research into the medical practices of the people in the villages surrounding his hospital. Both he and the schoolteacher used part of their time to establish and cultivate relationships with the people they had come to serve. In this way they learned as much as they could about the people's lives and concerns and sought to contextualize their relationships with them by expressing receptor-oriented love.

We note that Jesus' training school was relational. Ideally, then, the institutions we start and continue as means of communicating Christ would be relationally based. Apprenticeship and discipleship are non-formal educational institutions, with the relationships between the participants crucial to their effective functioning. If we have the privilege of starting or participating in a school, why not do it Jesus' way? It was not by accident that He called His disciples at the same time, choosing only twelve to enter His school. These men were to first *be with Him* in close relationship, and then go out and communicate what they had learned, including healing and freeing people from demons (Mark 3:13–15). By choosing and working with the fairly small number of followers who would be closest to Him, Jesus was simply recognizing that human limitations don't permit us to relate closely to very many people at a time.

In Jesus' school, the focus was on learning to minister, not simply on learning to *think* about ministry, as it is in our educational institutions. Jesus and His apostles *did things together*, giving them concrete life experiences to discuss and analyze. In addition, Jesus' disciples were second-career people: they had already learned much about life by participating in secular occupations. This is a factor we should not miss when we are recruiting disciples.

Many of the societies we go to as witnesses already have an apprenticeship or discipleship approach to training their people for various occupations. Wise contextualizers will seek to find such structures and adapt them for use within—and sometimes in place of—the Western institutions that are so typical of mission-generated Christian communities.

CONCLUSION

What this is about, then, is a culturally appropriate expression of love toward God and a receptor-oriented love between Christians in both ingroup and outgroup interactions. This is a love that is both sincere at the sender's end and interpreted as love at the receptor's end. From a missionary's point of view, we need to practice receptor-oriented love toward the people we seek to reach.

To advocate appropriate loving relationships seems easy. But to practice them, especially cross-culturally, involves a number of complexities brought about by cultural differences. The ideals of Scripture are fairly clear. The application of these ideals in the cultural contexts of the peoples of the world who have not known Christ is considerably more difficult. I hope this discussion will help us to be aware of some of those difficulties and to overcome them in our ministries.

CHAPTER 12
PARTNERING WITH GOD

I don't call you slaves, I call you friends.
John 15:15

Take my yoke upon you.
Matthew 11:28–29

We evangelicals spend a lot of energy learning who God is. We study the Scriptures diligently to find out everything we can about God. We learn about His character and His characteristics. He is righteous and good; He is omnipotent, omnipresent, and omniscient; He is loving; He cares for us and values us. All of this is good. We need to learn as much as possible about God. But I think we have often neglected a major part of what He intended for us to experience.

On the whole, I believe we evangelicals have tended to misconstrue what it means that God is omnipotent. Many have assumed that God's omnipotence means that He can do anything He wants to do, anytime He wants to do it. If this is true, then God really doesn't need us. So prayer, worship, fasting, baptism, the Lord's Supper, and all other rituals are just religious observances with little or no relationship to the realities of life around us. And since God can do whatever whenever, what we do makes no difference, unless it be for us to grow in our faith and to bring a few others into saving faith. For everything belongs to Him anyway, and we're just along for the ride until He decides to wrap things up.

If this is our understanding, we've missed the fact that God seems to have put certain limits on Himself. He is indeed omnipotent, so He cannot be limited by anything outside Himself. But He can make rules for Himself that limit Him in certain ways; and He seems to have done so when He gave human beings free will. These limits are not absolute, because we know that He wins in the end. And even in the interim, He sets limits on such things as abuse and temptation (1 Cor 10:13). But we know from Scripture that God doesn't always get His way on the earth. For instance, He doesn't want people to go to hell—He is "not willing that any should perish" (2 Pet 3:9)—but the Bible tells us that many *will* perish in spite of what God wants.

And in the Lord's Prayer, Jesus prays that God's will be done—as though it is not a sure thing (Matt 6:10).

I believe Scripture shows us some of the rules God has made for Himself (though perhaps not all of them), and in this chapter I want to discuss a rule that I believe to be a major one. I'll call it "Partnership."

The rule is this: God chooses to do His work in the human arena mainly in cooperation (i.e., being yoked) with a human partner. We are told that the Jews of Jesus' day regularly did their heavy work with two oxen. One was a strong ox, the other a weaker one—perhaps an apprentice or an old ox. The strong ox shouldered most of the load, and the weaker one walked half a step behind. Jesus used this analogy in Matthew 11:28–30, inviting us to be yoked to Him as the weaker ox was yoked to the stronger.

Or, to put it negatively, God regularly withholds things He wants to do in the human arena until humans get involved in bringing it about. Therefore, what happens on earth is very often the result of what humans decide it to be.

There are many examples of this rule in Scripture and life. No one is saved without choosing to enter a relationship with Jesus. God's choice in the matter of salvation is obvious. Our choice is the one that determines whether the relationship is activated or not. Jesus will not save us unless we choose to relate to Him. With regard to forgiveness, He doesn't forgive us unless we ask Him to and, according to Matthew 6:14–15, unless we forgive those who have hurt us.

With regard to prayer, we are encouraged to ask (John 16:23–24), and we get the impression that He withholds things from us until we ask Him for them, even though He already knows what we will ask for (Matt 6:32). With regard to healing, Jesus spoke of the importance of our faith if we are to be healed (e.g., Luke 17:19; 18:42).

Thus, there is an important human dimension in our relationship with Jesus. He seldom, if ever, overrules our choices. We partner with Jesus in salvation, in forgiveness, in prayer, and in healing.

PARTNERSHIP IN SCRIPTURE AND BEYOND

I believe it was partnership that God had in mind when creating Adam and Eve. They were to partner with God in running the created universe—God on one side of the yoke, humans on the other. Adam was to rule, linked to God with but one condition governing their relationship: obedience. Ever since, God has been working in partnership with people. When God's human partners obeyed, things went well. When they disobeyed, things did not go well.

A few generations after Adam and Eve, when wickedness abounded on the earth, God partnered with Noah to rescue humanity. Then He partnered with Abraham to create a people of God. Then with Joseph to save those people from famine.

God partnered with Moses' mother and sister to keep him from being killed, and with Pharaoh's daughter to raise him. Then, due to a mistake on Moses' part, God waited forty years to deliver His people from oppression. Since Satan has to follow the same rule of partnership that God does, there ensued a contest between God's partner (Moses) and Satan's (Pharaoh). And even though Moses messed things up a bit by getting Aaron involved, God conceded, and He and His partner Moses pulled off an enormous victory.

To conquer the land of Canaan after the death of Moses, God's chosen partner was Joshua. When it came to ruling the nation of Israel, He partnered with various leaders during the time of the judges (e.g., Gideon, Samson), the prophets (e.g., Samuel, Elijah, Isaiah, Jeremiah), and the kings (e.g., David, Solomon).

Then, in the fullness of time, God looked for a woman to partner with Him to bring Jesus into the world. And Mary agreed. But there was someone in power—Herod—who partnered with Satan to kill Jesus. When God visited Mary's husband in a dream, Joseph partnered with God to rescue the Child and His mother.

Then came God's ideal partner—God's only perfect partner: Jesus. Here was One would not try to get God to change His mind, as Moses had done by involving Aaron. I believe, however, that there was a change of plans when Jesus returned to Nazareth with His parents after they found Him with the elders in the temple. I think Jesus was supposed to remain in the temple and probably start His ministry earlier, but He chose to obey His earthly parents. Although in Gethsemane Jesus pleaded for another way to carry out God's plan, He ultimately went to the cross in obedience to the Father.

After the resurrection and ascension of Jesus, God's partners were the disciples, the Apostle Paul, and other New Testament writers. Centuries later, Luther, Calvin, and the other Reformers became God's partners, followed by people like Wesley and Whitefield and Moody and Billy Graham—right down to us in the present day.

SATAN HAS TO OBEY THE SAME RULE

As I have mentioned above, Satan has to obey the same rule of partnership. He also needs human yokefellows, people who will partner with him to tempt, deceive, and mess up whatever it is that God wants to do.

Satan deceived Adam into disobeying the one rule God had given him. Thus, at least for a little while, Adam became Satan's partner, and since he was the father of the human race, he passed on to all of us a tendency to partner with Satan. We are all infected with a spiritual inheritance known as the sin nature.

We can trace satanic partnerships down through history: Cain, who partnered with Satan to murder Abel; the people of Noah's day, whom God destroyed because of their wickedness; the Egyptian ruler who didn't abide by the agreement the previous pharaoh had made with Joseph to protect the children of Israel; Saul, the first king of Israel; the rulers of the Divided Kingdom and several of the kings of Judah; King Herod, who tried to kill Jesus as a baby; the Pharisees, who opposed Jesus; Pilate and the Romans, who killed both Jesus and the early Christians; evil rulers throughout human history, including Hitler and Stalin in the twentieth century; and everyone (known or unknown) who has served the devil in any way.

AN IMPORTANT IMPLICATION OF THE PARTNERSHIP RULE

A major part of the warfare between God and Satan takes place in the human arena, and as Jesus' partners, we are involved with Him in spiritual warfare. God won the ultimate victory through His partnership with Jesus, and it looks like He also wants to defeat Satan through us, God's people who now fill Jesus' shoes on earth. So the war is waged between God's partners and Satan's partners. This is what seems to be behind Satan's tempting of Adam and Eve—to steal God's partners and get them on his side.

But God wants to prove that He can defeat our enemy, Satan, and his human partners with the assistance of His partners—those who believe in Jesus. We're even told in Romans 16:20 that God will crush the enemy under *our* feet.

My hunch is that before God created humankind, Lucifer had been in charge of the universe, and that God created us and gave us what had been Satan's domain. In the very first chapter of the Bible we are told that God blessed Adam and Eve and told them to "fill the earth and subdue it" (Gen 1:28). So Satan went to work to try to get back his lost territory—and while tempting Jesus, he claims to have done so: "And the devil said to Him, 'All this authority I will give You, and their glory; for this has been delivered to me, and I give it to whomever I wish. Therefore, if You will worship before me, all will be Yours'" (Luke 4:6–7 NKJV).

WHAT DOES THIS MEAN FOR US?

If we are partners with a God who is at war, we are at war as well. It seems as though God has chosen not to wage war without His partners, and He depends on us to hold up our end of the yoke. He calls us and commissions us to partner with Him to defeat the enemy.

We defeat Satan by winning people to Christ. God doesn't do it alone (Mark 16:15; Acts 1:8). Like Jesus, we also defeat Satan by healing people. God usually doesn't do it alone (Luke 9:1; John 14:12). Like Jesus, we defeat Satan by casting out demons. God doesn't do it alone (Luke 9:1; John 14:12). Like Jesus, we defeat Satan by teaching people under the guidance of the Holy Spirit. He doesn't teach alone (Matt 28:20).

When we partner with God, we enable Him to do what He wants to do. There seem to be a lot of things that God wants to happen, things that don't get done unless we do them (with His help). If we are partners, things don't go God's way (or ours) without us doing our part.

God's kingdom is ours as well as His. I believe this is what He had in mind for Adam and what He demonstrated in Jesus. Jesus lived in total obedience to the Father, never using the privileges of His divinity but partnering with the Father and being guided and empowered by the Holy Spirit.

WHAT DOES THIS HAVE TO DO WITH CONTEXTUALIZATION?

God wants to partner with us in mission. He has shown that He values us greatly and trusts us with His mission on earth. When we work obediently and intelligently with Him, great things happen. We can join with the heroes of the faith by partnering with God to accomplish His plan for humanity.

God respects people and wants them to thrive within the only way of life they have ever known: their culture. For this reason, I believe He supports a culture- and person-positive approach to witness—an approach that honors the people He loves and the way of life they have created for themselves. Therefore, when churches value people and enable them to feel at home in life and worship, they are partnering with God to do His will.

CONTEXTUALIZATION OF POWER

CHAPTER 13
SPIRITUAL POWER
A MISSIOLOGICAL ISSUE

Most of the world is heavily involved in enslavement to and manipulation of spiritual powers. Those seeking to encourage insider ministry need to recognize this as a major focus in pre-Christian life. In addition, once one is attuned to this fact, even a casual observation of the world Christian scene leads to the realization that a large percentage of the world's Christians participate in what I have called "dual allegiance." That is, finding within Christianity as it has been presented to them little or none of the spiritual power they crave to meet their needs for healing, blessing, guidance, and deliverance from demons, they continue their pre-Christian practice of visiting shamans, priests, diviners, temples, shrines, and the like for spiritual power. They may attend church faithfully and be truly committed to Christ on Sundays. But if they wake up ill on Monday, off they go to the shaman, because they know there's no healing in the church and the hospital is too slow and expensive.

This being so, it seems strange that we find virtually no discussion of spiritual power in publications concerning contextualization. Missionaries, development workers, and others who seek to help cross-culturally, since they come largely from the West, have for the most part ignored this facet of biblical teaching and social concern. Perhaps the same Western worldview blindness that has plagued missionaries working in areas saturated with consciousness of the spirit world has also affected our theorizing about contextualization. And just as that blindness has kept the missionaries from ever learning to deal adequately with the problems raised, it keeps us from addressing them in our theoretical treatments. Nor do we give the attention we should to the great need to help Christian converts deal with spirit world problems in ways that are both biblically and culturally appropriate.

Where are the discussions concerning biblically legitimate and culturally appropriate approaches to such areas of Christian experience as warfare prayer, deliverance from demons, healing, blessing and cursing, dedications, visions, dreams, concepts of the territoriality of spirits, angels, demons, and the like? Shouldn't we be discussing the contextualization of a Christian approach to spiritual warfare? What are the scriptural principles applicable to every cultural situation, and what are the cultural variables in this important area? Something as important to non-Western and, increasingly, to Western Christians needs to be discussed and dealt with.

THE BIBLICAL VALIDITY OF DEALING WITH SPIRITUAL POWER

Though ivory tower theoreticians have questioned the concept of spiritual warfare, it is an important biblical reality and, for those of us who are practitioners, a continual existential reality (see Kraft 2015). Jesus treated Satan and demonic forces as real foes, frequently casting out demons and thus freeing people He called "captives" and "oppressed" (Luke 4:18). Such language is warfare language. Furthermore, Jesus calls Satan "the ruler of this world" (John 14:30). In a similar vein, Paul refers to Satan as "the evil god of this world" who blinds people to God's good news (2 Cor 4:4). This fact also leads John to say that "the whole world is under the rule of the Evil One" (1 John 5:19).

Like most of the world today, biblical peoples saw the world as populated by enemy spirits that could cause trouble if they were not properly appeased. Unfortunately, through most of their history, the people of Israel chose to deal with these spirits as the animistic peoples around them did rather than as God had commanded them to. God constantly warned His people against worshiping the gods (read: demons) of the nations around them, and He punished them when they disobeyed. We know that our God is a patient God. He has demonstrated this countless times in His dealings with human beings. But there are areas of life—especially those related to the counterfeiting of His power-oriented activities—in which He has made it clear that there is to be no compromise. This has to be factored in at every point in any discussion of God's relation to spiritual power.

Take, for example, what God says in 1 Kings 11 (especially vv. 9–13) concerning the penalty Solomon will have to pay because he has disobeyed God by turning to other gods. God is angry with Solomon and takes the kingdom away from his son because of his idolatry. Similarly, in Acts 5:3, Peter asks Ananias why he "let Satan take control" of him so that he would lie to the Holy Spirit about the price of the property he had sold. And in 1 Corinthians 10:20,21 we are warned against eating what has been offered to demons. This warning is repeated even more sternly in Revelation 2:14,20.

But Jesus came "to destroy what the devil had done" (1 John 3:8), and He gives His followers "power and authority to drive out all demons and to cure diseases" (Luke 9:1) and to do the other works that He Himself did while on earth (John 14:12). We can't be either biblical or relevant to most of the peoples of the world without a solid approach to spiritual power.

A PERSONAL INADEQUACY

"What can we do about evil spirits?" This was a burning question among the Nigerian leaders I was attempting to guide. But I, their missionary, knew virtually nothing about the subject. My three-volume seminary theology textbook had only two references to Satan, and none to demons. That's about all I had learned about the enemy kingdom and its activities, despite the prominence of that subject in Scripture. So my Nigerian friends were on their own. I couldn't help them.

But now, more than fifty years later, God has led me into regular and frequent open conflict with demonic "rats," with the aim of setting captives free. I deeply regret that I didn't know in the late 1950s what I know now. In that setting, I contributed to the growth of a "dual allegiance" church. That memory plus my present experience has led me to commit myself to raising this issue wherever possible in missiological circles, in hopes that future generations will be better able to deal with spiritual power than I was.

SPIRITUAL POWER IN BALANCE

In any discussion of contextualization in relation to spiritual power, we need to keep our focus balanced. We have spoken in a previous chapter of the need for contextualizers to do their work in three crucial dimensions. As pointed out there, these dimensions are (1) our allegiance/relationship to Christ, with all the love and obedience that entails; (2) the understanding that comes from continually experiencing His truth; and (3) the spiritual power Jesus gives us to use as He used it, to express His love and bring freedom to others.

Dealing with spiritual power, though prominent in Scripture, is never an end in itself. It must always be balanced by concern for our relationship with God and for God's truth. When Jesus' followers came back from a power-filled excursion into the towns and villages of Galilee, reporting with excitement that "even the demons obeyed us when we gave them a command in Your name" (Luke 10:17), Jesus cautioned them and pointed them to something more important. That more important thing is our *relationship* with the God who provides the power. According to Jesus, this relationship, which results in our names being written in heaven (Luke 10:20), is to be an even greater cause of rejoicing than our power over demons.

So, as crucial as the power issue is both scripturally and contextually, the relationship issue is even more important. As evangelicals, of course, we've recognized the importance of emphasizing the need for a commitment to Christ resulting in a freeing and saving relationship with Him. In focusing on spiritual power, then, we must be careful not to de-emphasize or neglect all the love and the other fruits of the Spirit that that relationship entails.

Nor dare we neglect the issue of truth. Jesus spent most of His time teaching, demonstrating, and leading His followers into truth. In keeping with the implications of the Greek word for truth, this is to be an experienced truth, not simply intellectual truth. The continual experiencing of that truth, then, leads to ever-deepening understanding, both of the truth dimension of Christianity and also of the power and relationship dimensions.

For this experienced truth dimension is, according to John 8:31,32, based on obedience to Jesus within the context of relationship. And as Jesus explains in John 15:1–17, all bearing of fruit—including the fruit of spiritual power—is dependent on our abiding in Christ. We are therefore to encounter people and the enemy in contextually appropriate ways with a balance of allegiance, truth, and power encounters (see Kraft 1991). Any approach to Christianity that neglects or ignores any of these three dimensions is an incomplete and unbalanced Christianity.

As mentioned previously, although evangelical Christianity has usually been deficient in dealing with spiritual power, it has been strong on the truth dimension. And it has focused to some extent on allegiance and relationship, though in practice this allegiance/relationship has often been treated largely as a byproduct of truth and knowledge. Pentecostal and Charismatic Christianity have generally been more relevant to the peoples of the non-Western world through their emphasis on spiritual power, but they have often compromised their strength through an overemphasis on tongues and emotion and/or a negative attitude toward the cultures of the receptor peoples.

When we look at these three dimensions in relation to Western evangelical missionary work, we come up with a chart such as the following:

	ALLEGIANCE	TRUTH	POWER
Traditional Power	Wrong Allegiance	Counterfeit Truth	Satanic Power
Western Christianity	True Allegiance	God's Truth	
Biblical Christianity	True Allegiance	God's Truth	God's Power

TABLE 13.1. Neglect of the power dimension in Western Christianity

Since the power dimension has not been dealt with by the advocates of Western Christianity, the people to whom they minister continue to go to their traditional sources of power, even though they have pledged allegiance to Christ and are learning biblical truth. And even if they have experienced God's power, they may not realize that God wants them to relate to Him exclusively. Any attempt to rectify this situation must involve applying biblical emphasis and guidelines to the missing dimension.

SECULARIZATION OR A BRIDGE FROM POWER TO POWER?

Western Christian witness, having largely ignored spiritual power issues, has tended to unwittingly recommend secularization as the antidote to traditional approaches to obtaining spiritual power. For example, Western secular medicine and hospitals are offered as the answer to health problems, and secularizing schools as the right way to deal with what Westerners perceive as ignorance. Secular approaches are applied to everything from agricultural techniques to church management and leadership, not to mention insights into culture and communication that largely leave out the activity of the Holy Spirit.

With this approach, is it any wonder that mission-planted churches around the world are deeply involved in secularizing their members? I believe it was Lesslie Newbigin who said that Christian missions have been the greatest secularizing force in all of history. Without our intending it, our strategy has been to secularize in order to Christianize.

What this approach has produced is secular churches like most of those in the missionaries' home countries, churches that depend almost entirely on the power of secular techniques and structures to replace traditional methods of blessing, healing, teaching, and organizing. There is, of course, a certain amount of power in these techniques. But they are stronger on human and/or naturalistic power than on spiritual power, even though it often replaces what people have traditionally sought in spiritual ways. For example, for most of the traditional peoples of the world, healing was (or still is) a spiritual matter, not a secular one. So is agriculture and human and animal fertility. In the West, however, we have secularized each of these areas.

Douglas Pennoyer (1990) suggests that secularization can assist Christian evangelization by breaking the domination of evil spiritual power in people's lives. While this may be true in some cases, I'm afraid that secularization has for many peoples clouded rather than assisted much of what a scriptural approach to conversion should engender. It has done this by changing the subject. What ought to have been presented as a change from one spiritual power source to another spiritual source (i.e., from satanic power to that of Jesus) has been depicted as a change from interpreting things spiritually to interpreting things secularly.

Directing people from a pagan power source to the true God as the source is, I believe, the shortest bridge for power-oriented people, since it involves little or no conversion from spiritual power to secular power. Instead, the conversion is from one spiritual power source (Satan) to another (God), as it was for Abraham.

The cultural results of an approach that focuses on such change of power source are likely to be forms of Christianity that look very similar to their pagan predecessors but have a different power source. The Christian practitioners would look similar to native shamans and other healers, but they would work only in ways appropriate to biblical Christianity, and only under the power of the true God. The places and times of worship, and the ways in which worship and other rituals are conducted, would look as much like their pagan predecessors as the places and rituals Abraham captured for the true God looked like theirs.

As with Abraham's descendants, the people of Israel, the practices and personnel would undoubtedly change over time to be less like their pagan models, especially where these God-exalting practices prohibit such God-condemned activities as divination. But they would start at points familiar to the people rather than with foreign practices that give the impression that God's whole system has to be imported. And when prohibited practices in the spiritual power area are replaced, let the substitution be a spiritual power substitution, not a secular one. I will speak more specifically about such substitutions in the following chapter.

RELATIONSHIP BETWEEN SPIRIT AND HUMAN WORLDS

In dealing with spiritual power cross-culturally, there are a variety of basic principles to be made explicit. Among these is the scriptural fact that there exists a close relationship between what goes on in human life and what goes on in the spirit realm. We learn from the discussion between God and Satan in the first chapter of Job, and again from Jesus' statement that Satan wanted to sift the apostles like wheat (Luke 22:31,32), that Satan is anxious to assert himself to disrupt our lives. The instance of an answer to prayer being delayed by a demonic being (Dan 10:13), and what Paul says about Satan blinding unbelievers (2 Cor 4:4), tells us that the enemy can sometimes be successful in thwarting God's plans.

Even so, we learn from the ministries of Jesus and His disciples that we can thwart at least some of the enemy's plans by casting demons out of people. In addition, the angels (and presumably demons as well) are watching us as we carry out our activities (Eph 3:10; 1 Tim 5:21; 1 Pet 1:12).

SATAN THE CONTEXTUALIZER

Satan is an excellent contextualizer. He does an expert job at meeting people at the point of their felt needs in culturally appropriate ways. The fact that he often does so through deceit is not usually recognized. I am told that there is a Japanese volcano where people have erected signs imploring the spirits not to allow it to erupt again. There are also shrines and a temple there at which visitors can add their petitions to those of decades' worth of earlier visitors. Satan's ability to deceive in Japan in contextually appropriate ways is enhanced by the fact that the language shows no adequate distinction between ordinary spirits and a High God, as was discussed in a previous chapter. Ordinary spirits and God are all called *kami* and generally considered to be of the same nature and capriciousness. Attempting to appease the *kami* of the volcanic mountain is therefore not seen as essentially different from what Christians do on

Sundays, except by the handful of Christians who have gone deeply enough into biblical Christianity to understand the difference.

In addition, our enemy has duped a large percentage of the world's population into believing that ancestors continue to participate in human affairs. All he needs to do now to be culturally relevant is to assign demons to impersonate those who have died. Likewise, with regard to reincarnation, he has long since convinced people of the logic of the recycling of persons. All he has to do in this matter is to assign demons to recount for people the details of the lives of real people who lived in the past, as if these lives were their own former lives. Very convincing, and very contextualized. And since people have such a felt need for spiritual power, how better to gain control than by giving certain ones (such as shamans) that power? Of course, shamans are aware that in repayment for the use of that power during their lifetime they will die a horrible death. But they consider it worth the cost for the power and prestige they receive.

In addition to these larger areas of satanic contextualization, demonic beings are quite skilled at providing for "smaller" felt needs for such things as money, position, fame, control, revenge, and the sense of security and being wanted. But all of these come with an eventual price tag attached.

I once read a letter from a woman who had made a pact with the devil, bargaining for power, prestige, and wealth. She promised him in writing that if he would give her these things, she would give him her first son and every first son from then on in the families of her descendants. According to the report I heard, it can be shown now, about three generations later, that each of the first sons in this woman's family have suffered major problems of one sort or another—problems of the kind that lead one to suspect that her pact with the devil is still in effect.

SATAN'S PREDICTABILITY

A principle that becomes apparent when we study the enemy's tactics is that the ways in which he works are quite predictable. I believe we can deduce from Scripture that angels are sterile and uncreative. Therefore, instead of originating things or ideas, Satan and his hosts spend their time counterfeiting and damaging those things that God has brought into existence, stealing from God's creation because they lack creative power of their own. They can influence people who are creative and thus, through deceit, gain some ability to originate. Whatever creativity Satan has, like his power in other areas, comes from the humans he deceives.

While he depends on this stealing of human talents, Satan's activities tend to be easily recognizable by those who understand the ways in which he works. For example, I have often been able to figure out how a demon has been functioning by simply asking myself the question, "If I were a demon (or Satan), what would I do in this situation?"

Perhaps this is what Paul was getting at in 2 Corinthians 2:11 when he stated that "we know what [Satan's] plans [or devices or schemes] are." It is fairly obvious, for instance, that the devil works in terms of human constants such as pride and the desire for prestige, position, and power. He is active in promising such things, allowing good to happen for a time and then "closing in" on people, making them pay for whatever he has given them. Predictably, he will deceive people into believing his promises and accepting his gifts, which he does more often by telling partial and twisted truths than by outright lying. But his gifts only counterfeit the things God gives, since he has no good thing of his own making to give. Thus, he will counterfeit healing gifts (even deliverance) as well as the gifts of prophecy, wisdom, knowledge, and even tongues.

Biblical Christianity, as we saw in chapter 6, is intended to be a relational faith, not a religion. Since Satan cannot offer what God does, he counterfeits spiritual reality by producing religious systems that are quite logical once people believe the basic lie or deceit underlying them. For example, once one has accepted the idea that one life is not enough to accomplish all that we're meant to accomplish, what could be more logical than to believe that people get recycled through incarnation? Or to believe that because a baby looks like dead grandpa, he is a reincarnation of grandpa? And is it not logical to worship something inside or outside of human beings once one has concluded that whatever lies beyond the grave is unknowable? Similarly, once one has believed that ancestors remain a part of the living community after death, it is logical to assume that negative things that happen today are the result of revenge taken by dissatisfied ancestors. We note, however, how predictable it is that our enemy will always in some way direct attention to humans, spirits, or created objects under his control as the objects of worship, and never to the Creator of all (see Rom 1:16–25).

Doctrinally, the counterfeit religious systems are disturbingly similar to what God has revealed in Judeo-Christianity. Advocating righteousness, truth, peace, gentleness, and other admirable virtues seems so much like what Jesus taught. How can those systems be wrong merely because they leave out the need for a relationship with Jesus? And what, many people ask, is the difference between the Christian belief that God became one of us in the Incarnation and the concept of reincarnation in Hinduism? Satan has made sure that just about every Christian doctrine and ritual has its parallels in the religions of the world, parallels that imitate God's truth and make sense to the people who practice them. And animistic systems are amazingly similar from one part of the world to another, leading us to suspect that there is a single mind behind them.

Since Satan's objective is to counter God and disrupt His creation, it is predictable that he will attempt to turn good things into bad (or at least unattractive), make bad things worse, and get people who insist on pursuing good things to go after them in obsessive ways. In tempting people, the devil will seldom simply oppose things, choosing instead to raise questions about rightness, fairness, and the like, as he did in the Garden of Eden. He prefers to work in terms of deceit rather than with outright lies.

Another satanic predictability, playing off a human vulnerability, is that once he has planted a deceit or a lie, he seems to "train" humans to perpetuate that untruth themselves. Thus, the deceit on which reincarnation and ancestor cults are based gets perpetuated within the human community generation after generation, probably requiring little help from the satanic beings themselves. And since meanings are difficult to change, something that we will discuss further below, the staying power of such lies is great.

Therefore, when considering Satan's activities cross-culturally, we need to look for the many quite predictable things. We must recognize, however, that these predictabilities will be in terms of the ways of thinking and behaving of the receptor society, whether or not they fit our own logic. That is, Satan contextualizes his deceit. In Western societies, for example, where people are quite unaware of spiritual reality, Satan likes to capture people through apparently innocent games such as Dungeons and Dragons, through membership in apparently constructive organizations such as the Freemasons, and through philosophical or psychological ideas that appear erudite and innocent. In non-Western, family-oriented societies, what could be more logical than the satanic lie that one's ancestors are still alive and participating in the lives of their descendants? Or that it would be better to be with one's ancestors when one dies, even if they are in hell, than to go to heaven? Or that people get reincarnated after they die?

CROSS-CULTURAL CONSTANTS

As in all of life, beyond the differences in cultural understandings and expression, there are certain basic things that are the same across cultures. In working for God, one such basic is obedience, preceded by listening to Him and following His leading, whether in life in general or in bringing freedom to captives. With regard to Satan's kingdom, the basics include relating to how Satan lures people, how he influences and/or enters them, and the kinds of strategies he uses to keep them under his influence. In addition to these basics concerning God and Satan, the fact of simply being human involves basics relating to such things as how we use our wills, our capability for relating to the spirit world, and our vulnerability to temptation, deceit, and the like.

That both God and Satan work in partnership with people in terms of their culture is a constant we can expect to find in every cultural context. Underlying this is the fact that both God and Satan have plans for any given people and their culture, and they work with human will to seek to accomplish those plans. Although it is apparent that Satan has tremendous influence on the human scene, we learn from Scripture—especially from Jesus' life, death, and resurrection—that God is working out His own purposes in the background and that Satan's ultimate defeat is certain. We can therefore expect to find both Satan and God working in every cultural context.

Satan's representatives, both human and demonic, are obviously working hard to expand his kingdom, but we believe that God is not inactive in any cultural situation. According to Romans 1:16–2:16, He is working through the human conscience and people's culture so that, whatever excuses those who choose Satan's way may give, they will be accountable to God for their disobedience.

PERSON AND CULTURE

In dealing with culture, it is always important to distinguish cultural structure from the persons who operate that structuring. Contextualization studies usually focus on the structuring, leaving implicit the fact that it is people, the insiders, who produce and operate that structuring. Culture does not run itself. Culture simply lies there, like the roads we drive on or, to use a metaphor we have mentioned before, like the script of a play, memorized but regularly altered by the actors for a variety of reasons, some good, some not.

In dealing with spiritual reality, it is important to recognize that both humans and spirit beings are involved in the way cultural structuring is used. Most cultural structuring is capable of being used either for good or for evil. For example, such things as status and prestige, which are provided by a society on the basis of birth and/or achievement, can be used by those who have them either to help others or to hurt them. The fact that given people have status and the power that goes with it is not in and of itself a bad thing, but Satan entices people to use their status to hurt others, while God gently prods His people to use their status and the authority and power that go with it to assist the powerless.

But in each case, the spiritual being (whether God or Satan) works with people, and in terms of the cultural structuring in which they are involved. This is why, in dealing with spiritual warfare (as with all studies of contextualization), our focus needs to be on *people* within culture, not simply on culture itself.

Nevertheless, the important place of human habit must be recognized. Culture seems to have power over people because they follow cultural guidelines through force of habit. That is, *the apparent power of culture is in reality the power of human habit.* Thus, any attempts to change culture are really attempts to change human habits. The structuring is a function of the script that is, for the most part, followed fairly closely by the actors out of habit (once they have memorized it). The script is, however, often creatively changed by them, either because they forgot the lines, or because something didn't go as planned, or because they simply chose to be creative. When we find enemy influence contextualized within sociocultural patterns that are habitually followed by people, we must appeal to people to change their habits so that they will use either their present cultural patterns or changed ones for godly purposes. The point is, our appeal is always to *people* to change habits, with or without a change in structure. We cannot appeal to an impersonal thing like a cultural structure or pattern.

EMPOWERMENT OF CULTURAL FORMS

A very important issue in any discussion of contextualization is the difference between cultural forms and their meanings. By "forms" we mean all of the customs and structures, visible and invisible, that make up a culture. By "meanings" we mean the personal interpretations that yield a people's understandings of these forms. The forms are the various parts of culture. The meanings exist, not in the forms themselves, but in the people who use those forms. Meanings are attached by people, according to the agreements of their group concerning what the forms signify.

By virtue of the fact that people participating in the same sociocultural group agree about what significance to attach to each cultural form, they can communicate with each other. If they did not agree, they could not communicate. This is the problem faced by people who speak different languages. While language groups use essentially the same sounds, sounds are organized differently in every language. Therefore, members of one language group cannot accurately interpret words in another—even words that sound familiar to them—since they are not in on the agreements of the speakers of that other language. They have been taught to agree with the members of their own language group what particular combinations of sounds mean, but they will not know the agreements of the other group without learning their language. Language learning, like all culture learning, is a matter of learning the agreements concerning the meanings that the new group habitually attaches to the sound forms they use when communicating with each other.

A major problem in contextualization is that of changing the meanings of familiar forms. In seeking to assist people to accept and practice Christianity in terms of their own cultural forms, we are assisting them to use those forms for new purposes and therefore to attach new or modified meanings to them.

When John the Baptist began to use baptism within the Jewish community to initiate people into his renewal movement, he was reinterpreting a form that was well-known as a way of initiating Gentile converts into Judaism. This cultural form was also used by Greek mystery religions as an initiation ceremony. When the early Christians decided to use it to signify initiation into the church, they were largely following John's lead, since they assumed that Christianity was to remain within Judaism. Consequently, when the rite of baptism was used in Gentile territory, the meaning was more in keeping with the one signified by its use in initiating Gentiles into Judaism. In both cases, the meaning was partly the same as that of previous practice and partly a modification of that meaning. Similarly, Jesus took the Jewish Passover meal and reinterpreted it into what we call the Lord's Supper. In addition to these cultural forms, the early church reinterpreted a host of Greek words such as *theos* (God), *ekklesia* (church), *kurios* (Lord), *agape* (love), and others.

But cultural forms can also be *empowered* by spirit beings. God regularly flows His power through words such as "in Jesus' Name" and the commands we give to demons. When such words are conveying God's power, we call them "empowered language forms." James recommends that we use anointing oil to bring healing to the sick (Jas 5:14), but if the oil is to be effective, it needs to be dedicated in the name of Jesus and thus empowered. The elements used in the Lord's Supper can (and should) also be dedicated and thus empowered for specific purposes such as blessing and healing. Paul's handkerchiefs and aprons were empowered so that people received healing through them (Acts 19:12), as was Jesus' robe (Luke 8:43–48).

In many non-Christian societies, it is common for certain people to dedicate the things they make to spirits or gods, especially if those items are to be used for religious purposes or in dangerous pursuits. In the South Pacific, for example, those who made the large canoes used for fishing and/or warfare regularly dedicated them to their gods. I suspect they still do, even if they call themselves Christians. When such things are dedicated to satanic spirits, they are empowered by those spirits. Many a missionary and traveler who bought or was given dedicated items has experienced difficulties springing from the fact that by placing those objects in their home, they have unwittingly invited in enemy spirits.

Nevertheless, breaking the power of such objects is usually not difficult. Since we have infinitely more power in Jesus Christ than such objects can contain, we simply have to claim His power to break the enemy's power in the object. After doing this, I usually go on to bless the object in the name of Jesus. The problem with satanic empowerment is not whether we have the power to break it but overcoming our ignorance so that we can discern when it is there and know what to do to break it.

In contextualizing the power of Christ, it is important to disempower whatever has been empowered with satanic power before attempting to use it. Satanic power can be broken over rituals, buildings, carvings, songs, and almost any other custom or artifact a people wants to capture for God's use. Although many will counsel us to refuse to use whatever the enemy has used, I believe we are to *capture* cultural forms, not reject them merely because the devil has been using them. But we shouldn't try to use them until the power is broken. That would be unwise in the extreme.

The bigger problem, however, is the *meaning* problem. It may take two or three generations before the pre-Christian meanings associated in people's minds with a given object can be fully replaced. People often want to throw away every vestige of their culture that reminds them of their old involvement with shamans, rituals, and evil spirits. But in its place they tend to borrow foreign stuff, to which they often attach dubious meanings (such as sacredness simply because it is not understood), and which signals that God wants them to be foreigners in their own country rather than to capture their traditions for Christ. Since we Westerners have so poorly understood the spiritual power dimensions of our movement, we have often gone along with and even actively encouraged the converts' desire to dissimilate. This has produced a Christianity that is as powerless as ours in the West and thus unattractive to the people around them—except as the source of such things as prestige, status, and power.

Nevertheless, we should not give up, especially since the danger posed by secularization is so great. Perhaps we have not learned how to build the short bridge between animism and Christianity very well, but we should at least have learned by now that a secularized Christianity (the usual form at home and in missionized lands) is a long way from the Bible in the area of spiritual power. When people have learned to depend on secular medicine without the power of God, instead of either seeing medicine as a gift from God or receiving direct healing through prayer, they have moved away from the spirituality of the Scriptures, and it is difficult to reintroduce the spiritual meaning.

LEVELS OF WARFARE

Spiritual warfare has to be waged on at least two levels. The lower level is what I call "ground-level warfare." The upper level is ordinarily known as "cosmic-level warfare" (called "strategic-level warfare" by Wagner). Ground-level warfare involves dealing with spirits (demons) that inhabit persons. My experience suggests that personal spirits or demons are of at least three kinds: family, occult, and "ordinary."

1. **Family Spirits** (resulting from dedications to family gods)
2. **Occult Spirits** (resulting from occult allegiances)
3. **"Ordinary" Spirits** (attached to sinful attitudes and emotions)

TABLE 13.2. Ground-level spirits (those living in people)

Family and occult demons usually seem to be stronger than the "ordinary" demons, but dealing with them is essentially the same as dealing with ordinary demons. Family and occult spirits (including the spirits of non-Christian religions) gain their power when people consciously or unconsciously dedicate themselves to them. These spirits are passed down from generation to generation, even after the practice of dedication has ceased (e.g., because a person has become a Christian). "Ordinary" spirits are those that empower emotions such as fear, shame, and anger, plus problems such as lust, suicide, rebellion, and the like. Demons can only inhabit people by legal right, which is given through means such as dedication or wallowing in sinful emotions. In each case, there is a human cause that gives the spirits access.

At the cosmic level, we are dealing with at least five kinds of higher-level spirits, which I have labeled *territorial, institutional, vice, nature,* and *ancestral.*

1. **Territorial Spirits** such as those over nations mentioned in Daniel 10:13,21 (called "Prince of Persia" and "Prince of Greece"); spirits over regions and spirits over cities
2. **Institutional Spirits** such as those assigned to churches, governments, educational institutions, occult organizations (e.g., Scientology, Freemasonry, Mormonism), non-Christian religions (e.g., the gods of Hinduism, Buddhism, and animism), temples, and shrines
3. **Vice Spirits** such as those assigned to oversee and encourage special functions, including vices such as prostitution, abortion, homosexuality, pornography, gambling, war, cults, etc.
4. **Nature, Household, and Cultural Item Spirits** such as those residing in trees, rivers, homes, and cultural items such as dedicated work implements, music, cooking utensils, rituals, artifacts used in religious worship, etc.
5. **Ancestor Spirits** or deceiving spirits believed by many to be their dead ancestors who still participate in the activities of the living community—in reality these are demons deceiving people.

TABLE 13.3. Cosmic-level spirits (the "power of the air," Eph 2:2)

Cosmic-level spirits are apparently in charge of ground-level spirits, assigning them to people and supervising them as they carry out their assignments by entering people or by tempting and harassing them from the outside.

Jesus, as we know, frequently encountered and cast out ground-level demons. But the evidence that He dealt with higher-level spirits is slim, except in His encounter with Satan himself (Luke 4:1–13). I suspect, though, that in confronting and defeating Satan in his own territory (the wilderness was considered the property of Satan at this time), Jesus broke much of Satan's power over at least that part of Palestine. Some have suggested that the demons afflicting the Gerasene demoniac (Luke 8:26–33) were territorial spirits. If this is so, they were concentrated in one man, like ground-level demons, and Jesus dealt with them in the same way He did with those whose assignment was purely ground-level.

Discussions of the contextualization of biblical understandings of the spirit world and spiritual warfare must take into account these levels of spirits and what to do about them. For more on this, see the following chapter.

CONCLUSION

In this chapter, we have surveyed some aspects of spiritual power that should be carefully but effectively dealt with in any consideration of appropriate Christianity and insider movements. It is unfortunate that in most contexts missionized by people from the West, these issues have not been taken seriously. Or, if they were taken seriously, the whole culture was condemned, as if the evil were in the customs of the people rather than in Satan and those serving him working behind the scenes. Since spiritual power was not dealt with properly, the converts have often moved into a "dual allegiance"—an allegiance to Christ without fully renouncing previous allegiances to traditional spirits and gods. This, and many other problems that have arisen because of the lack of attention to the contextualization of spiritual power, desperately needs to be faced and worked through if we are to discover answers that are both scripturally and culturally appropriate.

CHAPTER 14
APPROPRIATE CONTEXTUALIZATION OF SPIRITUAL POWER

In the preceding chapter I have asked the question, Where are the discussions concerning biblically legitimate and culturally appropriate approaches to spiritual power? It should be an important part of missiology to deal with cross-cultural issues such as the activities of demons, dedications, blessing and cursing, visions and dreams, concepts of the territoriality of spirits, angels and demons, and warfare prayer (see Kraft 2015). Given the prominence of these subjects in Scripture, we should be seeking scriptural principles concerning the treatment of such issues in the societies into which Christianity is being introduced.

It is a sad fact of Western missionary effort that these topics have usually been overlooked, leaving people to fend for themselves when dealing with the evil spiritual realities that surround them. Most of the peoples to whom we go as missionaries are keenly aware of the strong influence of evil spirits in their life and that of their neighbors. But new Christians, and many who have been following Christ for some time, need the help of outsiders who have both studied the Scriptures and also had experience with the evil spirit world themselves. Unfortunately, there are too few of such people around.

But things are changing. Several of us are now teaching courses on spiritual warfare, writing on the subject, and doing the works that Jesus promised we would do in relation to the evil spirit world (John 14:12; 20:21; Luke 9:1–2). Efforts such as these can, at the very least, point to ways of exploring the contextualization of a Christian approach to spiritual power.

THE DANGER OF OVERCONTEXTUALIZATION

Let me start with a warning. Although we will be taking spiritual warfare seriously given that there is both a need and scriptural precedent for it, we must bear in mind that there are plenty of examples of people "going off the deep end" in this area. Whether out of unfamiliarity with the spirit world or from the uncritical adopting of pre-Christian ways of dealing with spirit world problems, or for some other reason, many have fallen into unacceptable practices—practices that don't fit scriptural guidelines and often don't even measure up to common sense.

I use the term "overcontextualization" to signify situations in which people have come to practice at least parts of their Christianity—and in this case, specifically techniques relating to spiritual power—in ways that fit in with the surrounding culture but fail to measure up to biblical standards. Appropriate Christianity balances cultural appropriateness with scriptural appropriateness. An overcontextualized Christianity may lose that appropriateness at the scriptural end, though it may serve well the culturally inculcated desires of any given society.

While it is of great importance to see the use of spiritual power contextualized, it is equally important not to overdo it. What I mean is that there are several ways in which people have gotten into spiritual power and carried their emphasis too far. One of the perversions that is widespread in America is the so-called "Name it, claim it" or "Word faith" heresy. This approach teaches that if we generate enough faith and with it claim anything we might happen to want, we can manipulate God into doing our will. We can thus gain material things, healing, or whatever strikes our fancy. God wants us to be prosperous, say the advocates, so all we have to do is to produce the faith and He will grant us our desires. This is overcontextualization because it makes God captive to the American ideal of prosperity for all and seeks to use His power for human ends.

Another perversion is the one that holds that since God *can* heal without the use of medicine, we should not use medicine. There are, unfortunately, several deaths every year in the United States because people deny themselves or their children medical assistance on this premise. They fail to see that it is God who heals through doctors and medicine as well as apart from them, and that when we demand that God perform the healing in the way we prescribe, we are guilty of trying to manipulate Him to do our will in our way.

The opposite is also overcontextualization. Many Christians have so secularized their understandings of healing that they place all their faith in doctors and medicine and little or none in God. If someone is ill or experiencing emotional problems, their only thought is to get them to medical or psychological help, perhaps with a perfunctory prayer that God will lead the secular professional. If they pray in earnest at all, it is only after the secular means of healing have failed.

In many societies, Christian healers use the methods of shamans rather uncritically. In Korea, Africa, India, and other places, an unfortunately large number of pastors who seek to bring about physical healing and deliverance do so by violence, shouting, and other dramatic and very un-Christlike techniques in their ministries. I have heard of people being beaten in attempts to free them from demons both in Korea and in Africa. Certain American healers are also given to displays that make good drama but are quite unlikely to be methods Jesus would endorse.

Such methods are overcontextualizations because although they may be appropriate to certain subgroups within a society, they are not appropriate to Scripture. That is, they are manipulative and do not manifest the love, faith, and good sense that we see in scriptural personages such as Jesus and Paul.

ANIMISM VS. GOD-GIVEN AUTHORITY

Most of the world, including most adherents of so-called "world religions," practice what anthropologists and missiologists call "animism." According to this belief and the practices that go with it, the world is full of spirits that can hurt us unless we are careful to appease them. Animists may or may not believe in a High God. When they do, He is usually seen as benign and thus in need of little if any attention. However, all animists agree that the spirits need to be watched and kept happy so that they won't hurt them. In addition, animists believe (rightly) that evil spirits can inhabit material objects and places such as certain mountains (e.g., OT "high places"), trees, statues (e.g., idols), rocks (e.g., the Ka'aba in Mecca), rivers (e.g., the Ganges), territories, fetishes, charms, and any other thing or place that is dedicated to the spirits. Animists also believe in magic and the ability of at least certain people to convey power via curses, blessings, spells, and the like.

What the Bible says concerning spiritual power recognizes the validity of both the power and the power techniques practiced by animists. Scripture teaches us to use similar techniques based on similar principles, but with the true God as our source of power. The deceptive thing is that much of what God does and endorses looks on the surface like what animists do. There is a reason why this is so, and those without experience and understanding of what's going on in the interaction between the spirit world and the human world can easily miss it.

The reason why animism and Christianity look so similar is that the basic difference between them is not at the surface level. It's not in the cultural forms—both Christians and animists use many of the same techniques. It's in the source of power. In areas such as healing, dedicating, and blessing, for example, Christians and animists do essentially the same things, but the source of our power is God, the source of theirs is Satan. We learn both from Scripture and from practical experience that many if not all of the rules that apply to God's interactions with humans also apply to the ways the enemy interacts with us (see Kraft 1994; and chapter 12 in this book). For example, obedience to God in prayer, worship, sacrifice, and service enables Him to carry out His purposes in the world. Conversely, when people obey Satan in these same ways, Satan is enabled to accomplish his purposes. The importance of obedience, and the fact that this is a warfare issue, is thus underlined.

Again, animists believe that objects such as idols and implements used in religious rituals may be dedicated to gods or spirits and thus *contain* spiritual power. The Bible shows that objects can be dedicated to our God and thus *convey* His power (e.g., the Ark of the Covenant, Paul's handkerchiefs). On the surface, containing and conveying power look the same, especially since what animists believe to be power *contained* in objects is in reality satanic power *conveyed* by them.

To use another example, animist diviners, shamans, and priests can heal with the power of Satan, just as God can with His power. The fact that satanic healing will sooner or later lead to captivity and misery is not immediately apparent to the one being healed. More immediately obvious is the fact that God's healing leads to freedom and peace. But both types of healing look the same initially, and people who seek healing rather than the Healer are easily deceived, especially since demons often seem to work faster than God does.

Our authority as Christians versus the authority Satan can give his followers is an important issue at this point. Those who don't know the difference between what animists do and God-given authority to work in spiritual power accuse those of us who are working in God's power of practicing "Christian animism" (e.g., Priest et al. 1995). But when we exercise the power and authority Jesus gives us to do things animists do—healing, casting out demons, blessing people and objects, dedicating buildings, praying for rain or against floods, and such—we are not animists, because we are working in God's power, not Satan's. We are simply exercising the authority Jesus gave His disciples (Luke 9:1) and told them to teach to their followers (Matt 28:19).

We may summarize some of the major issues in this discussion in the following chart, which shows many of the contrasts between animism and God-given authority. Note that the primary expressions of each area will look very similar at the surface level. It is in the underlying power and motivations that they differ.

	ANIMISM	GOD-GIVEN AUTHORITY
Power Need (in order to utilize spiritual power)	Power believed to be *contained in* people and objects	God conveys His power *through* people and objects
	Felt need to learn how to manipulate spirit power through magic or authority over spirits	We are to submit to God and learn to work with Him in the exercise of power and authority from Him
Ontology (what is really going on)	Power from Satan: he is the one who manipulates	Power from God: He empowers and uses us
God	Good but distant, therefore ignore Him	Good, close, loving, and involved with us, therefore relate to Him

	ANIMISM	GOD-GIVEN AUTHORITY
Spirits	Fearful and can hurt us, therefore appease them	Defeated, therefore assert God's authority over them
People	Victims of capricious spirits who never escape from being victims	They are captives, but we can assert Jesus' authority to free them
Cost	Those who receive power from Satan suffer great tragedy later	Those who work with God experience love and power throughout life and eternity
Hope	No hope	We win

TABLE 14.1. Animism vs. God-given authority

Satan is very good at protecting himself from what he knows to be a power much greater than his. He knows that God has infinitely more power than he has and that Jesus passed this power on to us. His primary strategy, therefore, is to keep God's people ignorant and deceived so that we will not use God's power against him.

A very important first step in contextualizing spiritual power, then, is to help people to know who they are scripturally and how this identity is to be expressed culturally. Scripturally, we are the children of God, made in His image, redeemed by Jesus Christ to be heirs of God and joint heirs with Him (Rom 8:17). This gives us all the power and authority Jesus gave His followers to cast out demons and heal diseases (Luke 9:1); to do the works Jesus Himself did (John 14:12); to be in the world what Jesus was (John 20:21); and to crush the enemy under our feet (Rom 16:20). Therefore, if we are to be true to Scripture, we need to follow Jesus' example, always using His power to show His love.

Christians in non-Western societies, like us in the West, will be accountable to God to resist traditional cultural models for the exercise of power. We need, rather, to discover or create models that will be interpreted by cultural insiders as consonant with Scripture. Appropriate ways of exercising power in love in cross-cultural contexts may look quite different from the appropriate expressions in Western societies, and many Euro-Americans set a poor example of scriptural contextualization in this area. We have often shown captivity to our home cultural models in our approaches instead of working out scripturally appropriate use (capture) of traditional customs, with or without modification.

DEMONIZATION

An important issue to deal with in every society is "ground-level" demonization. There will always be a high percentage of people (unfortunately including many Christians) who are hosting demons, especially in societies where babies are dedicated to spirits or gods before or soon after birth. In such societies, we can expect the percentage of demonized people to be about 100 percent, since dedication invites the demons to inhabit the children. How demons behave in any given society, and how what they do and don't do differs from society to society, are fitting subjects for research.

At the ground level, the casting out of demons by the authority of Jesus Christ appears to be cross-culturally valid. Although I have seldom been able to simply command demons out as easily as Jesus seems to do in the Gospels, I have been successful in confronting and defeating them in Jesus' name in several different cultural contexts.

My experience in ministering to demonized people of other societies leads me to conclude that the basic principle of "dual causation" is cross-culturally valid. This principle holds that demons can live in a person only if there are problems within that person to which they can attach themselves, thus gaining a legal right to be there. The dual causation, then, is to recognize that there is both a human cause (the internal problem to which the demons are attached) and a spirit problem (the demons themselves). Dealing with demons in people of other societies requires us to deal with the internal problems as well, just as it does with Westerners.

The analogy I use to describe demons is that they are like rats, because rats live where there is garbage. Demonic "rats" gain their rights and their strength from the spiritual, mental, and emotional "garbage" in the life of the person they inhabit. That garbage may be spiritual, such as dedication to spirits. Or it may be mental, such as believing lies. Or it may be emotional, such as wallowing in fear, anger, shame, hatred, or lust. When a person is carrying such garbage, it gives demons entrance, allows them to stay, and gives them power.

Whether in the West or cross-culturally, then, dealing with the garbage in people is the most important aspect in the process of fighting demons at the ground level. Demons must have legal rights to inhabit people, and those rights are a function of the garbage. The garbage is therefore more important to deal with than the demons, although both problems must be dealt with if the person is to be set free. When the garbage is dealt with first, the demons are weakened and leave quietly when they are challenged (see Kraft 1992b, 1993, 2010, 2015). Still, they seldom if ever leave on their own—they usually need to be cast out. I have demonstrated the validity of this approach in casting out several thousand demons. As we will see, this "rats and garbage" principle also applies to cosmic-level spirits.

As mentioned in the preceding chapter, our enemy is good at contextualizing. He will adapt his approach to the problems and concerns that are most prominent in a given society. A major part of his strategy is to do his work without being noticed, especially in areas where there might be Christians who know how to combat demonization. Another of his preferred ways of working is the practice of making negative things worse and getting people to go overboard on positive things. Yet the things

Satan pushes in each society will differ for maximum effectiveness in his attempts to deceive and disrupt.

In Asian societies, for example, where the relationship between mothers-in-law and daughters-in-law is a difficult one, demons will often be active in pushing mothers-in-law to be oppressive and daughters-in-law to hate them. In African societies, where fear of the unknown is endemic, demons will push all the buttons they can to heighten this fear so that people continue to visit diviners (where demonic influence is increased) for relief. In the Americas, Asia, and Europe, where male domination of women and children is culturally inculcated, the enemy kingdom is very active in increasing the abuse and the pain experienced by women and children. And we can speak of satanic enhancement of racism, suppression of women, and social class oppression in many parts of the world. The thing that all such examples have in common is that the seed from which Satan works to produce harmful fruit is culturally appropriate.

With regard to the techniques people use for dealing with demons, the enemy is also active in seeing to it that culturally appropriate excesses are regular occurrences. As mentioned previously, in places like Korea and Africa, it is common to hear of deliverance sessions that involve beating the demonized person to get the demons out. It is possible that such attempts at deliverance may be orchestrated by Satan himself. I know of two situations in which demonized Koreans died as a result of such beatings, thus fulfilling a demon's intent to destroy those he inhabits.

The appropriate and proper approach to getting people set free from demons in any society seems to always be the same: deal with the spiritual and emotional garbage to weaken the demons, then kick them out. Fighting physically with them is never a good idea. And even when it is necessary to physically restrain a demonized person, it is God's power wielded through words, not power wielded through physical force, which gets the demons out.

While I have found this approach to be cross-culturally valid, there can be problems. Asians and persons of many other shame-based societies, for example, often find it very difficult to admit things they have said or done that have given rights to the demons. This often springs from a worldview value that holds that if a problem is hidden or denied, it will simply go away if one waits long enough. This is not true, of course. On the contrary, the longer people hold onto deep problems, the more such problems fester deep within and affect their lives.

Since God is a God of truth, no matter what the culture, people have to "come clean" and be willing to deal with the things they have done, and the things that have been done to them, if they are to be healed. And this holds true regardless of how culturally strange it might be for people to admit these disagreeable things and to forgive those who have hurt them. As in the West, it is especially a person's reactions to things done to them that must be dealt with, so that the heavy emotional loads such reactions produce may be brought to Christ and laid at His feet (Matt 11:28). The hurtful events cannot be undone. What happened, happened. But with the help of the Holy Spirit, reactions such as anger, bitterness, fear, and especially unforgiveness can be given to Jesus, bringing emotional healing. When such things are brought to Him, the demons have nothing more to cling to and are easily banished.

DEALING WITH FAMILY SPIRITS OR OCCULT SPIRITS

Several years ago I was working to bring "inner healing," including freedom from certain demons, to a Chinese missionary in her early fifties. In addition to the fairly "normal" problems to which demons were attached, such as hate and anger, she was carrying "family" demons that she had inherited from her parents. The demons had been strengthened when her parents dedicated her at a temple as a newborn and when they took her to a temple as a child for healing. She was also carrying demons that had entered when she was practicing Chinese martial arts under a "master" who, without her knowledge, dedicated all he did to demonic spirits. The lady had no idea that things like these, which had happened so long ago, could be responsible for the daily (and nightly) torment she experienced. She believed in the existence of demons but had until recently been believing the lie that demons cannot live in Christians, especially dedicated ones such as those who served as missionaries.

Fortunately, unlike others who had tried to deliver her, I have worked with enough Chinese people (as well as Koreans and Japanese) to know that just about every child born into non-Christian Chinese families—and even many born into Christian families—are dedicated by their mother, grandmother, or some other close relative. Such dedications both empower the inherited family spirits and add new spirits. The name and exact date of the baby's birth (often even the time of day) is written down and taken to a priest to be registered with the gods of the temple. Though many Chinese families claim not to believe in spirits anymore, this is often done "just in case."

It is usually easy to break the power even of long-standing family demons, since the power of Jesus is so great. We simply claim Jesus' authority over the vows, curses, dedications, sins, and other ways in which rights have been given to demons by the person's ancestors; this I have done innumerable times. The issues that remain relate to the canceling of all permission the person—or anyone in authority over them—has given to demons in any of the ways the ancestors had done. This usually involves dealing with demons attached to emotional reactions such as anger, hatred, unforgiveness, and fear. Once each of the areas of permission has been dealt with, the demons go quietly at our command.

We can count on finding family spirits in anyone who is within three or four generations (or more) of the routine dedication to gods or spirits and/or has received healing from such gods or spirits. This means that we can expect family spirits in nearly all Asians, Africans, Latin Americans, South Pacific islanders, American Indians, and many Euro-Americans. Anyone within three or four generations of conversion from Hinduism, Buddhism, Islam, Shinto, or animism, or any occult organization such as Mormonism, Freemasonry, Scientology, or Jehovah's Witnesses, is likely to be carrying family and/or occult spirits.

Occult spirits are dealt with in the same way as family spirits. We look for things such as curses, dedications, and sins that have given the demons rights, and break their power, then we cast the demons out. Like family spirits, occult spirits can unfortunately be inherited down to at least the third or fourth generation, and probably longer in some cases. So if a person had a father or grandfather who was a Freemason, or a mother or grandmother who was into Christian Science, we can expect demons from those sources to be living in the person we are working with even though they have personally never been involved in these occult organizations.

COSMIC-LEVEL SPIRITS

Most of the world believes there are specific spirits attached to nations, regions, mountains, rivers, and other geographical features. We find this understanding in the Old Testament, where the Baal gods were considered to have control of the plains while Yahweh was supposed to be merely a mountain god. In the events recorded in 1 Kings 20:23–30, we see Yahweh angered at this belief on the part of the Syrians and therefore giving Israel a victory on the plains.

One of the spinoffs of the belief in territorial spirits is the understanding that a person who enters the territory of a given god must show respect to that god. The Bible constantly depicts the Israelites honoring the Baals and other gods when they were in territory believed to belong to these gods. For example, we see in Hosea 2:8 that Israel attributed her prosperity to Baal instead of to Yahweh. And King Solomon, to cement relationships with the surrounding countries, married women from Ammon, Moab, Edom, and other places, even though this clearly violated the Lord's command. Furthermore, he erected altars to his wives' gods to show honor to their countries. By keeping his wives and their relatives happy in this manner, Solomon made peace with Israel's enemies. But in so doing, he sacrificed the favor of Yahweh (1 Kgs 11:1–11).

Westerners tend to think that such beliefs need not be taken seriously, since these so-called gods are not gods at all but imaginary beings empowered only by superstition. The Bible, however, shows God and His people taking such spirits seriously, though we are warned against giving them honor or fearing them because the true God is greater and more powerful than these servants of Satan. If we are properly related to the true God, we have the authority to protect ourselves from other gods and to confront and defeat them when necessary.

I hold the position that people who have been under the sway of territorial spirits for generations have a great deal of understanding of what territory the spirits have influence over and what the results of this influence are. Consequently, any approach to Christianity in such areas will need to recognize the reality of the spirits over the area and seek to understand their assignments. We can then deal with them by taking away their rights as we work with the true God to retake territory that is rightfully His. See Wagner (1991) for case studies dealing with territorial spirits.

Experiments going on in Argentina and elsewhere in the world suggest that a direct approach to warring against cosmic-level spirits can be successful. As with ground-level warfare, however, it is most important to deal with the spiritual "garbage." Thus, issues such as confession of sin, repentance, reconciliation, and unity ("corporate garbage") are the first order of business if our praying against territorial bondage is to be successful. In his chapter in my book *Behind Enemy Lines* (1994), Ed Silvoso reports on the success of such an approach in Resistencia, Argentina, where for three years he led a comprehensive spiritual attack aimed at breaking the power of the territorial spirits over the city and opening the people up for evangelism. That approach involved getting the pastors (the spiritual "gatekeepers") to repent of their sins and their disunity and to unite; training pastors and lay church leaders in spiritual warfare; praying; repentance, reconciliation, and prayer marching; and, after two years of such preparation, all-out evangelism. The results have been spectacular.

Some have criticized such efforts to wage war at the cosmic level, pointing out that Jesus never seemed to concern Himself with any level above ground level. Could it be, though, that the Holy Spirit is simply leading us in our day (maybe the last days) into more of the "all truth" that Jesus promised in John 16:13? And could it be that by cleaning up so much of the ground-level garbage and praying as much as He did—in private, as well as in John 17—Jesus was contributing greatly to the breaking of satanic power at the cosmic level? From what those engaged in cosmic-level warfare are discovering, it seems clear that most of what it takes to effectively confront higher-level spirits takes place at ground level. I am referring to such things as confession of sin, repentance, reconciliation, and the need for spiritual gatekeepers to work in unity.

Whether or not a certain strategy to confront cosmic-level spirits is scriptural, we cannot argue against the scriptural sanction of such things as repentance, unity, and intercessory prayer, which are felt to provide the key to breaking the power of higher-level spirits. Disunity, lack of repentance, and failure to fast and pray may be seen as the cosmic-level "garbage" on which cosmic-level "rats" feed.

An important technique developed by spiritual warfare activists such as George Otis Jr. (1993, 2001), John Dawson (1989), Ed Silvoso (1993), C. Peter Wagner (1993), and others is known as "spiritual mapping." This is an approach to discerning and identifying the cosmic spirits over the areas charted in the preceding chapter, as a step toward developing strategies to oppose and defeat them.

Spiritual mapping is much like what God told Moses to do when He commanded him to send spies into the Promised Land to discover the situation Israel would face as they attempted to take the land. Such spying, a standard feature in warfare of any kind, is a major component in developing strategies for attacking the enemy. It should certainly be a part of any attempt to contextualize spiritual warfare.

GODS, IDOLS, AND DIVINATION

Our efforts to contextualize spiritual power must take into account the strong negative tone of God's pronouncements concerning compromise with regard to other gods and spirits and the ways in which their power is engaged. I will first point out several of the prohibited areas and then discuss what may be done about them.

God's ideals in this area are quite clear from Scripture. The Old Testament, especially, is an excellent source from which people today can learn what is and is not allowable. Most of the world's peoples today share with the peoples of biblical times the understanding that the world is populated by evil spirits and that higher level spirits are in charge of territory (see Dan 10:13,21). God never counters that belief, but He is very much against His people honoring these spirits.

For example, it is not acceptable to God when it is assumed—as it was in biblical times and is in many societies today—that when we enter the territory of any given spirit, we should be polite and recognize that spirit's right to control the territory. As mentioned earlier in this chapter, God got angry and taught the people a lesson when it was assumed that He was only powerful in the mountains but not on the plains (1 Kgs 20:23–30).

Both the Old and New Testaments are clear that the worship of any god but the true God is not permitted. We are to worship no god but Yahweh (Ex 20:3), and to neither make nor worship idols because, as the Lord declared on Mt. Sinai, "I am the Lord your God and I tolerate no rivals" (Ex 20:5). And among the many warnings against idolatry in the New Testament is the command at the end of 1 John: "My children, keep yourselves safe from false gods!" (5:21).

Perhaps the clearest indication of what God feels about His people having relationships with other gods is found in the story of the Israelites at Peor in Numbers 25. God was incensed when the leaders attended feasts with Moabite women, "where the god of Moab was worshipped" and where "the Israelites ate the food and worshipped the god Baal of Peor" (vv. 2,3). So strongly was God's anger roused by this that He commanded that those who had participated in the idolatry be killed publicly (v. 4). And when one of the men openly challenged the prohibition by taking a Midianite woman into his tent, God commended Aaron's grandson, Phinehas, for killing the man and his Midianite lover. "Because of what Phinehas has done," declared the Lord, "I am no longer angry with the people of Israel.... He and his descendants are permanently established as priests, because he did not tolerate any rivals to Me and brought about forgiveness for the people's sin" (vv. 11,13). Thus, it is clear that contextualization of idolatry is impossible for Christians.

Several other forbidden practices are listed as the reasons why God gave His people the right to drive out the inhabitants of Canaan. In Deuteronomy 18:9–13, many of these practices are recorded and labeled "disgusting." They include sacrificing children, divination, looking for omens, using spells or charms, and consulting spirits of the dead. The text says, "God hates people who do these disgusting things, and that is why He is driving those nations out of the land as you advance" (v. 12).

So it is clear that many common pagan practices involving spiritual power are forbidden. God does not tolerate appeasing pagan gods or spirits or seeking information, health, wealth, or blessing from them. His answer to the quest for these things is to relate to Him in love and trust, allowing Him to provide the blessings we need.

What such total condemnation says to today's "dual allegiance" Christians is frightening. The majority of Christians in non-Western contexts—and many in Western contexts as well—probably find so little spiritual power in Christianity that they regularly seek help from non-Christian power sources. In most of the world, the kind of Christianity people have received has been strong on the intellectual and spiritual distinctives of Western evangelical Christianity but virtually powerless in healing, deliverance, blessing, and the other areas traditionally covered by pagan shamans and priests. Unable to get these needs met within Christianity, many Christians (including pastors and other church leaders) continue to visit traditional power brokers.

Since Scripture is very clear that God tolerates no rivals, seeking out these other gods and spirits is a serious matter—even more so if it constitutes worship. I believe, however, that God does take into account the ignorance of such people and their missionaries. We find in 2 Kings 5 that He also takes pagan authority relationships into account. After Naaman was healed and committed himself to the God of Israel, he asked the prophet Elisha how he should now behave when required by his master to accompany him to a pagan temple. "I hope that the Lord will forgive me when I accompany my king to the temple of Rimmon, the god of Syria, and worship him," he says (v. 18). Elisha simply responds, "Go in peace" (v. 19), indicating that God would understand the situation and not hold it against Naaman.

In attempting to see biblical Christianity contextualized, we recognize that God brooks no rivals. Although He allowed Israel's belief in the existence of many gods to continue for some time (see Ex 20:3's reference to "other gods"), He insisted that there be no compromise with regard to allegiance. There were to be no rivals, and certainly no contacting of spirits or dead people. However, as we have noted before, places of worship, and even rituals and transition rites such as circumcision and baptism previously used for pagan purposes, can be captured, disempowered, purified, and used to honor the true God. This is what Israel did with pagan worship rituals and ceremonies. They took over the use of high places as places of worship to the true God, and even blood sacrifices were infused with new meaning.

Nearly all the customs used by the early Israelites came from their pagan background and were captured for Yahweh. In the New Testament, baptism had pagan roots, as did many key terms—"Lord," "church," "grace," "love," and most of the other words used for important Christian concepts.

ANCESTORS

As mentioned before, I believe ancestor cults to be satanic contextualizations carried out through demonic deception. Probably all people, especially those in societies that are strongly family-oriented, are greatly concerned about what happens to their loved ones when they die. What a stroke of genius on Satan's part to convince people that their loved ones are still alive (which is true) and that they continue to actively participate in human life (which is false)! By so doing, demons are able to work freely, disguised as ancestors. And since they already know everything about that ancestor, they can do an excellent job of impersonation and, in the process, exert great control over the people they deceive. Demons posing as ancestors have the power to give and to take away. Thus they bind people to false beliefs and the rituals that go with them in a way that is hard to break free of.

Given the appropriateness of such contextualization from Satan's point of view, the question to be raised is, what can we do about it? Most of those who believe in ancestor reverence have long since bought the lie that it is really their loved ones who are receiving and responding to their attention. And it is not easy to get them to understand that what they have been believing for generations is a lie. Nor is it easy to convince the academics who, with no experience with the demonic world themselves, argue interminably on the basis of pure theory about whether or not ancestors, demons, or Satan are real. Our enemy has done a good job of deluding, or at least confusing, the academics. Their lack of agreement unfortunately affects the practitioners and would-be practitioners, causing doubt and uncertainty in their efforts to preach and teach and in their attempts to wage war against evil spiritual forces operating at the ancestor level.

Those who argue that ancestors are conscious of and can influence what goes on in human life support their theory with the account of King Saul's excursion to the medium in Endor (1 Sam 28:3–19). But I believe that this event, and Moses and Elijah's appearing at the Transfiguration of Jesus (Luke 9:28–31), are best interpreted as specific times when God allowed deceased people to return for specific purposes. They have, I believe, nothing to do with the possibility that ancestors are conscious of and interacting with human life. And although the statement that "we have this large cloud of witnesses round us" (Heb 12:1) may mean that the deceased are able to watch us, it gives no indication that they can participate in human life.

So we have no scriptural encouragement to believe that the dead interact with the living. And, in fact, we are warned sternly not to attempt to contact the dead (Lev 19:31; Deut 18:11). The practice of diviners seeking information about this life, and especially about the future, from the deceased is well-known, both in Scripture and in contemporary societies. It is a form of divination called "necromancy." God's attitude toward this practice is stated in the strongest terms in Deuteronomy 18: "The Lord your God hates people who do these disgusting things, and that is why He is driving those nations out of the land as you advance" (v. 12).

People who regard ancestors as participants in the living community are deceived, but how can we tell them that and still expect them to listen to our message? And when people have for generations offered sacrifices and performed other acts of worship to these supposed ancestors, the problem of how to present Christianity to them is compounded greatly. "Where are my ancestors now?" they ask, often adding that they want to be with them for eternity even if they are in hell. With regard to where they are now, I believe we can take some encouragement from God's gracious response to Abraham when he asks, "Will not the Judge of all the earth do right?" (Gen 18:25). And Jesus' parable of the rich man and Lazarus (Luke 16:19–31) speaks directly to the issue of eternity. According to that story, if any of our ancestors are in hell, they will desperately want us, the living, to avoid going there too.

To free people from satanic deception in ancestral matters, we will have to deal with demonization from early childhood. Any commitment to enemy spirits is an invitation for them to live inside a person. And since a commitment such as ancestor worship has been going on for generations, with accompanying dedications of each newborn, what we are dealing with are ancestral family spirits inherited from a person's parents. These need to be banished. So do the spirits inhabiting ancestral tablets or other paraphernalia associated with the reverence and worship accorded them.

The difficulties involved in dealing with change of meaning, however, are another matter. Will people agree to speak to Jesus, asking Him to convey any messages He chooses to the ancestors? Will they replace the pictures of ancestors with that of Jesus, or place His in the center and the others in secondary places? And even if they do, are the meanings in their minds sufficiently changed? We know of the experiments in Papua New Guinea designed to present Jesus as the Great Ancestor, but are they working? And are they theologically valid? We need to hear of more experiments in this area.

REINCARNATION

I once asked a demon if reincarnation was one of the things they did to deceive people. He answered something like, "Of course. We know people's lives in detail. It's easy for us to simply tell people someone else's life as if it was their own past life." This is how they fool Westerners into believing something that was, until recently, only believed by a few in the West. It's even easier to deceive Hindus, who for centuries have philosophized the recycling of lives. As with many of his activities, Satan has trained them to perpetuate his deceit themselves, without much, if any, help from him.

Scripture is clear that "everyone must die once, and after that be judged by God" (Heb 9:27). There is, therefore, no scriptural allowance for anyone to be reborn into another earthly existence. God has created each of us unique and eternal. This belief, therefore, like idolatry and divination, cannot be contextualized. Dealing with the demons of reincarnation may be the first step toward freeing people from this lie.

SHRINES AND DEDICATED PLACES

It is important that we recognize Satan's ability to heal and bless those who come to places dedicated to him. For too long Christians have tried to ignore Satan's skill at counterfeiting and the attraction it has for many who want enough spiritual power to enable them to live their lives reasonably well.

I have previously shared the story of my visit to a Shinto shrine with a Japanese friend. As people entered and poured water over the statue in that shrine, my friend and I asked them what it was they sought. Their answers included blessings for marriage and school examinations, healing of various ailments and relationships, fertility for themselves or loved ones, and other such things. Jesus is concerned about all of these things, I thought as I stood there. How great it would be if the churches sponsored shrines where people could receive prayer in His name for such requests. Japanese people are used to going to places of power at times convenient to them rather than at set times such as Sunday morning. So even if such needs are prayed for in church (and they often are not), Christian shrines would be more appropriate places to deal with them.

Such shrines would, of course, differ in several respects from normal Shinto shrines. For one thing, the land on which they stand would be spiritually cleansed of satanic power and dedicated to God. In addition, there would be people to pray for those who come, not simply a statue to pour water over. Visitors who express further interest would be invited to attend the regular Sunday services and meetings held on other days at the sponsoring church. They would also be given literature explaining the faith further, and the shrines would be advertised on the trains, just as other shrines are. Those who pray for people could include young people, thus providing the youth with a kind of ministry for which they would usually have to wait several years.

Thus, these shrines would look to the Japanese like places where their power needs can be met. They would not look like foreign incursions into Japanese life, where knowledge about a foreign religion is dispensed but the power people seek in religious activity is missing.

Such an approach might be suggested for other areas of the world as well. Many of the world's peoples are accustomed to frequenting shrines to satisfy their quest for spiritual power. In some Muslim countries, it is customary for people to seek spiritual power at the tombs of saints—even of *Hindu* saints! Might not some adaptation of that custom for Christian witness be appealing to these peoples?

Obviously, wherever such an approach is attempted, the land and any buildings taken over will have to be spiritually cleansed and then blessed with the power of Jesus. Traditional customs for dedicating buildings and property are likely to be adaptable for such purposes, but the power behind the dedications would be that of the true God, not of the traditional gods or spirits.

FORBIDDEN CUSTOMS

Understanding which customs God is against is the easy part of our consideration. It is much more difficult to work out how to handle such customs in contemporary situations in a way that is loving and does not distract from the main message of Christianity. We have learned, for example, that simply condemning customs such as polygamy and the consumption of native alcoholic beverages has given Christianity a disagreeable reputation in many places. Unfortunately, such rules have kept many out of the kingdom, because they were focused on secondary cultural changes supposedly required by God rather than on the centrality of a relationship with Christ.

The Old Testament shows how strongly God is against such customs as divination and the worship of other gods, but the messages that make these points are directed to Jewish people. It is not surprising that God would want to warn those whom he calls His people about falling into pagan practices and attitudes. But is His attitude on such matters the same toward those just coming out of paganism who may still believe and practice certain things from their pre-Christian lives? Can God be patient with sub-Christian beliefs and practices in the spiritual power area, just as He is with sub-ideal practices (e.g., polygamy, common law marriage) in other cultural areas?

We again turn to the account of Naaman the Syrian, whom God healed of leprosy through Elisha (2 Kgs 5), as potentially relevant here. As Naaman was about to return to his country after being healed, he requested

> two mule-loads of earth to take home with me, because from now on I will not offer sacrifices or burnt offerings to any god except the Lord. So I hope that the Lord will forgive me when I accompany my king to the temple of Rimmon, the god of Syria, and worship him. Surely the Lord will forgive me! (vv. 17,18)

"Go in peace," responded the prophet, presumably indicating that God would allow such a concession.

Given that God requires primary allegiance to Himself (Ex 20:3), can we assume from the fact that Israel accepted the existence of many gods for some time that God will allow this today? I believe we can. But these other gods and allegiances (e.g., family) must be seen as secondary. A Christian's primary allegiance can only be to the true God. It might not be too difficult for those who believe in multiple gods to add Yahweh to their pantheon, even to put Him in first place. Perhaps even those who worship their ancestors would be willing to put God above them, as Israel did when they used the phrase "the God of Abraham, Isaac, and Jacob." The Israelites, no doubt, like many animistic peoples, would have gladly worshiped Abraham, Isaac, and Jacob. But to keep that from happening, *they learned to focus on the God of these revered ancestors rather than on the ancestors themselves as objects of worship.*

As with all conversion and cultural transformation, once people have decided to adopt a new custom, the crucial thing is the pressure for continued movement in the right direction (see chapter 10). For this to happen, a people's decision to make Yahweh or Jesus number one must be followed by the process of greater and greater insight into and acceptance of God's ideals. And often this requires someone or something to keep the pressure on. If the people are highly motivated, that motivation coming from inside of them is usually sufficient pressure. But if such motivation is missing, outside agencies will be needed. Nevertheless, pressure or no pressure, without the growth the result will not be appropriate Christianity.

An illustration from language learning will help make the concept of "point plus process" clearer (see also chapter 9). In the first few weeks of a person's attempt to learn another language, they may not pronounce words very well and will make numerous grammatical mistakes. Still, their teacher will encourage them by saying they are doing well, even though there are many mistakes. But if that person is making the same mistakes after five or ten years, the judgment will be different. Language learners are expected in the early stages to be bold and try to speak, even if they make many mistakes. But they are expected to improve in fluency over time, assisted by internal pressure (the motivation to be understood) plus or minus external pressure (encouragement from those helping in the language learning process). So it goes for group and individual converts: they are expected to grow in their ability to practice their new faith, but they will need internal plus or minus external pressure to keep growing.

As I have written in *Christianity in Culture* (1979), conversion is a directional thing. To be a Christian is to be one who is growing toward greater Christlikeness, not simply one who appears to live like a Christian or identifies as such. It is not so much the position a person is in that makes them a Christian as the direction in which they are headed. Thus, the thief on the cross, in response to Jesus, turned and headed toward Him. And he was saved. The Pharisees, on the other hand, who believed most of what Jesus taught and conscientiously practiced the commands of the Old Testament, were headed in the wrong direction because their motivation was not right. And they were lost.

In this all-important area (as in all other areas), I believe God is willing for those who have not known Him to start with nothing more than a commitment to Him, making Him their primary allegiance. From this flows the growth in understanding what that commitment means concerning the changes needed in the secondary allegiances and cultural practices of the individual or group. Practices such as ancestor worship, belief in reincarnation, seeking healing from shamans, and divination in all of its many forms are to be turned away from as soon as possible, but not as a precondition for salvation. There is only one precondition: faith commitment to God through Jesus Christ.

Are the rules different for those who have been recipients of God's revelation, such as the Hebrews, than for those who have not received such an advantage? I believe they certainly are. Though the faith requirement—commitment to Jesus—is the same, the knowledge available to converts makes a big difference in what is expected of them behaviorally. Though all are expected to change over time, the kind and amount of change will depend on where a person or group starts in that process. The thief on the cross started at a very long distance from ideal Christian belief and behavior, with only one qualification for salvation—faith in Jesus. The believing Pharisees (and there were many) started their life of faith in Jesus with much of the expected behavior already habituated. And both the believing thief and the believing Pharisees were saved on the basis of their faith allegiance to Jesus—a faith allegiance that started them moving in a Christward direction that meant salvation for them.

DEVELOPING FUNCTIONAL SUBSTITUTES

Once faith in Jesus is pledged, though, a lot of the ensuing growth may depend on whether or not other customs are developed to replace the customs that are judged to be inappropriate for Christians. A sad fact of mission history is that missionaries often condemned customs without suggesting alternatives that would serve the function the pre-Christian customs had served. With regard to the power customs, this has usually resulted in people continuing to practice their pre-Christian customs, often in secret from missionaries or other outsiders. In places like Latin America, such pagan customs take place quite openly—even in the church buildings.

The first and most important custom to be replaced is, of course, the primary faith commitment to gods, spirits, family, ideas, movements, or whatever else the person or group's primary allegiance had been. For it is this commitment that creates the dividing line between Christian and non-Christian. But certain customs related to this allegiance need to be replaced as well. The custom of seeking assistance from a pagan shaman or priest is one. New converts need to learn how to appeal to the true God instead of to false gods for their needs.

And this is the area where missionary Christianity has failed most miserably, by not providing functional substitutes to replace the customs of the receiving peoples. Often the habit of going to shamans has been condemned but all that has been put in its place is a weak appeal to God in prayer, or simply the use of a secular Western technique such as medicine or fertilizer—but no rituals; no authoritative use of the power of Christ to heal or bring fertility; no blessing of fields or animals or of couples seeking children; no enthusiastic worship. Not that we should ignore secular techniques—but we should honor God by appealing to Him first, before using medical, agricultural, or other techniques that He has led people to discover.

For most of the peoples of the world, things like healing, fertility, and protection from misfortune are *spiritual* things, not simply the human manipulation of physical substances, as we think of them in the West. And any such manipulation, if it is to adequately function as a substitute for their pagan custom, needs to be conducted with primary concern for the spiritual nature of the problem and wrapped in meaningful ritual. If this is not done, the people are left with a void in their experience that they will probably seek to fill by returning to their pre-Christian practices.

An example of this would be the way funerals are conducted in areas where missionaries have worked. Pagan funerals usually involve a great deal of interaction with the spirit world, and when such activity has been forbidden to Christian converts, they typically satisfy themselves by doing much of that activity in secret. How different things would be if a study were to be made of the pagan funerals, and functional substitutes developed for each aspect of the activity so that the felt needs of the people are met rather than ignored. The traditional concern over the involvement of the spirit world in death needs to be taken seriously and Christian answers worked out in culturally appropriate rituals, so that the bereaved will be satisfied that the spiritual dimensions of life that death brings to the fore have been adequately addressed. If this is not done, people will often expect retribution from the spirits or gods that have not been properly appeased.

The belief that ancestors are involved in funeral exercises needs to be taken seriously, and substitute understandings and rituals need to be developed. As mentioned above, I believe it is possible to honor ancestors in culturally appropriate ways just as long as God is recognized as primary. When the ancestors are not given what the people believe is their due, any subsequent misfortune that may strike the family is attributed to the fact that the ancestors' desires were not attended to.

An example of dealing with the spiritual dimensions of conversion in culturally appropriate ways can be found in the Issan region of northeastern Thailand. Under the wise guidance of Evangelical Covenant missionaries, the churches in this region have captured a custom used by the people to show their allegiance to spirits. The custom involves tying a string around the wrist as a symbol of several things, including dedication to spirits and friendship commitment to other people. This custom is now used by the Christians to symbolize conversion and love for one another. The traditional cultural felt need for such a ritual is thereby satisfied, though the meaning of the ritual has been changed for Christians. This capturing of a traditional ritual is reminiscent of the way God led Abraham to capture the ritual of circumcision and to change its meaning.

When it comes to divination, the problem of finding a functional substitute is made more difficult by the fact that God condemns the practice out of hand. We are forbidden to use any of the forms of divination to discern the future (see Deut 18:9–13). However, God Himself gives the spiritual gifts of prophecy, words of knowledge, and spiritual discernment (1 Cor 12:27,28). Christians can be taught to seek these gifts, to practice them, and to use them as God leads. Some will discover that God has gifted them in these areas and that they are able for the sake of the Christian community to function in many of the ways the diviners function, and with greater accuracy. Those gifted in this manner may even find themselves regularly consulted, as diviners are, when something lost needs to be found or special advice from God is desired.

Dealing with magic and magical expectations can be another troublesome area. The essence of magic is to expect that if certain things are said or done, the desired result will be automatic. The great temptation is for people (Westerners included) to try to control God through words or rituals regarded as efficacious for getting Him to do our will. The key change here is to help people recognize that the Christian life is to be a life of submission to God, not of controlling Him. This submission does of course involve the authority He gives us in ministry, which, though not magic, can be far more powerful. Another key to dealing with the realm of magic is to make people understand that although they may think they are able to control things through magic, what is really happening is that they are unconsciously submitting to satanic power.

What I am suggesting, then, is that we give solid attention to developing Christian functional substitutes for the customs traditional people practice in the exercise of spiritual power. Many of the churches in missionized areas are, of course, already secularized in these matters—at least on the surface. We once ran into a situation on the island of Chuuk (Truk) that is probably typical of such churches worldwide. My wife asked a group of about fifty pastors' wives if traditional power was ever used in their churches. Without hesitation they replied, "Yes, of course!" They added that they themselves regularly went to traditional spirits when they needed a quick answer to their problems. "The true God is too slow," they said.

I would suggest that we look for the ways in which spiritual power is sought, even in westernized churches, and if necessary help Christians meet their power needs in ways that are more appropriate to the Bible. Many of them have been secularized and are not expecting God to work in power. They need to become more scriptural. Others have been meeting their power needs underground in traditional ways. These need to be helped to discover that the powerful God of Scripture is still alive and doing powerful things in the present.

If the witness of Christ that we desire is to have an impact on the world's power-oriented peoples, we need to be presenting a Christianity with power (see Kraft 2005b). Jesus, working with a power-oriented people, used signs and wonders as a major part of His strategy, and He has passed this power on to us (John 14:12). Let's learn to do His work in His way. Let's move from powerless, secular Christianity into biblical Christianity, which is always three-dimensional. Neglecting the power dimension of our faith has, I believe, cost us millions of converts to Christ. We must not let that continue to happen.

CONCLUSION

In this chapter I have tried to discuss several aspects of the spiritual power dimension of the Christian faith. This is by far the most neglected of the three dimensions for those of us who have gone out from the West as cross-cultural witnesses. Though it is in many respects a very difficult area to deal with, we should not continue to neglect it. Ours is a faith that can flow through the forms of any culture, even those considered "religious." The contextualization of the spiritual power dimension needs to be thought through that power customs, as well as the other areas of people's lives, can be captured for Christ.

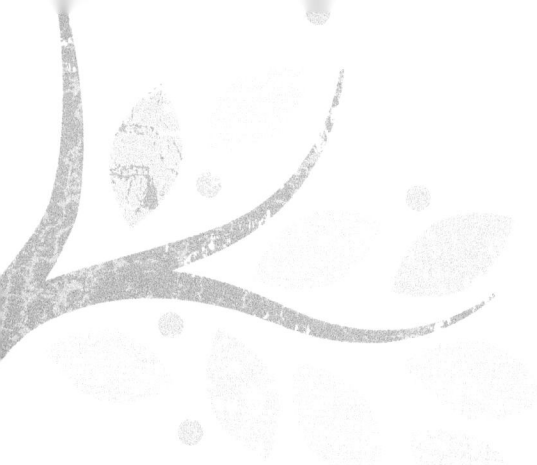

CHAPTER 15
POWER ENCOUNTER

This chapter is different from the previous chapters in that it is part case study, part a study of the concept of *power encounter*, and part a tribute to the late Alan Tippett, my senior colleague at Fuller Seminary to whom we owe the concept. It is a revision of an article I wrote to honor Dr. Tippett, which was originally published in the *Australian Journal of Mission Studies* (volume 8, number 2, December 2014).

In studying the entrance of Christianity in the South Pacific, Tippett noted that the main contextualizing factor experienced by the Pacific islanders was *the contest between the traditional spiritual powers and Jesus Christ, with the people turning to the winner.* This he termed "power encounter," developing the idea most fully in his book *People Movements in Southern Polynesia* (1971).

Tippett observed that in the early days of Christian work in the South Pacific the acceptance of the gospel usually occurred when there was an "encounter" between the Christian God and the traditional deity or spirit, in which it was demonstrated that the power of the true God is greater than that of the other deity. Such a demonstration was usually accompanied by a visible desecration of the symbol(s) of the traditional deity by its priest or priestess, or by a king who served that deity. In performing such an act, the priest, priestess, or king who was previously devoted to that deity declared that they were rejecting its power and instead pledging allegiance to the Christian God, on whom alone they would henceforth depend for protection, healing, and other favors, especially including protection from any reprisals from the traditional deity.

What Tippett found was that the beginnings of the acceptance of Christ in the South Pacific usually involved encounters between Christ and the people's gods. When Jesus won such encounters, the islanders turned to Christ in culturally appropriate larger or smaller groups—what we call "people movements." They did not come one by one. Nor were they reasoned into conversion. Culturally, they were both group- and power-oriented. Underlying these movements of people to Christ were power encounters, because "in a power-oriented society, change of faith had to be power-demonstrated" (1971, 81).

KEY POINT

What we are dealing with is an encounter or confrontation between the false gods and the true God. The power of the true God is demonstrated, the people see that their gods can do nothing against the true God, and the group converts.

This encounter takes place at two levels: the human level and the spirit level. At the *spirit level*, the most powerful God wins and protects those who have defected—whether the individual, the family, or the larger group—from the revenge of the weaker god/spirit. At the *human level*, a representative of the false god defects—either as an individual or on behalf of the group—by desecrating the symbol (e.g., animal, fish, wooden carving) that represents the god, thereby challenging the false god in the name and power of Jesus Christ to retaliate. If there is no retaliation, the true God has won.

A WIDER USE OF THE CONCEPT

Tippett's concern was a historical one: he was primarily interested in the place this concept had had in the introduction of Christianity in the South Pacific. But those of us concerned with spiritual warfare in the present found the concept worthy of wider application. We began using the term "power encounter" with a much broader meaning than Tippett had originally envisioned, and he saw no problem in our using the concept in this way.

John Wimber, Peter Wagner, and I have used the term to label healings, deliverances, or any other "visible, practical demonstration that Jesus Christ is more powerful than the spirits, powers, or false gods worshiped or feared by the members of a given people group" (Wagner 1988, 150). The concept of "taking territory" from the enemy for God's kingdom is seen as basic to such encounters and a major insider method of winning power-oriented people to Christ.

The power encounters in Scripture are between the true God and the gods the Israelites encountered as they took over the Promised Land. The people of Canaan were classic animists, following a plethora of deities attached to trees, bodies of water, land, and various other items and places. Usually, however, a single deity (often known as Baal) presided over the lesser ones, and it was this deity who had to be challenged in a power encounter.

We find specific encounters mentioned throughout Scripture. In the Old Testament we have Moses against Pharaoh in the deliverance of Israel from Egypt; David against Goliath; and Elijah against the prophets of Baal. Another such instance is the success of the Israelite armies against God's enemies when they went into battle in faithfulness to Him. When Israel was unfaithful they usually lost—except when God was avenging Himself against the army of Aram in the events recorded in 1 Kings 20:13–30. On that occasion, the army of Aram had insulted God by claiming that He was only a god of the mountains. So even though Israel's king was the wicked Ahab, God avenged Himself by granting His people a victory.

In the New Testament, we see Jesus engaging in power encounters by delivering people from evil spirits (e.g., Mark 5:1ff; 9:14ff; Luke 4:33; 9:37; Matt 8:16; 17:14) and His followers doing the same (e.g., Acts 4:7–10; 5:16; 8:7; 16:18). In one particularly impressive power encounter, the result was that the converts burned their books of magic (Acts 19:19)—books that had an incredible monetary value.

Even temptation can be considered a power encounter. Throughout the Old Testament we see Israel facing the constant, strong temptation to turn away from the true God and to the animistic gods. Prominent examples include Gideon, who, after he had won a great victory for Yahweh, retired and returned to the pagan gods of his father; and Solomon, who allowed his pagan wives to get him to follow their gods.

The history of the kings of Israel and Judah, then, is an account of which god or gods the Israelites would follow. Each king has a "report card" evaluating his reign, a report card with but a single entry: whether that king followed Yahweh and was therefore a "good" king or whether he followed the animistic god(s) and was therefore an "evil" king who "sinned against the Lord" (e.g., 1 Kgs 16:25,26,31–33; 2 Kgs 8:18,27; 10:29–31). Notice that all of the Northern Kingdom kings followed animistic gods, and several of the Southern Kingdom (Judah) kings also fell into the "evil" category.

All of the contests between the true God and counterfeit gods involve encounters in which the superior power of the true God is demonstrated. Thus, *Jesus' entire ministry can be seen as a massive series of power confrontations between God and the enemy.* The apostles and their disciples continued the ministry of exercising the "authority and power over all demons and all diseases" given by Jesus to His followers (Luke 9:1). And those who take up God's power today, encountering demons and defeating them, fulfill Jesus' prophecy in John 14:12 that we would do His works and more.

The use of power encounters was a prominent means of attracting people to God in Jesus' day, and as His followers we are expected to use His approach to witness. We have been given the ability to work in Jesus' name as He did, in love and power.

A PASSAGE FROM TIPPETT

To further illustrate this important aspect of appropriate insider witness, we turn to one of Tippett's accounts in *People Movements in Southern Polynesia*:

In common with other people of Oceania, the Samoans believed that the only real and effective way of proving the power of their new faith was to demonstrate that the old religion had lost its powers and fears....

The *aitu* [god] of [King] Malietoa was a fish called *anae*, a kind of mullet. On the appointed day the forbidden food was set before Malietoa. The incident created tremendous excitement. Friends and distant relatives had come from afar to witness the daring spectacle. Many expected all who ate to drop dead there and then. Those of the family who were to share the experiment were in some cases so frightened that they dowsed themselves with oil and salt water as possible antidotes to the mana [power] of the *aitu*. But Malietoa and a few others with him took no precautions. As a power encounter it had to succeed or fail on its own merits. By partaking as a social unit the encounter involved both Malietoa as an individual and his family as a group. They ate. The excitement subsided. No evil befell them. Thereafter for many the *lotu* [Christian faith] was true and the *aitu* was false. Malietoa's sons could endure the separation for no more than three weeks, and then pleaded for the family's permission to take the same step.

This incident led many people to dispense with their personal *aitu* or break the taboos, and to put themselves under the instruction of the Christian teachers. The movement gained momentum. Chiefs took the initiative; and thus it was that when [the missionary] Williams arrived after twenty moons, he found villages all around the coast where large groups had eaten or desecrated their *aitu*, built chapels, and were awaiting the return of Williams with more teachers. Their gods had been discarded, evil spirits had been cast out, and the houses swept—and were empty.

For the second example I have chosen one that concerns an inanimate and inedible *aitu*. It is the case of the war god, Papo, whose considerable power was concentrated in a venerated shrine, a piece of matting that was attached like a battle flag to a war canoe going into action. At the *fono* (council) of this group it was determined that they destroy the shrine and put on the white cloth or armband. The shrine would either have to be burned or drowned in sea water (recognized methods both widely used throughout Oceania). The matter was debated at length by the group, which decided to tie a stone to the matting shrine, and, taking it on a new canoe (i.e., not one dedicated to war, in itself an act of desecration), throw it overboard in the deep sea. Several chiefs, Fauea among them, set off to do this so that the shrine of Papo might be visibly and ceremonially drowned.

These two incidents, in which the deities and persons involved can be identified and documented, demonstrate that the locus of power was regarded as the shrine of the god, and conversion to [the Christway] had to be an ocular demonstration of encounter at this point. There were, no doubt, scores of important features in the total complex, but in the final analysis decision to quit paganism and become [a Christ-follower] was a dynamic demonstration on the level of [spirit reality]. This was so on the level of the individual, as it was also of the group. In the case of the group there had to be . . . discussion and agreement. . . .

Laulii, a Christian Samoan who lived nearer to those times than ours, described conversion in these terms of encounter with the *aitu* by saying that when any Samoan "resolved to declare himself a [Christ-follower], he commenced by killing and eating" his *aitu*—grasshopper, centipede, octopus, bat, snake, eel, lizard, or parrot, as the case might be. I note that Laulii conceives this as an individual act. Yet it was a public act and would usually be at the family meal when the taboo creature was served up before the whole family. From evidence in other areas we would expect the family to eat the family *aitu*, and the individual his own personal *aitu*, if this distinction existed as it did in some places.

The question of what pressures might be exerted to achieve unanimity is a serious one in some communities; but in Oceania such pressures operated more against conversion than for it. Sometimes persons who agreed with the common decision were nevertheless quite frightened about the power test, as we have seen in the oil and sea water antidote incident, and this is why the period of Christian instructional follow-up is so important. Perhaps it is true that some would be swept into the movement with the crowd, but this was never exploited by Protestant missionaries and they were most vocal about its undesirability. (1971, 163–66)

As another example, Tippett refers to the experience of the Tahitians under King Pomare II, who had asked for Christian baptism in November 1811 but was refused by the missionaries because he was not deemed ready to become a member of the church. Between then and July 1812, Pomare came to realize that some dynamic encounter was required, not only to convince his own people of the truth but also to convince the missionaries of his sincerity. The missionaries made him wait seven years for baptism, not because he lacked sincerity, but because he needed more instruction. In the instance quoted below, the king's actions are without question the flowering of his hearing and believing the Christian message.

> Pomare had, for some time past, shown his contempt for the idols of his ancestors, and his desire to be taught a more excellent way. . . . The natives had watched the change in his mind with the most fearful apprehension. . . . They were powerfully affected on one occasion when a present was brought to him of a turtle, which was always held sacred, and dressed with sacred fire within the precincts of the temple, part of it being invariably offered to the idol. The attendants were proceeding with the turtle to the [temple], when Pomare called them back, and told them to prepare an oven, to bake it in his own kitchen, and serve it up, without offering it to the idol. The people around . . . could hardly believe the king was in a state of sanity. . . . The king repeated his direction; a fire was made, the turtle baked, and served up at the next repast. The people of the king's household stood, in mute expectation . . . of the god's anger. . . . The king cut the turtle and began to eat it, inviting some that sat at meat with him to do the same; but no-one could be induced to touch it. (1971, 16)

In a society that feared the spirits, Pomare risked his life by challenging the only spiritual powers they had ever known. And his people stood around waiting for the spirits to take revenge by killing him.

This was a classic power encounter, and it resulted in the conversion of many. What is more, the conversion took place in keeping with the people's custom: they changed allegiance to the more powerful god, and they all followed their king together.

Another example concerns a Tahitian priest named Patii, who served several gods symbolized by wooden images. After considering changing allegiance over a period of time, Patii eventually decided to convert and lead his followers to change gods. He convened a meeting at which a large number of his followers gathered, and instructed his servants to build a fire. Then he ceremoniously disrobed each idol and addressed it directly, saying he was no longer following it. Next he threw each article of clothing, and eventually the wooden idol itself, into the fire. As he did this, Patii pointed out to the spectators the inability of each god to resist the superior power of the true God.

Again, the people stood by apprehensively, expecting the gods to take revenge by killing the priest. Many of them feared for their own lives as well. But when nothing evil happened, the people converted.

Tippett gives several additional examples of rituals marking the change of allegiance in the South Pacific. For instance when the people in the Solomon Islands decided against their traditional gods, they ceremonially buried their ancestral skulls, which had hitherto been the focal points of their allegiance to the gods. In West Irian, as the gospel message spread through the Baliem Valley, it became the norm to burn fetishes as the people changed allegiance. In Tonga, the converts publicly desecrated and hung their idols. In Samoa, a group that had been studying Christianity demonstrated their change of allegiance by eating the sacred fish in a non-ceremonial way. There were no negative results in any of these instances.

KINDS OF POWER ENCOUNTERS

The first kind of power encounter may be called *face-to-face confrontation*. Some of these confrontations are unsought, as with the attack on Jesus in Nazareth (Luke 4:28–30). Others are open challenges, such as those between Moses and Pharaoh (Ex 7–12), Gideon and the Midianites (Judg 7), and Elijah and the prophets of Baal (1 Kgs 18:18–40). The South Pacific examples cited above also fall in this category.

When the concept is expanded to include contemporary encounters, we see representatives of the true God commanding healing and deliverance as open challenges or encounters designed to defeat the enemy. These encounters are *visible* challenges.

In addition, there are quite a few types of *invisible* power encounters, where the challenges are largely through prayer and asserting the authority given us by Jesus (Luke 10:17; John 14:12). These challenges materialize into insider spiritual battles over territories, systems, institutions, churches, schools, political organizations, and the like. There are battles over territories (countries, cities, regions); issues (prostitution, homosexuality, abortion); relationships (families, friendships, work relationships); individual behavior (lying, lust, self-will); and demonization (individuals, institutions, whole societies). There are even power encounters between the Covenant Box and God's people in the Old Testament. See 1 Samuel 5 for an encounter with the god Dagon (vv. 1–8) and encounters at Gath and Ekron (vv. 8–12).

Wherever we turn, the conflict between God's kingdom and Satan's is obvious to those who have eyes to see what is going on in the spirit realm. God reveals Himself in these encounters as a God of power who works within the culture.

RESULTS OF POWER ENCOUNTERS

The results of power encounters are mixed. Though power encounters were an important part of people movements in the South Pacific, they did not always result in people movements. People did not always respond positively to the power demonstrations.

Because our Western Christianity is largely powerless, we might assume that if people see the power of God in action, they will automatically begin to follow the God who wins the encounter. We might assume that the normal response is as follows:

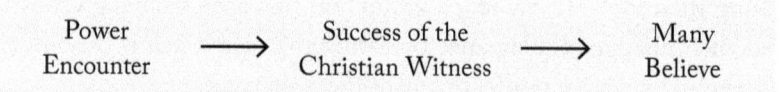

FIG. 15.1. Ideal response to power encounter

What we often miss is the fact that animistic peoples are used to seeing demonstrations of spiritual power. They are also used to inviting any power to help them. They are not used to going exclusively with one god or spirit. They will accept blessings or healings from one spirit today and from another tomorrow, even if tomorrow's spirit is weaker than today's.

In the short term, the power encounter may make a great impression and bring in a large number of converts. Over the long term, however, many people simply accept the defeat of their god and go right back to it. Note the situation recorded in 1 Kings where the Israelites went right back to Baal despite Elijah defeating the prophets.

Elijah → Demonstrates God's Power → Elijah Flees + Jezebel Appoints New Prophets, but God's Remnant Is Encouraged

FIG. 15.2. Israelite response to power encounter

Families often ostracize those who convert. As Tippett recounts, in Tonga a convert's family threw a feast for their god and ceremonially disinherited the convert. By so doing, they sought to protect themselves from the anger of their family deity (1971, 97). One chief, however, thwarted such a return to the old gods by calling for a feast and blessing the food in the Christian manner. This disqualified the food from serving as a pagan offering.

Even those who conduct a power encounter often get discouraged or compromise. After the spectacular victory on Mount Carmel, Elijah fled in fear to the wilderness and asked God to take his life (1 Kgs 19). And Gideon, after heading the defeat of the Midianites, returned to his village, made an idol, worshiped it, and thus led Israel astray (Judg 8). A power encounter can also be followed by religious or political institutions rising up against God's witness, resulting in persecution, opposition, suffering, and even death. Even though people may believe and convert, the witness usually has to suffer some consequences.

HOW ARE POWER ENCOUNTERS UNDERSTOOD?

There are several meanings attached to power encounters by those who observe them. I have pointed out above that not everyone who observes a power encounter is swayed from their previous loyalty. For many animists, power demonstrations are more or less routine. Their gods compete with one another and the winners attract the most followers. But these contests between the gods and the choices made by their followers are internal, taking place within the society.

Along comes the powerful god of another society that is more powerful than the indigenous gods. The people may acknowledge that god's superiority, but they may not change their allegiance. They are simply recognizing that the gods of another society are more powerful than their own, but the reasoning is that those gods' power works within the society that honors them and perhaps occasionally in other contexts as well. And this is not enough evidence for them to switch allegiances.

Thus, when the white man's God comes into contact with the gods of certain animistic societies, He may be recognized as more powerful than the local deities, but the people may show no inclination to convert. This could be because they make allowances for the powerful God of the whites, feeling that they are eligible only for the power of their own gods and ineligible to appeal to this God because He belongs to the whites and cares for them only.

Or the power encounter may be successful (from our point of view) and the people choose to follow the God who wins the contest, but this is usually done at risk of revenge by the gods they have forsaken. We have seen several examples of this response in the cases cited above.

When such a conversion happens, it is a very significant event. Those who turn away from the greatest power they have ever known do so at considerable risk. They are turning away with the expectation that their tribal god will try to kill them. Indeed, observers almost always await the backlash from their god, and the foremost question in their minds is whether the new God will be able to protect them.

The motivation is important here. Tippett suspected that at least some of the animist kings chose to follow the new God for political reasons. In their thinking, they were attempting to gain greater power to establish their thrones.

Or the new God could be filling a void. For example, we are told that the animist gods in Hawaii had died. There was no encounter here in the sense in which we have been discussing power encounters since the gods had lost their power. The Christian God, once introduced, filled a void that had been created when the traditional gods died.

PROCESS LEADING TO POWER ENCOUNTER

Power encounters typically do not happen without some prior experience that alerts people to the possibility of one. There is usually a period of observation, sometimes reports of encounters that have taken place elsewhere. Generally, some sort of agent is needed to make a people aware that such an encounter can occur. In the South Pacific, the missionaries often served this purpose. In other cases, nationals who had travelled to places experiencing a power encounter returned to tell their people about it, thus creating awareness and stirring hunger for the same experience.

Beyond learning about power encounters, there needs to be a willingness on the part of political or religious leaders—those who have authority over a population—to challenge the powers they have traditionally worshiped and depended on. And the stakes are high. That's why such confrontations often attract a crowd of onlookers, who watch expecting the worst.

These people are well acquainted with spiritual power. They probably have experienced many power demonstrations over the years, and their experience of the power of their deities makes them very fearful of what might happen when those deities retaliate. They often fully expect their gods to strike the challengers dead. When such retaliation does not happen, it is a powerful statement that the God of the Christians is powerful enough to protect the challengers.

In each instance of such an encounter, when the Christian God won, the people had to make a choice. They could either change their allegiance or ignore the results of the encounter. Some did ignore the significance of the encounter and continued to follow their traditional gods because, as mentioned above, they believed that they had their gods and the whites had theirs. Sadly, the fact that the Christian God was the true God was not the decider.

The scriptural parallel to this is in 1 Kings 20:13–30, where we see the Israelites defeating the Aramites in engagements in the hills. The king of Aram and his counsellors attribute Israel's victory to the fact that their God is a mountain god. Therefore, if the Aramite army could entice the Israelite army down onto the plain, they would defeat them. This analysis angers and insults God, leading Him to empower the much smaller Israelite army so that they win the confrontation on the plains. When the true God is in the encounter, His side wins.

THE MESSAGE FOR US

Jesus said we're to do what he did (John 14:12). His whole ministry was a series of power encounters—it featured power demonstrations in abundance. With this in view, the anemic Christianity of many non-Charismatic churches does not look like His.

Charismatics and Pentecostals are to be commended for including spiritual power in their approach, but it is regrettable that many Charismatics have abandoned power ministry, often in what appears to be an attempt to be seen as respectable.

It is ironic that in these days of secular Christianity, God has called non-Charismatics like Tippett (or me) to seek to restore to our faith the power dimension that was so important to Jesus. With his keen eye for historical fact and its implications for the present, Tippett uncovered a truth the contemporary church needs to listen to.

Another non-Charismatic, James Kallas (a Lutheran NT scholar), points out that there are two basic themes in the Synoptics and Pauline Epistles. He labels these the "Godward View" and the "Satanward View." Kallas claims that in these two sections of the New Testament, 80 percent is devoted to the Satanward View (power Christianity) and only 20 percent to the Godward View (love, forgiveness, faith, peace, etc.). *Both messages are there, but the one that most of Christianity neglects is the more frequent one statistically* (Kallas 1966). I can neither verify nor dispute these figures, except to suggest that neglecting the majority of the NT is a serious mistake, especially if we claim that ours is a Bible-centered faith.

Jesus engaged in power encounters and gave His disciples—which includes us—the authority and power to cast out demons and heal (Luke 9:1,2), and to train others to do the same (Matt 28:20). His aim was to free people from the enemy (Luke 4:18,19). His method was power wrapped in love. We are to go into the world as witnesses. But what many miss is that Jesus told His followers to wait for power before going (Acts 1:8).

In addition, we are to communicate the gospel as Jesus did (Mark 16:15) and to make disciples as Jesus did (Matt 28:19). He said, "As the Father has sent me, so I send you" (John 20:21)—to do the things he did. The normal Christian life means doing what Jesus did: teaching, healing, casting out demons, blessing, and forgiving. All of these involve spiritual power and power encounters.

Jesus' style, then, is also to be imitated. He didn't get excited or over-emotional, except in his compassion. On occasion He cried from pity, or was upset that people weren't paying attention to the message. He taught and healed with authority but wasn't loud. He didn't shout, knowing that neither God nor Satan is hard of hearing. With quiet authority, Jesus simply spoke things into being, and that authority was a challenge to the religious leaders, winning their hatred and eventually bringing about His death. He also leveled an all-out attack against Satan's power, and this too figured in His death.

There is a warning to be heeded here. When we get into spiritual power and challenge spirit power, we will win opposition from both human and spirit entities, just as Jesus did. As we have seen in this chapter, this is also what happened to those in the South Pacific who dared to take on the forces of darkness. We are at war, and it is a power game. We can expect wonderful victories if we engage—and no victories if we continue to practice secular Christianity. But there will be a Christianity that reflects the ministry of Jesus if we incorporate power encounter expression in our faith.

APPENDIX
THE DEVELOPMENT OF CONTEXTUALIZATION THEORY IN EURO-AMERICAN MISSIOLOGY

The term *contextualization* has not had a long history as the preferred label for the ideal toward which we evangelicals strive as we communicate the gospel to the peoples of the world. It wasn't until the late 1970s that it displaced *indigenization* as the label of choice. What follows is a brief history organized into seven "stages" of how this came about, followed by a list of what I see as unresolved issues in contextualization studies.

STAGE 1: CULTURAL ENCOUNTER

In the earliest days of the modern missionary era (i.e., roughly since William Carey went to India in 1792), the basic concept European and American missionaries carried with them may be labeled *cultural encounter*. Taking the gospel to non-Western peoples was assumed to be an encounter between the "Christian" culture of Euro-America and the "pagan" cultures of the non-Western world. The cultures of non-Western peoples—and especially their religions—were seen as evil and needing to be stamped out if the gospel was to be effective. To replace the forms of these religions, the early missionaries felt called to substitute a purified form of our Western approach to Christianity.

Though both Protestant and Catholic missionaries approached mission with this "encounter" mentality, they differed with respect to the brand of European culture they imposed. Protestants imported austere Northern European customs surrounding organizational and doctrinal concerns, while Catholics imported the more expressive customs of southern Europe within which were packaged a great concern for ancient ritual and allegiance to Rome.

Both streams of missionaries recognized the presence and activity of Satan in non-Western societies (though they largely ignored it in their own) and proceeded to fight his evil influence. They erroneously assumed, however, that the enemy's presence invalidated just about every aspect of non-Western cultures as potential vehicles of God's love and grace. So they sought to defeat the enemy by converting so-called *pagan* peoples to the Western ways they assumed were Christian. The problem, as the missionaries saw it, was that non-Western peoples were so blinded by the devil that they couldn't think properly. They must therefore be taught how to think before the missionaries could expect any results from their witness. The watchword thus became *"Civilize in order to evangelize* (Christianize)."

Discussing the background from which these early missionaries came, mission historian Wilbert Shenk states,

> The seventeenth-century New England Puritan missionaries largely set the course for modern missions. They defined their task as preaching the gospel so that Native Americans would be converted and receive personal salvation. But early in their missionary experience these New Englanders concluded that Indian converts could only be Christians if they were "civilized." The model by which they measured their converts was English Puritan civilization. These missionaries felt compassion and responsibility for their converts.
>
> They gathered these new Christians into churches for nurture and discipline and set up programs to transform Christian Indians into English Puritans. From this emerged the slogan, "Civilization and Christianity," which was shorthand for saying that native peoples and their cultures had to be made over in the likeness of European culture. They assumed that European culture was synonymous with Christian culture. Therefore, to be a Christian required that the convert adopt European culture. All other cultures were "heathen" and depraved. Christianization was the same as civilization. (1980, 35–36)

The missionaries considered Western institutions such as schools, hospitals, and churches as means to an end: that of getting non-Westerners to think like Euro-Americans and, in the process, to become truly Christian. The assumption they worked on was similar to that of one of my missionary colleagues, who, around 1958, said to me regarding the Nigerian church, "We have had two thousand years of experience with Christianity; we know how things ought to be run."

In addition, Western missionaries tended to assume that producing Christianity in non-Western lands was entirely their responsibility, with little or no participation from the receiving peoples in the process. In their eyes, the natives were like children, needing constant instruction, direction, and supervision as they moved along the road to civilization.

STAGE 2: THREE SELFS (FORMAL INDIGENEITY)

Toward the middle of the nineteenth century, even without the benefit of formal anthropological training, various missionaries began to develop an awareness of their own ethnocentrism and domination. The writings of Henry Venn (1840s) and Rufus Anderson[1] on the Three Selfs—self-support, self-governance, and self-propagation—were an attempt to change things, though mostly at the superficial form level. The central idea was to allow the nationals to be in charge of their own churches.[2]

From 1856 to 1893, John Nevius was rigorously applying Three-Self principles in China. He put the principles in writing sometime in the mid-1880s and helped implement them in Korea after 1890 as the famous "Nevius Plan."

As early as 1879, William Taylor's *Pauline Methods of Missionary Work* sparked an interest in revisiting the apostolic missionary enterprise as a model for the Christian church. Taylor was a precursor of Roland Allen, who, a generation later, published his *Missionary Methods: St Paul's or Ours?* ([1912] 1953) and *The Spontaneous Expansion of the Church* ([1927] 1956). Sidney Clark's *The Indigenous Church* (1928) espoused a similar approach.

Three-Self theory was considered enlightened missiology for nearly a century. Alan Tippett, in pointing to Venn's contribution to missiological theory, says,

> Over a century the missionary world has had this basic theory of mission before it. Because God spoke to the missionary world through Venn's writings we have no one to blame but ourselves for our preference for paternalistic and foreign missions and the problems that have emerged from our policy. (1973, 155)

On the Roman Catholic side, the tendency was to speak of *accommodation*, since their polity requires the continuation of a given ecclesiastical system that is always intended to be an import, though they admit that the model may be locally modified. Even with certain accommodations to the surrounding culture, the Roman Catholic ideal is a kind of *form indigeneity*, requiring the introduction of certain cultural forms in areas such as worship, the Mass, and baptism.

Up to this point, both Protestants and Catholics had usually assumed that missionaries were to take an existing system to the ends of the earth. And while they knew there would inevitably be accommodations and adjustments of that system, be it Methodist, Presbyterian, Baptist, or Roman Catholic, few questioned that the governance, doctrines, ceremonies, teaching structures, and just about all else were to be imported.

During this period, enlightened missionaries began to advocate and to a certain extent implement the change from foreigners running the system to nationals running the system. But it was still a foreign system they were operating. The indigeneity was,

---

1. For a list of the work and works of Rufus Anderson, see Beaver 1967, 39–44.

2. Whether or not the national leaders exerted enough actual power in the *control* of their churches was another matter. The important aspect was the *impression* of self-governance that the elevation of selected indigenes into *positions* of leadership provided.

therefore, with few exceptions, simply a matter of the forms of Christianity in the hands of nationals; the meanings were still largely foreign.

STAGE 3: EARLY IMPACT OF ANTHROPOLOGY

In the 1940s and '50s, with roots going back as far as the turn of the century in Europe (especially among Roman Catholics) and the 1920s and '30s in America, the findings of anthropology started to be felt in missiological thinking. Missionary training institutions began to teach anthropology as a way of sensitizing outbound missionaries to the cultures of the peoples with whom they were going to work.

Among the first such institutions to introduce anthropology courses were the Kennedy School of Missions at Hartford Seminary Foundation (late 1920s, early '30s); Wheaton College and Wycliffe Bible Translators[3] (both dating back to the 1930s); the Jaffray School of Missions at Nyack, NY, and the Toronto and Meadville language and culture summer programs run by the American Bible Society (early 1950s).

A very influential source of anthropological insight among evangelical[4] missionaries and missiologists during the 1950s and '60s was the bimonthly journal *Practical Anthropology*. This publication, started in 1953 by Robert Taylor, then professor of anthropology at Wheaton College, aimed at getting the anthropological message out to missionaries. It limped along for the latter half of 1953 and all of 1954 until the American Bible Society Translations Department (under the leadership of Secretary for Translations, Eugene Nida) took it over, with William Smalley being appointed as editor in 1955. The publication influenced a whole generation of missionaries through the perceptive writings of Smalley, Nida, William Reyburn, Jacob Loewen, and others. In 1973, *PA* was absorbed into *Missiology*, the journal of the newly established American Society of Missiology.

The popularizing of anthropological and communicational insights related to missionary work owes a great deal to Eugene Nida, whose personal influence began to have great impact in the 1940s. Nida's spellbinding lecturing and writing style served to awaken the missionary community to cultural realities and how they influence the work of the gospel around the world. Two of his books, *Customs and Cultures* (1954)

---

3. The case of WBT was a little different in that the organization emphasized the *linguistic* side of what was then one area of specialization—namely, *linguistic anthropology*. It took Wycliffe quite a few years to make the study of *cultural* anthropology a major component of their training programs for Bible translators (1980s onwards).

4. A number of Catholic cross-cultural workers also received a good deal of help from the articles in *PA*. Though the contributors to *PA* were largely evangelicals, their focus was on contextualizing the biblical message, not on advocating a particular brand of evangelicalism.

and *Message and Mission* (1960), were especially helpful and constitute obligatory reading for missiologists/missionaries even today.

The significance of anthropological input for the discussion of contextualization cannot be overemphasized. Up until the 1960s and '70s, anthropology was virtually the only field of study that focused on the validity of non-Western cultures. Although the most effective missionaries were those who learned to respect the cultures of the peoples among whom they worked, it was only as we began to incorporate the insights of anthropology into missionary thinking that we gained a theoretical perspective from which to counter our natural ethnocentrism. This perspective enabled us to improve our understandings in at least three crucial areas: the implications for life and witness of the cultural involvements of the people we seek to reach; the implications of our own involvement in culture; and our ability to probe and penetrate in new ways the cultural dimensions of biblical revelation.

Not all anthropological teaching was relevant to the task of Christian witnesses. We had to learn to temper anthropology's commitment to a nearly absolute relativism with biblical truths concerning a Creator who sustains the universe, and who offers a solution to the sin problem underlying the cultural difficulties that anthropologists can only describe. But by applying anthropological insight to the biblical revelation, we learned that the Creator interacts with humans *within* the cultural worlds they (we) have created. This insight, then, enabled us to make sense of the times when God worked differently in the Old Testament than in the New because He was adapting His approach to the culture of the people He was working with. We began to understand biblical texts like 1 Corinthians 9:19–22, in which Paul states his commitment to adapt culturally in order to witness effectively, as an articulation of God's own approach to humans through culture. The development of such insights into the relationships between God, culture, and human beings helped us move into deeper understandings of how to handle the Christian witness in a world of richly diverse cultures.

STAGE 4: BEYOND "FORM INDIGENEITY"

The publication of William Smalley's "Cultural Implications of an Indigenous Church" in *Practical Anthropology* (1958) was a major breakthrough in our thinking about indigeneity and contextualization. Up to this point, the assumption of most of those who wrote on the subject seemed to be that if we simply turn our institutions (e.g., churches, schools, medical facilities, development projects) over to nationals to govern, support, and propagate, all would go well. Smalley challenged this assumption. He noted that in his mission, and in many others that had committed themselves to Three-Self indigeneity, the nationals running things were doing their jobs in what was often an uncritical commitment to *Western* principles. Given this fact, Smalley asked whether a church run by nationals according to Western patterns was truly indigenous. He concluded that an "indigeneity" solely at the form level was no indigeneity at all, even when the nationals were operating the system. He proceeded, then, to define a truly indigenous church as

> a group of believers who live out their life, including their socialized Christian activity, in the patterns of the local society, and for whom any transformation of that society comes out of their felt needs under the guidance of the Holy Spirit and the Scriptures. . . . An indigenous church is precisely one in which the changes which take place under the guidance of the Holy Spirit meet the needs and fulfill the meanings of that society and not of any outside group. (1958, 55–56)

The business of Christianity, Smalley asserts, whether in matters pertaining to church structures, doctrinal formulations, the way we live, or any other part of our biblical faith, is to follow the leading of the Holy Spirit according to patterns that are meaningful to those inside any given society. Patterns and institutions imported from outside, no matter how meaningful they might be to the missionaries or how long they have been in force, cannot be seen as indigenous, even if they are run by nationals.

In the late 1950s, we evangelical Protestants who were struggling to understand the relationship between Christianity and culture had little awareness of what was going on in Roman Catholic circles. But even with the limitations of the Roman Catholic approach noted above, their voices were not totally silent during this period, especially after Vatican II. Characteristic of the best of Roman Catholic thinking was Louis Luzbetak's *The Church in Cultures* (published in 1963, revised and expanded in 1988). Luzbetak, an anthropologically trained missioner who worked in Papua New Guinea, demonstrated in his book that he was very much in touch with both Roman Catholic and informed Protestant thinking on this subject, including all that was published in *Practical Anthropology*.

The 1970s were an important period in the history of contextualization theory and practice. The mood in missiological discussions during this decade was that we should be advocating an approach to the relationship between Christianity and culture that was more dynamic than the "form indigeneity" concept. Seeking to advance our thinking along this vein, Alan Tippett of Fuller's School of World Mission wrote a chapter titled "Indigenous Principles in Mission Today" in a book called *Verdict Theology in Missionary Theory* (1969, rev. ed. 1973). In this chapter, Tippett dealt with quantitative, qualitative, and organic church growth and suggested that we should focus on the *quality of selfhood* when discussing whether a church was truly indigenous or not. He suggested that we look for a dynamic, indigenous quality in six areas: self-image; self-function; self-determination; self-support; self-propagation; and self-giving. Tippett stated,

> When the indigenous people of a community think of the Lord as their own, not a foreign Christ; when they do things as unto the Lord meeting the cultural needs around them, worshipping in patterns they understand; when their congregations function in participation in a body, which is structurally indigenous; then you have an *indigenous* Church. (1973, 158)

In my 1978 Willowbank paper on Dynamic Equivalence churches, I expressed the concern we were feeling in that decade over the use of the word *indigenous*. I said,

> Strictly speaking, "indigeneity" is not necessarily the most appropriate label for the ideal toward which we strive. A church *totally* indigenous in appearance, function, and meaning would be no different from the rest of the culture. Christianity, because it comes into a culture from the outside, is inevitably intrusive to a certain degree. There is "no such thing as an absolutely indigenous church in any culture," observes Smalley ("What Are Indigenous Churches Like?" *Practical Anthropology*, 1959, Vol. 6, 137). Nevertheless, we will employ the term "indigenous church" (as Smalley does) to signify an expression of Christianity that is both culturally authentic and genuinely Christian. (Stott and Coote 1980, 214)

As a further indication of our dissatisfaction with the term *indigenous*, my co-editor Tom Wisley and I decided to name our collection of readings on the subject *Readings in Dynamic Indigeneity* (1979). By 1979, some of the more open evangelical thinkers had started using the term *contextualization*, but it was still highly suspect to the more conservative (including the group that was helping fund our book). After several serious discussions concerning the title, Wisley and I concluded that the evangelical groups we sought to reach would probably reject the book if we used the new term. Thus our title, and the following words in the introduction:

> Two recent articles (Coe 1973; Taber 1979) have raised the issue of the terminology that we use to label the subject matter of this volume. Both of these authors suggest that the older term "indigenization" connotes a static view of what is desirable for the church while "contextualization" connotes a more dynamic concept. They have a point.
>
> We believe, however, that the crucial distinction that these authors are bringing to our attention lies deeper than any mere surface level change from one term to the other. Which label one prefers is secondary to how one conceives of the process. While it may be true, as Coe and Taber contend, that most of those employing the older term, indigenization, had an inadequate, more static view of the way

Christianity is to become a part of a new culture, it is by no means true that most of those now speaking of contextualization hold a very different view. The problem, as we see it, lies in whether the process is conceived of as basically a matter of 1) preformulation, transfer and modification within the receiving culture of a given system or 2) the creation within the receiving culture of something new which is the result of fertilization from outside but may bear little formal resemblance to the source culture system.

It is the latter concept that we recommend in this volume, whatever the label attached. Our aim is to bring about "dynamic equivalence" to God's processes made explicit in the Scriptures. . . . We have no disaffection for the term contextualization. Indeed, we use it freely, especially with reference to theologizing. (Kraft and Wisley 1979, xix–xx)

STAGE 5: TRANSITION TO CONTEXTUALIZATION

Prior to the above publication, in a World Council of Churches consultation, Shoki Coe formally introduced the term *contextualization*. His presentation was published in 1973 as "Contextualizing Theology" in *Theological Education*, and reprinted by Gerald Anderson and Thomas Stransky in *Mission Trends* no. 3 (1976). In the article, Coe stated that

indigenization tends to be used in the sense of responding to the Gospel in terms of traditional culture. Therefore, it is in danger of being past-oriented. Furthermore, the impression has been given that it is only applicable to Asia and Africa, for elsewhere it was felt that the danger lay in over-indigenization, an uncritical accommodation such as expressed by the culture faiths, the American Way of Life, etc. But the most important factor, especially since the last war, has been the new phenomenon of radical change. The new context is not that of static culture, but the search for the new, which at the same time has involved the culture itself. . . .

So in using the word *contextualization*, we try to convey all that is implied in the familiar term *indigenization*, yet seek to press beyond for a more dynamic concept which is open to change and which is also future-oriented. (Anderson and Stransky 1976, 20–21)

As noted above, the fact that the term surfaced in World Council circles troubled many evangelicals, especially those at the more conservative end of the spectrum. An early though grudging acceptance came from Bruce Nicholls in his 1979 book, *Contextualization: A Theology of Gospel and Culture*. Nicholls started by presenting so many cautions about the term and the concept that one was led to believe he was against both. But by the end of the volume he had become positive and accepting. Bruce Fleming, however, in the publication of his thesis at Trinity Evangelical Divinity School entitled *Contextualization of Theology: An Evangelical Assessment* (1980), made no such accommodation to the term. Fleming critically evaluated the origination and development of the concept within ecumenical circles, taking a negative stance toward the term but accepting most of the concept under his proposed label *context-indigenization*.

Among the significant events of the 1970s was the publication of several specific attempts at contextualization of theology by representatives from the Two-Thirds World. Many of these were from a liberal theological perspective, which increased the suspicions of the more conservative evangelicals in the US (e.g., Nicholls, Hesselgrave) that the whole exercise was a threat to biblical Christianity. Much of their reticence was, I believe, justified. These were the days when Liberation Theology, especially in Latin America, and Black Theology (e.g., James Cone, *Black Theology and Black Power*, 1969) in the US were gaining popularity.

The reticence of North American evangelicals was especially understandable as a reaction to liberation theologians who often seemed more concerned about what they defined as liberation than about being faithful to Scripture. For example, while we may sympathize with their desire to be free of domination by Euro-American theological thinking, we cannot endorse the way the Bible is treated by such Latin American theologians as Gustavo Gutierrez (in *A Theology of Liberation*, 1973) or Juan Segundo (in *The Liberation of Theology*, 1975, Spanish; 1976, English). Likewise with certain Asian theologians, such as C. S. (Choan-Seng) Song in *Third-Eye Theology* (1979), and at least some of the authors in Gerald Anderson's collection *Asian Voices in Christian Theology* (1976).

Nevertheless, some of these authors, along with Japanese theologian Kosuke Koyama, bear careful reading, even if one disagrees with their interpretations (see Koyama's insightful *Water Buffalo Theology*, 1974). So do works by John Mbiti from Africa (see *New Testament Eschatology in an African Background*, 1971). More cautious voices from Africa were those of John Pobee (1979) and Kwame Bediako (1992, 1995).

A particularly sharp reaction against theological contextualization in Africa came from Byang Kato, who served for several years, before his untimely death, as the leader of the Association of Evangelicals of Africa and Madagascar. Kato was a conservative Nigerian who studied theology at Dallas Theological Seminary and published his doctoral dissertation in 1975 under the title *Theological Pitfalls in Africa*. However, by the time of his death the following year, he was beginning to recognize some validity to the motivations behind the contextualization movement, and rumor has it that in one of his last (unpublished) presentations, he was fairly positive toward the need for contextualization. Perhaps it was this recognition that led him to apologize to John Mbiti shortly before his death for some of the criticisms he had published in his book (see Kraft 1978a).

In the US, Carl Armerding edited a largely negative evangelical reaction to Liberation Theology, entitled *Evangelicals and Liberation* (1977). It included essays by Harvie Conn, Steven Knapp, Kenneth Hamilton, and Clark Pinnock.

In spite of such reactions from some conservative evangelicals, the climate began to change during the mid- and late 1970s. As we began to take seriously the broadening of the concept beyond the earlier discussions surrounding indigeneity, first the more open and then the more conservative evangelical missiologists among us began to overcome our prejudices toward the ecumenical origins of the term *contextualization*, and to find both the term and the discussion useful and instructive. We have never condoned the way some seem to dilute the authority of the Scriptures (e.g., Song, Segundo) as they propose new approaches to contextualization, but we join them in seeing the value and necessity of the process of contextualization.

STAGE 6: EVANGELICAL ACCEPTANCE OF THE CONCEPT OF CONTEXTUALIZATION

Although evangelicals had considered *indigeneity* the ideal term for decades, we now abandoned that word in favor of the new term and the broader concept it was intended to signify. At the School of World Mission, Fuller Seminary, we initiated what was probably the first professorial position with the term *contextualization* in its name when we appointed Dean Gilliland an assistant professor of the contextualization of theology in 1977.

Typical of the new mood, several events important to this discussion happened the following year. First, the entire January 1978 issue of *Evangelical Missions Quarterly* was devoted to the topic. In the lead article, "Contextualization: Is It Only a New Word for Indigenization?," James Buswell suggested that the issues we are dealing with require a broader perspective than that encompassed by the word *indigenization*. He then suggested that we use the term *inculturation* when dealing with the witness dimension of Christianity, *indigenization* when the contextualization of the church and its leadership are in view, and either *contextualization* or my own term *ethnotheology* for the production of appropriate theology.

Buswell's article was followed by one by F. Ross Kinsler, "Mission and Context: The Current Debate about Contextualization." Pushing beyond the controversy over the term *contextualization*, Kinsler pointed out that we need to recognize that our discussion has to get to deeper issues such as (1) the very nature of the gospel, (2) the question of syncretism, (3) tradition and renewal, and (4) the apparent conflict between biblical theology and contextual theologies.

In "Contextualization: A New Dimension for Cross-Cultural Hermeneutic," Harvie Conn (1978) suggested that we develop a *contextual hermeneutic* that addresses two important questions to the church: "How are the divine demands of the gospel of the kingdom communicated in cultural thought forms meaningful to the real issues and needs of the person and his society in that point of cultural time? How shall the man of God, as a member of the body of Christ and the fellowship of the Spirit, respond meaningfully and with integrity to the Scriptures addressing his culture so that he may live a full-orbed kingdom lifestyle in covenant obedience with the covenant community?" (Conn 1978, 43).

In my article entitled "The Contextualization of Theology," I tried to demonstrate that contextualization is a *biblical* process, results in theologies none of which are absolute, and is a risky enterprise. My concluding statement was as follows:

> What is the contextualization of theology? That is what happens whenever the given gospel, the message of Christ, is reinterpreted in new cultural contexts in ways equivalent to the ways in which Paul and the other Apostles interpreted it from Aramaic into Greek thought patterns. Contextualization of theology must be biblically based if it is to be Christian. It may take place in a number of different ways—such as sermons, hymns, poems, discussions, art, and many other ways. Contextualizing Christian theology is risky, but is not as likely to lead to syncretism as is the preservation of antique forms of theologizing and the importation of these forms into contexts in which they are not appropriate. No theology is an absolute representation of the mind of God. Appropriate contextualizations, produced by Spirit-led interpreters of God's word, enable them to present the Christian message within a biblically allowed range of variation in such a way that today's peoples will respond to Christ as those in the first century did. (1978b, 36)

Then, from January 6–13, 1978, under the auspices of the Lausanne Theology and Education Group, the Willowbank Consultation on Gospel and Culture was convened. The subject of the consultation was broader than the topic of contextualization—extending to such things as the definition of culture, the nature of inspiration, the normative nature of Scripture, culture and the communication of the gospel, conversion, the church in culture, and even Christian ethics and lifestyle—but the concern for contextualization was evident throughout.

In the Report of the Consultation, insight into the Willowbank scholars' view of contextualization comes to the fore when the matter of understanding God's Word for today is discussed. The Report states that a contextual approach to understanding the Bible

> takes seriously the cultural context of the contemporary readers as well as of the biblical text, and recognizes that a dialogue must develop between the two.
>
> It is the need for this dynamic interplay between text and interpreters which we wish to emphasize. Today's readers cannot come to the text in a personal vacuum, and should not try to. Instead, they should come with an awareness of concerns stemming from their cultural background, personal situation, and responsibility to others. These concerns will influence the questions which are put to the Scriptures. . . . We find that our culturally conditioned presuppositions are being challenged and our questions corrected. . . .
>
> In this process of interaction our knowledge of God and our response to his will are continuously being deepened. The more we come to know him, the greater our responsibility becomes to obey him in our own situation, and the more we respond obediently, the more he makes himself known.
>
> It is this continuous growth in knowledge, love and obedience which is the purpose and profit of the "contextual" approach. Out of the context in which his word was originally given, we hear God speaking to us in our contemporary context, and we find it a transforming experience. This process is a kind of upward spiral in which Scripture remains always central and normative. (Stott and Coote 1980, 317)

In dealing with the church in culture, the Report suggests that the criticisms of models of indigeneity were not so much applicable to "the ideal itself, but [to] . . . the way it has often been applied." Nevertheless, "a more radical concept of indigenous church life needs to be developed, by which each church may discover and express its selfhood as the body of Christ within its own culture" (1980, 329).

The Report then recommends the *dynamic equivalence* model for contextualizing churches—an issue I had discussed in the paper I presented at the Consultation.

> Just as a "dynamic equivalence" translation . . . seeks to convey to contemporary readers meanings equivalent to those conveyed to the original readers, by using appropriate cultural forms, so would a "dynamic equivalence" church. It would look in its culture as a good Bible translation looks in its language. It would preserve the essential meanings and functions which the New Testament predicated of the church, but would seek to express these in forms equivalent to the originals but appropriate to the local culture. (Stott and Coote 1980, 330)

The year 1978 also saw the publication of three significant pieces by Charles Taber. The lead article in the January issue of the (unfortunately short-lived) journal *Gospel in Context*, edited by Taber himself, was entitled, "Is There More Than One Way to Do Theology?" He argued that although all theologies are to be subject to Scripture, they are also to be conditioned by the culture in which they function. The same month, Taber published "The Limits of Indigenization in Theology" in *Missiology*. Bevans and Thomas say of that article,

> A seminal article outlining six propositions regarding the doing of theology in context and seven criteria for measuring indigenous theology, noting that as far as form and methodology go, there are no a priori limits which can be imposed on Christian theology. (1991, 108)

Taber also contributed a chapter entitled "Contextualization: Indigenization and/or Transformation" to *The Gospel and Islam* (ed. McCurry) that year. In this chapter, Taber helpfully (though at times more hopefully than realistically) contrasted contextualization with indigenization in six ways, contending that

> Indigenization . . . was a step in the right direction, but it did not go far enough, especially if we are to take seriously the 20th century context. Contextualization extends and corrects indigenization in the following directions.
>
> 1. Indigenization tended to focus exclusively on the cultural dimension of human experience. . . . Contextualization recognizes the importance of this dimension but insists that the human context to which the gospel is addressed also includes social, political, and economic questions: wealth and poverty, power and powerlessness, privilege and oppression. . . .
>
> 2. Indigenization tended to define culture in rather static, traditional terms. The various aspects of culture are "given," and they sit there while the gospel works around them. There was insufficient appreciation for the flexibility and changeableness of culture. . . .
>
> 3. Indigenization tended to think of sociocultural systems as closed and self-contained; the type of society was the small tribal group, isolated by distance and jungle from outside influences. . . . Today groups and societies relate to each other, trade with each other, fight each other, and defeat and exploit each other within a vast politico-economic system which operates on a global scale. Our model must take into account this global system and its differential impact on the various groups, societies, and nations of the earth. . . .

4. Indigenization was almost by definition something that happened "out there" on the mission field; it had nothing to say about how the gospel related to the missionary's society and culture on its own home turf; it merely said that the missionary's culture was not for export. In fact, indigenization tended to take a rather too uncritical and optimistic view of *each* given culture in its home setting, and to see evil only in the imposition of an alien culture on groups in the "mission field.". . . But contextualization insists on two additional insights: that the demonic as well as the divine is manifest in all societies and cultures, and that the same processes of cultural confrontation and/or syncretism plague churches in the West as in any other place, and must be faced with the same attitudes and means.

5. Indigenization, on the whole, tended to deal with relatively superficial questions such as the "expression" of a gospel which was conceived to be "the same" in all contexts. Contextualization argues that there is indeed a sense in which the gospel is "the same" all over the world; but that universal dimension is much more remote from the surface level of verbal and symbolic expression than was previously acknowledged. . . .

6. [T]hough indigenization was intended to place responsibility, authority, and initiative in the hands of national Christians, it usually did so in only a part of the total missionary enterprise: the work of the local church. More complex operations, such as hospitals and major schools, were without question designed, financed, and controlled from the outside. Seldom . . . was the more fundamental question asked, whether the very concept behind these efforts was itself sound. . . .

Contextualization, then, is an attempt to capitalize on the achievements of indigenization, to correct its errors and biases, and fill in its gaps. It is the effort to understand and take seriously the specific context of each human group and person on its own terms and in all its dimensions—cultural, religious, social, political, economic—and to discern what the gospel says to people in that context. . . . Contextualization takes very seriously the example of Jesus in the sensitive and careful way he offered each person a gospel tailored to his or her own context. . . . (1978a, 144–46)

Soon after, in 1979, my book *Christianity in Culture* appeared. In it, I attempted to advance what we now would call contextualization theory by suggesting that new insights into Bible translation theory be looked at as a model for how Christianity as a whole should look in any given culture. Specifically, I suggested that the Bible translators' ideal of *dynamic equivalence* be the model for all other aspects of Christianity as well.

The first rule of translation, said J. B. Phillips, is that a translation should not sound like a translation but, rather, like an original work in the receiving language. By analogy, I suggested in my book that churches ought not to look like imports but, rather, like original works in their own cultures. I then applied this principle to several aspects of Christianity, suggesting how we might achieve dynamic equivalence transculturation (e.g., preaching), dynamic equivalence theologizing, dynamic equivalence conversion, dynamic equivalence cultural transformation, dynamic equivalence leadership principles, and the like.[5]

In the section of *Christianity in Culture* in which I discuss dynamic equivalence theologizing, I was greatly helped by Daniel von Allmen's article entitled "The Birth of Theology" (1975), in which the author parallels Pauline contextualization with contemporary contextualization. As I have written, von Allmen

> sees all theologies . . . including Pauline theology, as the result of "contextualization" done by certain people within a group to meet the needs of that group. Missionaries, translators, and those who "sang the work that God had done for them" (1975:41) provided the raw materials for theologizing in the early churches. These consisted of expressions of need, translations and transculturations (including preaching) of the message in Greek, and partial preliminary formulations in culturally appropriate fashion. (1979, 295)

A key point made by von Allmen is that a proper theology is not simply some sort of adaptation or contextualization of an existing theology. He says,

> Any authentic theology must start ever anew from the focal point of the faith, which is the confession of the Lord Jesus Christ who died and was raised for us; and it must be built or re-built (whether in Africa or in Europe) in a way which is both faithful to the inner thrust of the Christian revelation and also in harmony with the mentality of the person who formulates it. There is no short cut to be found by simply adapting an existing theology to contemporary or local taste. (1975, 50)

---

5. In "Signs of Progress in Contextual Methodology" (1981), Louis Luzbetak described *Christianity in Culture* as "a landmark in missiological theory" and suggested that my book and the work of Robert Schreiter (published as *Constructing Local Theologies* in 1985) were signs of hope in the process of understanding and working toward truly contextualized Christianity.

STAGE 7: SINCE 1980

Contextualization studies have increased greatly among both Protestants and Roman Catholics since 1980. Bevans and Thomas's helpful bibliography, published in the January 1991 issue of *Missiology,* lists thirty-two significant studies, twenty-five of which were written in the 1980s. Only three of the earlier seven were published before 1978. Twelve of the twenty-five studies are from Roman Catholic perspectives, including an eleven-volume collection of papers presented at a conference on inculturation held in Jerusalem in 1981 (Crollius 1982).

In a valuable attempt to respond to and go beyond *Christianity in Culture,* Harvie Conn published *Eternal Word and Changing Worlds* in 1984. In preparation for that book Conn, who had solid theological and missionary credentials, worked hard to educate himself anthropologically. Thus he was able to wed theological and anthropological insights in a very helpful fashion, providing evaluation of old approaches and suggestions for new approaches to theologizing and theological education.

In 1985, Robert Schreiter published his experiment with a semiotic approach to contextualization entitled *Constructing Local Theologies*. In this work he presents an insightful but very complex approach to producing local theologies and shows a preference for the term *localization* in place of contextualization.

The year 1987 saw the publication of Paul Hiebert's seminal article "Critical Contextualization," in which he articulated what many of us had assumed but not stated so clearly: that Christians need to critically assess the *scriptural validity* as well as the *cultural appropriateness* of each Christian practice. A dangerous and unbiblical extreme is to consider anything that is indigenous as automatically worthy of incorporation into Christianity. The biblical authors were not uncritical of cultural practices; neither should we be. Our drive toward relevance should not obscure the fact that we are to be tethered to the Bible.

The 1989 publication of David Hesselgrave and Edward Rommen's *Contextualization* provides an indication of how the more conservative wing of Christian thinkers were receiving several of the above explorations. This book contains, for example, a pretty harsh reaction against myself and several others.

On the Roman Catholic side, Louis Luzbetak's revised and expanded *The Church and Cultures* (1988) is in reality an introduction to missiology within which the author has enfolded his earlier anthropology text. It updates and expounds his helpful understandings of contextualization.

At least four other valuable Roman Catholic contributions appeared during this period. Eugene Hill's article on "Inculturation" in *The New Dictionary of Theology* (1987) surveys the subject and argues that Jesus' incarnation demands contemporary inculturation. Aylward Shorter's *Toward a Theology of Inculturation* (1988) provides a valuable overview of Roman Catholic theological thinking on the subject. Peter Schinneller's *A Handbook on Inculturation* (1990) is an introduction to the theology and practice of contextualization for the non-specialist. Another guide for practitioners is Gerald Arbuckle's *Earthing the Gospel: An Inculturation Handbook for the Pastoral Worker* (1990). These works demonstrate to the evangelical world both the centrality of the Bible and a sound concern for cultural appropriateness in the thinking of Roman Catholic missiologists.

In *The Word among Us*, edited by Dean Gilliland, the faculty of Fuller's School of World Mission provide statements on a wide variety of contextualization issues. In a statement of evangelical commitment to our subject, Gilliland says,

> The conviction behind this volume is that contextualization, biblically based and Holy Spirit-led, is a requirement for evangelical missions today. Contextualization is incarnational. The Word which became flesh dwells among us. It clarifies for each nation or people the meaning of the confession, "Jesus is Lord." It liberates the church in every place to hear what the Spirit is saying. Contextual theology will open up the way for communication of the gospel in ways that allow the hearer to understand and accept. It gives both freedom and facility for believers to build up one another in the faith. Contextualization clarifies what the Christian witness is in sinful society and shows what obedience to the gospel requires. These are the components of a theology for mission that meets the needs of today's world. (1989, 3)

A very useful book by Stephen Bevans, *Models of Contextual Theology*, was published in 1992. The author, a Roman Catholic, contends that by now enough contextualization studies have been done to enable us to categorize and classify them. So he attempts to take stock of and organize the various approaches by placing them in five categories or models, which he calls the Translation Model, the Anthropological Model, the Praxis Model, the Synthetic Model, and the Transcendental Model. The book, though not without the kinds of limitations one would expect of such an ambitious venture, is an excellent attempt to organize and synthesize both Protestant and Roman Catholic approaches.

Emblematic of the importance missiologists attach to this subject, contextualization has become one of the most frequent topics appearing in missiological journals. Various issues of *Missiology* have either been devoted to contextualization or contain significant articles on the subject. The January 1991 issue, entitled "Contextualization in Mission," and the January 1997 issue, entitled "Contextualizing the Gospel," are exclusively devoted to this subject. Each contains several useful articles, and the former also provides an excellent bibliography by Bevans and Thomas. Other missiological journals, such as *Evangelical Missions Quarterly*, the *International Bulletin of Missionary*

Research, and *International Review of Mission*, have also featured numerous articles on contextualization, culminating so far in Moreau's comprehensive volume (2012).

My focus in this book has been on concepts rather than the historical development of contextualization thinking post-1995 or so. Moreau does that well. I have therefore not interacted with much of the recent writing, choosing instead to deal with factors that enable us to understand what contextualization is and why it is needed. As the title suggests, this is a book of "issues," with an emphasis on what I see as important as we think about the subject of contextualization.

REFERENCES

Allen, Roland. (1912) 1953. *Missionary Methods: St. Paul's or Ours?* 3rd ed. London: World Dominion.

———. (1927) 1956. *The Spontaneous Expansion of the Church.* 3rd ed. London: World Dominion.

Anderson, Gerald, ed. 1976. *Asian Voices in Christian Theology.* Maryknoll, NY: Orbis.

Anderson, Gerald, and Thomas Stransky, eds. 1976. *Mission Trends* no. 3. New York: Paulist/Grand Rapids, MI: Eerdmans.

Anderson, Rufus. 1967. *To Advance the Gospel.* Grand Rapids, MI: Eerdmans.

Annacondia, Carlos. *Listen to Me, Satan! Keys for Breaking the Devil's Grip and Bringing Revival to Your World.* Lake Mary, FL: Charisma House, 2008.

Arbuckle, Gerald A. 1990. *Earthing the Gospel: An Inculturation Handbook for the Pastoral Worker.* Maryknoll, NY: Orbis.

Armerding, Carl, ed. 1977. *Evangelicals and Liberation.* Nutley, NJ: Presbyterian and Reformed.

Barnett, Homer. 1953. *Innovation: The Basis of Cultural Change.* New York: McGraw Hill.

Barrett, David B. 1968. *Schism and Renewal in Africa: An Analysis of Six Thousand Contemporary Religious Movements.* Nairobi: Oxford University Press.

Beaver, R. Pierce. 1967. *To Advance the Gospel: Selections from the Writings of Rufus Anderson.* Grand Rapids, MI: Eerdmans.

Bediako, Kwame. 1992. *Theology and Identity: The Impact of Culture upon Christian Thought in the Second Century and in Modern Africa.* Oxford: Regnum.

———. 1995. *Christianity in Africa: The Renewal of a Non-Western Religion.* Maryknoll, NY: Orbis.

Berlo, David. 1960. *Process of Communication: An Introduction to Theory and Practice.* New York: Holt, Rinehart & Winston.

Bevans, Stephen. 1992. *Models of Contextual Theology.* Maryknoll, NY: Orbis.

Bevans, Stephen, and Norman Thomas. 1983. Selected Annotated Bibliography on Missiology: Contextualization/Inculturation/Indigenization. *Missiology* 19, no. 1: 105–8.

Buswell, James. 1978. Contextualization: Is It Only a New Word for Indigenization? *Evangelical Missions Quarterly* 14: 13–20.

Clark, Sidney J. W. 1928. *The Indigenous Church.* London: World Dominion Press.

Coe, Shoki. 1973. In Search of Renewal in Theological Education. *Theological Education* 9: 233–43. Reprinted 1976 as Contextualizing Theology. *Mission Trends* no. 3, ed. Gerald Anderson and Thomas Stransky, 19–24.

Cone, James. 1969. *Black Theology and Black Power.* New York: Seabury.

Conn, Harvie. 1978. Contextualization: A New Dimension for Cross-Cultural Hermeneutic. *Evangelical Missions Quarterly* 14: 39–46.

———. 1984. *Eternal Word and Changing Worlds.* Grand Rapids, MI: Zondervan.

Crollius, Arij A. Roest, ed. 1982. *Inculturation: Working Papers on Living Faith and Cultures.* Vol. 1–11. Rome: Pontifical Gregorian University.

Dawson, John. 1989. *Taking Our Cities for God.* Lake Mary, FL: Creation House.

Deere, Jack. 1988. Being Right Isn't Enough. In *Power Encounters in the Western World*, ed. Kevin Springer, 101–15. San Francisco: Harper & Row.

Fleming, Bruce. 1980. *Contextualization of Theology: An Evangelical Assessment.* Pasadena, CA: William Carey Library.

Gilliland, Dean, ed. 1989. *The Word among Us: Contextualizing Theology for Mission Today.* Waco, TX: Word.

Goldschmidt, Walter R. 1966. *Comparative Functionalism: An Essay in Anthropological Theory.* Berkeley: University of California Press.

Guelich, Robert A. 1991. Spiritual Warfare: Jesus, Paul and Peretti. *Pneuma* 13: 33–64.

Gutierrez, Gustavo. 1973. *A Theology of Liberation.* Maryknoll, NY: Orbis.

Hesselgrave, David, and Edward Rommen. 1989. *Contextualization.* Grand Rapids, MI: Baker.

Hiebert, Paul. 1982. The Flaw of the Excluded Middle. *Missiology* 10, no. 1: 35–47.

———. 1987. Critical Contextualization. *International Bulletin of Missionary Research* 11, no. 3: 104–12.

Hill, Eugene. 1987. Inculturation. In *The New Dictionary of Theology*, ed. Joseph A. Komonchak, Mary Collins, and Dermot A. Lane, 510–13. Collegeville, MN: Liturgical Press.

Hodges, Melvin. 1971. *The Indigenous Church.* Rev. ed. Springfield, MO: Gospel.

Hoefer, Herbert. 2001. *Churchless Christianity.* Pasadena, CA: William Carey Library.

Kallas, James. 1966. *The Satanward View.* Philadelphia: Westminster.

Kato, Byang. 1975. *Theological Pitfalls in Africa.* Kisumu, Kenya: Evangel.

Kinsler, F. Ross. 1978. Mission and Context: The Current Debate About Contextualization. *Evangelical Missions Quarterly* 14: 23–29.

Koyama, Kosuke. 1974. *Water Buffalo Theology.* Maryknoll, NY: Orbis.

Kraft, Charles. 1978a. Christianity and Culture in Africa. In *Facing the New Challenges*. Kisumu, Kenya: Evangel.

———. 1978b. The Contextualization of Theology. *Evangelical Missions Quarterly* 14: 31–36.

———. 1979, 2005. *Christianity in Culture*. Maryknoll, NY: Orbis.

———. 1991. What Kind of Encounters Do We Need in Our Christian Witness? *Evangelical Missions Quarterly* 27: 258–65.

———. 1992a. Allegiance, Truth and Power Encounters in Christian Witness. In *Pentecost, Mission and Ecumenism: Essays on Intercultural Theology*, ed. Jan. A. B. Jongeneel, 215–30. Frankfurt: Peter Lang.

———. 1992b. *Defeating Dark Angels*. Grand Rapids, MI: Chosen Books.

———, ed. 1994. *Behind Enemy Lines*. Eugene, OR: Wipf & Stock.

———. 1995. "Christian Animism" or God-Given Authority? In *Spiritual Power and Missions*, ed. Edward Rommen, 88–135. Pasadena, CA: William Carey Library.

———. 1996. *Anthropology for Christian Witness*. Maryknoll, NY: Orbis.

———. 1997. *I Give You Authority*. Grand Rapids, MI: Chosen Books.

———, ed. 2005a. *Appropriate Christianity*. Pasadena, CA: William Carey Library.

———. 2005b. *Christianity with Power*. Eugene, OR: Wipf & Stock.

———. 2008. *Worldview for Christian Witness*. Pasadena, CA: William Carey Library.

———. 2015. *The Evangelical's Guide to Spiritual Warfare*. Grand Rapids, MI: Chosen Books.

Kraft, Charles, and Tom Wisley, eds. 1979. *Readings in Dynamic Indigeneity*. Pasadena, CA: William Carey Library.

Kraus, C. Norman, ed. 1980. *Missions, Evangelism, and Church Growth*. Scottdale, PA: Herald.

Luzbetak, Louis. 1963. *The Church in Cultures*. Techny, IL: Divine Word. Revised and enlarged in 1988, Orbis.

———. 1981. Signs of Progress in Contextual Methodology. *Uerluem* 22: 39–57.

Mbiti, John. 1971. *New Testament Eschatology in an African Background*. London: Oxford.

McGavran, Donald A. 1970. *Understanding Church Growth*. Grand Rapids, MI: Eerdmans.

Moreau, C. Scott. 2012. *Contextualization in World Missions*. Grand Rapids, MI: Kregel.

Nevius, John. 1958. *Planting and Development of Missionary Churches*. Philadelphia, PA: Presbyterian and Reformed.

Nicholls, Bruce. 1979. *Contextualization: A Theology of Gospel and Culture*. Downers Grove, IL: InterVarsity.

Nida, Eugene. 1954. *Customs and Cultures*. New York: Harper & Row.

———. 1960. *Message and Mission*. New York: Harper & Row.

Oliver, Roland. 1952. *The Missionary Factor in East Africa*. London: Longmans, Green, and Co.

Otis, George, Jr. 1993. An Overview of Spiritual Mapping. In *Breaking Strongholds in Your City*, ed. C. Peter Wagner, 19–48. Grand Rapids, MI: Chosen Books.

———. 1999. *Informed Intercession*. Grand Rapids, MI: Baker.

Pennoyer, F. Douglas. 1990. In Dark Dungeons of Collective Captivity. In *Wrestling With Dark Angels*, ed. C. Peter Wagner and F. Douglas Pennoyer, 249–70. Grand Rapids, MI: Chosen Books.

Pobee, John. 1979. *Toward an African Theology*. Nashville, TN: Abingdon.

Priest, Robert J., Thomas Campbell, and Bradford A. Mullen. 1995. Missiological Syncretism: The New Animistic Paradigm. In *Spiritual Power and Missions*, ed. Edward Rommen, 9–87. Pasadena, CA: William Carey Library.

Richardson, Don. 1974. *Peace Child*. Grand Rapids, MI: Baker.

Schacter, Daniel L. 1996. *Searching for Memory: The Brain, the Mind, and the Past*. New York: Basic.

Schineller, Peter. 1990. *A Handbook on Inculturation*. Mahwah, NJ: Paulist.

Schreiter, Robert. 1985. *Constructing Local Theologies*. Maryknoll, NY: Orbis.

Segundo, Juan. 1976. *The Liberation of Theology*. Maryknoll, NY: Orbis. Spanish ed., 1975.

Shaw, R. Daniel. 1995. Contextualizing the Power and the Glory. *International Journal of Frontier Missions* 12, no. 3: 155–60.

Shenk, Wilbert R. 1980. The Changing Role of the Missionary: From "Civilization" to Contextualization. In *Missions, Evangelism, and Church Growth*, ed. C. Norman Kraus, 31–58. Scottdale, PA: Herald.

Shorter, Aylward. 1988. *Toward a Theology of Inculturation*. Maryknoll, NY: Orbis.

Silvoso, Edgardo. 1993. Prayer Power in Argentina. In *Engaging the Enemy: How to Fight and Defeat Territorial Spirits*, ed. C. Peter Wagner, 109–15. Ventura, CA: Regal.

Smalley, William A. 1958. Cultural Implications of an Indigenous Church. *Practical Anthropology* 5: 51–65.

———. 1959. What Are Indigenous Churches Like? *Practical Anthropology* 6: 135–39.

Song, Choan-Seng. 1979. *Third-Eye Theology*. Maryknoll, NY: Orbis.

Stott, John R. W., and Robert Coote. 1980. *Down to Earth*. Grand Rapids, MI: Eerdmans.

Taber, Charles. 1978a. Contextualization: Indigenization and/or Transformation. In *The Gospel and Islam*, ed. Don McCurry, 143–54. Monrovia, CA: MARC.

———. 1978b. Is There More Than One Way to Do Theology? *Gospel in Context* 1: 4–10.

———. 1978c. The Limits of Indigenization in Theology. *Missiology* 6: 53–79.

Tippett, Alan R. 1971. *People Movements in Southern Polynesia.* Chicago: Moody.

———. 1973. Indigenous Principles in Mission Today. In *Verdict Theology in Missionary Theory*, rev. ed., 126–41. Pasadena, CA: William Carey Library.

Travis, John. 1998. The C1 to C6 Spectrum: A Practical Tool for Defining Six Types of "Christ Centered Communities" ("C") Found in the Muslim Context. *Evangelical Missions Quarterly* 34, no. 4: 407–8.

Venn, Henry. 1983. The Native Pastorate and Organization of Native Churches. In *Henry Venn—Missionary Statesman*, ed. Wilbert R. Shenk, Appendix I, 118–29. Maryknoll, NY: Orbis.

Wagner, C. Peter. 1988. *How to Have a Healing Ministry Without Making Your Church Sick.* Ventura, CA: Regal Books.

———. 1990. Territorial Spirits. In *Wrestling with Dark Angels*, ed. C. Peter Wagner and F. Douglas Pennoyer, 73–91. Ventura, CA: Regal Books.

———. 1991. *Engaging the Enemy.* Grand Rapids, MI: Chosen Books.

———. 1993. *Breaking Strongholds in Your City.* Grand Rapids, MI: Chosen Books.

———, and Pablo A. Deiros. 1998. *The Rising Revival: What the Spirit Is Saying through the Argentine Revival.* Ventura, CA: Gospel Light.

Whiteman, Darrell. 1997. Contextualization: The Theory, the Gap, the Challenge. *International Bulletin of Missionary Research* 21: 2–7.

Wimber, John. 1987. *Power Healing.* San Francisco: Harper & Row.

INDEX

A
Aaron, 167, 200
Abraham, 8, 35, 81, 151–52, 166, 177–78, 202, 205, 208
Adam, 8, 166–69
Africa, African societies, 7, 15, 19–21, 68, 85, 97, 135, 139, 141, 148, 153–54, 190, 195, 197
African Independent Churches, 47, 94, 97, 101, 122
allegiance/relationship dimension, 44, 56–57, 59–61, 67–68, 70
ancestors, 130, 148, 179–81, 186, 196, 207–8, 216
   cults, 181, 201–2
   reverence for, 9, 205
   spirits, 186
   worship, 201, 205–6
American Christianity
   absence of spiritual power, 57, 141
   individualism, 27, 47
   nationalism, 143
   Word faith and prosperity teachings, 190
American way of life, 22
animism
   in the ancient world, 174, 212–13
   concept of God, 152–53, 191
   contextualization of, 5, 114
   God-given authority vs., 191–93
   Japanese, 34
   and power encounter, 218–19
   spirits, 153, 191
appropriateness, 41–52, 147, 163
   defined, 42–43

Arabic, 5, 76, 113
Argentina, 65, 142, 198
Asia, Asian societies, 15, 97, 148, 195, 197

B
Baal, 68, 128, 197, 199, 212, 217–18
baptism, 24, 64, 68, 85, 115, 133, 136, 165, 183, 201, 215–16
   infant, 133
Barnabas, 13, 81
Barnett, Homer, 83
Behinemo people, 51
Berlo, David, 30–31
Bible translation, 69, 115, 122, 137, 140
   dynamic equivalence, 17, 36, 41, 126
   meaning equivalence, 21, 25, 36, 38–39, 41
Buddhism, 5, 12, 77, 81, 84, 98, 105–6, 114, 186, 197

C
C1–C6, 9, 105–9
China, Chinese society, 15, 85, 143, 196
Christo-paganism, 22, 99, 120
commitment dimension, 55, 60, 67. *See also* allegiance/relationship dimension
communication, 3–4, 7–9, 25–26, 28–33, 36, 38–39, 45, 55, 75, 81, 90, 99, 120, 131–32, 137, 139–40, 154, 158, 177
   communicational bridge, 4
   communicational heresy, 99
   incarnational, 3, 9
   theory, 7, 26, 32
Communion, 77, 115, 155, 165, 184
communism, 5, 79–80

contextualization
  adaptation vs., 5–6, 14, 22, 70, 73, 75–77, 81–87, 108, 114, 136, 194, 204
  anti-contextualization, 10
  critical, 44
  dynamics of, 26, 35, 111, 123
  negotiation of meanings, 29, 38–39
  overcontextualization, 189–91
  of power, 45, 69, 121, 175, 187, 189, 209
  process of, 31, 116, 125, 131
  studies, 8, 44, 55, 67, 182
conversion, 44, 57, 60–61, 65–68, 90, 132, 140–41, 148, 160, 177, 197, 205–6, 208, 211, 215–16, 219
  to culture vs. to Jesus, 7, 13, 21–23, 37, 75–76, 81, 85–86, 115, 117, 125–30
C-Spectrum, 106–7
culture
  characteristics of, 17
  deep-level, 14, 16, 18–19, 22, 26, 76–77, 86, 127
  defined, 14
  shock, 93
  subsystems of, 18–19
  surface-level, 14, 16, 18–19, 21–22, 24, 76–77, 127, 134
customs, 9, 14–17, 23–26, 35–36, 49, 69–70, 78, 81, 112, 116–17, 125, 127, 132, 134–36, 147–48, 150–51, 154, 183, 187, 193, 201, 204, 206–9
  forbidden, 204
  foreign, 7, 12

D
David, 8, 167, 212
Dawson, John, 198
Deere, Jack, 59
deity, 35, 211–12, 218
demons, demonization, 11, 48, 56–57, 60, 64–66, 68–69, 140–41, 156, 162, 168, 173–75, 178–79, 182, 184–86, 189–90, 192–97, 201–3, 213, 217, 221
devil. *See* Satan
discipleship, 9, 39, 62, 64, 67, 122, 162
Dye, Sally and Wayne, 51, 122
dynamic equivalence, 17, 36, 41, 126

E
East Africa, 34
Elijah, 68, 167, 212, 217–18
Elisha, 200, 204
Esther, 152
Europe, European culture, 21, 34, 76, 82, 120, 130, 135, 195
evangelicals, evangelicalism, 22, 41–42, 44, 47, 56–59, 85, 90, 126, 165, 175–76, 200
Eve, 166

F
freedom dimension. *See* power/freedom dimension
Fuller Theological Seminary, 92–93, 211

G
Galilee, 175
generational appropriateness, 108–9, 125–44
Gentiles, 13, 21, 75–76, 81, 114, 116, 183
Germany, German society, 13, 15, 76
Good Samaritan, 19, 155
Greek language and thought forms, 20–21, 23, 35, 59, 136, 149, 161, 175, 183–84

H
Hausa, 35, 108
Herod, 167–68
Hiebert, Paul, 44
Hindus, Hinduism, 5, 77, 84, 98, 100, 114, 180, 186, 197, 203–4

I
Ibibio, 20
incarnation, 3–4, 8–9, 12, 41, 180
inculturation, 20, 23, 25, 41–43, 48, 55, 92, 126, 130, 143
India, Indian society, 22, 44, 85, 135, 190
indigeneity, 41
indigenization, 20, 48, 55
indigenous forms and expression, 9, 21, 46, 108, 112, 219
insider movements, 3, 5–6, 9–10, 17, 21, 36, 73, 187
Islam, 5, 76, 83–84, 98, 100, 105–7, 114, 197

Israel (ancient), 30, 47, 152, 167–68, 174, 178, 197, 199–201, 205, 212–13, 218, 220

J
James, 60, 75, 184
Japan, Japanese society, 4, 6–7, 15, 34–35, 47, 49, 85, 114–15, 130, 135, 138, 141–43, 153–54, 178, 196, 203–4
Jerusalem Council, 75
Jews, Jewish culture, 13, 17, 21, 47, 75–77, 80–81, 114–16, 126, 133, 148, 152, 155, 166, 183, 204
Joseph, 8, 166–68
Judah, 119, 168, 213
Judaism, 77, 183

K
Kallas, James, 221
Kamwe, 108
Kenya, 135, 139
King, Roberta, 139
knowledge dimension. *See* truth/understanding dimension
Korea, Korean society, 15, 49, 51, 85, 94, 96, 135, 141–43, 153, 190, 195–96

L
Latin America, Latin American societies, 22, 85, 99, 120, 130, 197, 207
Lazarus, 8, 202
literacy, 85, 112, 122, 139–40, 154
localization, 25, 41–42, 48, 55, 126
Loewen, Jacob, 23
Lord's Supper. *See* Communion
Luther, Martin, 13, 167

M
Mary, 120, 130, 167
meaning equivalence, 36, 38–39, 41
Moabites, 197, 199
Moses, 8, 68, 149, 167, 199, 201, 212, 217
Muslims, 30, 81, 83–85, 101, 105–7, 113, 133, 135, 204

N
Naaman, 200, 204
nationalism, 109, 142–43
Nazareth, 64, 167, 217
New Testament. *See specific topics*
Newbigin, Lesslie, 177
Nida, Eugene, 133
Nigeria, Nigerian church, 20, 28, 34, 37–38, 51, 91, 94, 96, 100, 108, 118, 134, 136, 141, 149–50, 153, 155, 157–60, 162, 174–75
Noah, 8, 34, 166–67
nominalism, 47, 109, 142–43

O
Old Testament. *See specific topics*
Otis, George, Jr., 198
outsider problems, 89–97

P
paganism, pagan culture
  captured for God's use, 23–24, 35, 129, 152, 177–78, 201, 208
  divination and witchcraft, 22
  exchanging for Christian culture, 43
  funerals, 207
  gods and spirits, 35, 115, 128, 177, 200, 213, 218
  paganized Christianity, 120, 130, 207. *See also* Christo-paganism
Palestine (ancient), 50, 186
Papua New Guinea, 51, 122, 202
partnership
  with God, 116, 166–69, 181
  with Satan, 167–68, 181
Paul
  and Christlikeness, 8, 37, 119, 191
  as contextualizer, 13, 21, 75–76, 81, 114, 116
  partnership with God, 167
  spiritual power and warfare, 128, 174, 178, 180, 184, 192
Pennoyer, Douglas, 177
Peter, 13, 81, 174
Pharaoh, 68, 167–68, 212, 217
Philippines, 51, 96, 135
Phillips, J. B., 4
Pomare II, 215–16
Portugal, 120

power encounter, 62, 68–69, 71, 176, 211–21
power/freedom dimension, 44–45, 52, 55–62, 64–65, 67–68, 71, 176, 185, 209, 221

Q
Quran, 113, 137

R
receptors, 6–7, 11–12, 20, 26–34, 38–39, 42–43, 46, 77, 98, 113–16, 131, 135, 143, 149, 151, 157
  characteristics of, 27–30
recombination theory, 83–84
reincarnation, 179–81, 203, 206
relationship dimension. *See* allegiance/relationship dimension; commitment dimension
repentance, 21, 56, 59, 62, 68, 90, 198
Richardson, Don, 155
Roman Catholic missions, 22, 130
Rwanda, 160

S
Samaritan woman, 28
Satan, 12, 44, 48, 56, 64–65, 68, 114, 128, 167–68, 174–75, 177–82, 184, 186–87, 191–93, 195, 197, 201, 203, 217, 221
  satanic power, 57, 65, 87, 128, 134, 140, 143, 176–77, 184, 192, 198, 203, 208
Sawi people, 155
secularization, 34, 176–77, 185, 190, 208–9
Shinto, 5, 114, 197, 203
shrines, 35, 114, 173, 178, 186, 203–4
Sierra Leone, 128
Silvoso, Ed, 198
Smalley, William, 46
Solomon, 167, 174, 197, 213
Solomon Islands, 216
South Pacific, 47, 68, 85, 156, 184, 197, 211–12, 216–17, 220–21
Spain, 120

spiritual dimension, Western neglect of the, 10–11, 150
spiritual warfare, 10, 48, 65, 168, 173–74, 182, 185–86, 189, 198–99, 212
  levels of, 185–86
syncretism, 22–24, 99–100
Syria (ancient), 197, 200, 204–5

T
Tahiti, 215–16
Thailand, 85, 101, 107, 208
three crucial dimensions. *See specific dimensions*
Tippett, Alan, 46, 134, 211–13, 215–16, 218–19, 221
Travis, John, 105–6
truth/understanding dimension, 44–45, 55–60, 62–63, 70, 176

U
United Bible Societies, 140
United States of America, 15–16, 19, 21–23, 27–28, 47, 76, 92, 115, 117, 135, 141–42, 190

V
Vietnam, 19
von Allmen, Daniel, 45

W
Wagner, C. Peter, 185, 198, 212
Wesleyanism, 13
Whiteman, Darrell, 43, 89, 91–92, 132
Wimber, John, 212
worldview, 6, 13–24, 26, 59, 74, 76–81, 84, 119–20, 124, 127
  Christian, 85–86
  defined, 14–15
  Western, 173
Wycliffe Bible Translators, 122, 140

Y
Yir Yoront people, 20

www.ingramcontent.com/pod-product-compliance
Ingram Content Group UK Ltd.
Pitfield, Milton Keynes, MK11 3LW, UK
UKHW050416240426
12048UKWH00021B/1534